Praise for *Buying Buddha, Selling Rumi*

"Sophia Rose Arjana's *Buying Buddha, Selling Rumi* is a fascinating and wholly engrossing exploration of how 'mysticism,' as we know it in the West, circulates as a modern-day product of colonial structures of power. With deft prose, Arjana skillfully illuminates the historical invention of what she calls 'modern mystic-spirituality,' which is sourced from the Orient/East, and specifically from the teachings and traditions of Hinduism, Buddhism, and Islam. From the Dalai Lama to *Eat, Pray, Love*, tantric sex to Burning Man, and yoga to spiritual tourism, Arjana expertly exposes how Orientalist logics shape the ways Westerners have manipulated, watered down, and come to consume 'Eastern' religions to bolster their own individual physical, emotional, and/or psychological health. While every chapter is illuminating, especially cogent is Arjana's analysis in the chapter 'Rumimaniacs,' which grounds 'Sufism' in Islam and examines Rumi's (who was, undeniably, Muslim) popularity as the best-selling poet in the U.S. *Buying Buddha, Selling Rumi* is a much-needed interrogation of our notions of the 'mystical,' and an important read for anyone interested in the intersections of religion, culture, colonialism, and capitalism in the twenty-first century."

Sylvia Chan-Malik, Associate Professor, Departments of American Studies and Women's and Gender Studies, Rutgers, The State University of New Jersey

"In *Buying Buddha, Selling Rumi*, Sophia Rose Arjana provides a wide-ranging overview of the ongoing power and cultural significance of long-standing Western Orientalist tropes about 'the Mystic East.' This is an important work for anyone working on Asian traditions and their contemporary appropriation, transformation and commodification."

Richard King, Professor of Buddhist and Asian Studies, University of Kent

"Both scholarly and readable, *Buying Buddha, Selling Rumi* deepens our understanding of the way the West appropriates Eastern religion, excising elements that offend, and using an idealized picture of non-modern and non-rational religion to tell a story about Western desires. Using multiple examples, Sophia Rose Arjana describes the 'muddled Orientalism' that romanticizes and conflates Eastern religions, turning them into a source of spiritual products and disconnected experiences to be marketed to hip Westerners."

Jeffrey H. Mahan, Ralph E. and Norma E. Peck
Professor of Religion & Public Communication,
Iliff School of Theology

BUYING BUDDHA, SELLING RUMI

Orientalism and the Mystical Marketplace

SOPHIA ROSE ARJANA

Oneworld Academic

An imprint of Oneworld Publications Ltd

Published by Oneworld Academic in 2020

A CIP record for this title is available from the British Library

ISBN 978-1-78607-771-4
eISBN 978-1-78607-772-1

Typeset by Jayvee, Trivandrum, India
Printed and bound in Great Britain by Clays Ltd, Elcograf S.p.A.

Oneworld Publications Ltd
10 Bloomsbury Street, London, WC1B 3SR, England

For Wahyudin

CONTENTS

ACKNOWLEDGMENTS

This journey began nearly a decade ago in a doctoral seminar I took with Ted Vial, one of the smartest people I know. Ted, who was also my colleague for five years when we taught at the same institution, assigned Richard King's great book on Orientalism and India, which I have read and reread numerous times over the years. In another seminar, we read Charles Taylor's magnum opus on secularism and modernity. These two books, alongside many others, inspired this project, which looks at the ways that people living in modernity *do* religion while calling it something else—*mysticism* or *spirituality*—and the roles that Orientalism and the religious marketplace play in their articulations of human experience.

I was helped by many people along this journey who read drafts, made suggestions, and provided encouragement. I owe a special debt to Blayne Harcey, my writing buddy for many years, who read a draft of this book while en route to India and sent feedback from his temporary home in Nepal. To my other readers, Rose Deighton, Cyrus Ali Zargar, Julie Todd, Ted Vial, Emran El-Badawi, thank you, and to Jean Charney, my longtime editor, I am grateful for your friendship and meticulous critiques.

As I launched into the writing of this book, I received support from many of the wonderful people at Western Kentucky University. Among these, I would like to especially thank Jeffrey Samuels, my department head and colleague, our steadfast dean, Larry Snyder, and colleagues Andrew Rosa, Audrey Anton, and Elizabeth Gish.

Finally, I would like to thank my mom, my dear husband, and our children. Their love makes the world a better place.

Introduction

In the centre of a Catholic village of around 800 households in northern Germany is a small roadside shrine of the Virgin with the Infant. Behind it stands a building with a bright red roof, through the centre of which rises a "Hindu temple tower". It houses a German Heilpraktiker (healing practitioner) and his spa. One enters an enclosed courtyard through a curtain of multicoloured glass beads to be greeted by soft music, with Ayurvedic treatment wings for men and women on either side.

Harish Narindas[1]

The search for enchantment in the modern world rarely entails the decades-long religious labor of the early Christian desert fathers or the Buddha's lifetime struggle to achieve enlightenment. More commonly, modern mysticism is characterized by a kind of dilettantism, a lifestyle that consists of a CD of Deepak Chopra meditations on Rumi, a subscription to Oprah's magazine, and a yoga retreat in Bali. As we shall learn, Orientalism often plays a powerful role in these products and practices, seen in everything from Buddhist sex toys to the mystical tourism found in Thailand, Indonesia, and Morocco.

This book examines mysticism from several vantage points: historically, as a concept invented in Western academia;

theoretically, in its function as an arm of capitalism; critically, through its identification with Orientalism and other colonial projects; and materially, through many of its products and practices. The first three chapters deal with these historical, theoretical, and critical issues. The last three chapters focus on the material culture of popular mysticism, its ties to Orientalism, and the ways it is expressed in popular television and film. Later, in this introduction, I will outline these chapters, but first I want to foreground my work by touching upon some of the forces that shape modern mysticism—capitalism, colonialism, and Orientalism.

COLONIZATION, CAPITALISM, AND MODERNITY

Mysticism and its entanglement with the Orient is seen broadly in the consumer culture of North America and Europe. Popular code words like *mysticism* and *spirituality* are used to sell products and experiences to the bliss chique, casual Sufi, imitation Hindu, and hipster Buddhist.[2] Individuals can combine these traditions with others—like Kabbalah, African spirituality, and Native American mysticism—without ever being identified as part of a religious community. One of the appeals of Orientalized mysticism to spiritual seekers, which may include ex-Christians, self-declared secularists, and the *Nones*, the group who claim to be "spiritual, but not religious" (also called "metaphysicals"), is that it rejects religious hierarchies and the institutions that support them.[3] This is modern mysticism.

The search for religious meaning in modernity often involves the colonization of other cultures. This is often unintentional and unconscious, where consumers browse a kind of mystical flea market in which the bright, shiny, and colorful objects stand out. The Orient is, for historical and aesthetic reasons we shall explore in the following chapters, a confused hodgepodge of images and cultures, symbols, and traditions. The phenomenon I call *muddled Orientalism* sustains a marketplace populated with mystical and spiritual products and experiences. Modern mysticism exists in a system of cultural exchange born of colonial encounters and transformed into entrepreneurism, dilettantism, and spiritual voyeurism through the creative force of Orientalism.

The twenty-first century is characterized by capitalism, globalism, and consumption, all affecting the ways in which individuals explore and experience religion. Scholarship on religion and consumption has often focused on individuals consuming products that are identified with a specific tradition. For instance, American Hindus produce a large number of religious goods and also are active consumers of religious items. As one scholar notes:

> A vast array of objects and items carrying religious symbolism is associated with the everyday religious practices and rituals of Indian American Hindus, including sculpted and painted images of Hindu gods and goddesses, framed pictures, bells, incense sticks, deity-specific items, prayer altars, and more transient items like fresh fruits, flowers and leaves for making garlands and decorations.[4]

Hindus, Christians, Muslims, and Buddhists have rich histories of material culture, but as we shall learn, modernity has expanded the market for these products beyond the individuals located in distinct religious communities. Scholars describe this expansive space the *religious marketplace.*

Some religious practitioners are successful in the religious marketplace through their attentiveness to the economic and social trends of the time. Joel Osteen is one of several televangelists known for the prosperity gospel, which is "a powerful example of the economic system the aesthetic image prefers."[5] As Luke Winslow writes, the prosperity gospel is popular in part because it "resonates with the secular, economic, and aesthetic rationales already in place."[6] As one of North America's most successful *pastorpreneurs*, Osteen is both preacher and savvy businessman.[7] Not simply a Christian preacher, he is also a New Age spiritualist guru. Even though he identifies as a pastor and many of his customers are Christian, he combines "self-help, positive thinking, and the pursuit of happiness and prosperity with spirituality."[8] Osteen is a neoliberal capitalist who knows his market well, and he is not alone.

The religious marketplace is not limited to North America. Indonesia has several successful *pastorpreneurs*—who I call *imampreneurs*—including Aa Gym (Abdullah Gymnastiar), a popular Islamic preacher whose teachings include tolerance, cleanliness (*kebersihan ialah sebagian dari iman*, "cleanliness is next to godliness"), and prosperity (making money and having a good business sense).[9] Buddhism participates in this game as well. His Holiness the Dalai Lama "has appeared in advertisements for Mercedes Benz and Microsoft."[10] Osteen and Aa Gym sell their products to fellow Christians and Muslims, while the mystical entrepreneurs discussed in this book colonize imagery, practices, and symbols from other religions and sell them as something non-religious—as *mystical* and *spiritual*.

Osteen, Aa Gym, and the Dalai Llama all represent the ways in which religion functions in the marketplace as a *commodity*. Religions associated with the East—Hinduism, Buddhism, Islam—are also commodified. Their symbols are marketed by entrepreneurs and corporations and then consumed by everyone from non-religious spiritualists to ambivalent mystical seekers. These consumptive patterns often reflect the aversion felt by some individuals around organized, institutionalized religion. This rejection of religious identity often includes a distrust of authority. Mysticism and spirituality are innocuous terms that appeal to those seeking understanding, health, or personal growth, but who reject an overt religious identity. As we shall learn, the appeal of mysticism is situated in part in a kind of apathy with modernity—a search for magic in a disenchanted world.

The vague quality of mysticism often results in behaviors, or even a lifestyle, characterized by cultural colonialism. In the United States, African American culture is the most popular target of these practices. In rap and hip-hop music, white singers often use AAE (African American English) as part of their performative identity. Eminem is an example of "a non-native user performing the language in a native-like manner, commodifying blackness for increased profitability in the marketplace."[11] These kinds of practices are so widespread that they often go unnoticed. In the 2018 film *Crazy Rich Asians*, the character played by the comedian Awkwafina used African American speech as a comic ploy. Black culture is often so commodified and globalized that it is difficult to notice all the places it is found in music, film, and fashion. In this case, the appeal of Awkwafina's speech was due, at least in part, to the popularity of African American cultural forms in North American society.

MUDDLED ORIENTALISM

The religions of the Orient are colonized in different ways. The colonization is often sloppy—such as the Buddha quotes mistaken for Rumi verses of poetry. I call this careless mixing of images, terms, and tropes from the imagined Orient *muddled Orientalism.* At times one part of the Orient is transposed to another, representing the fictive nature of Orientalism. One literary example of this transposition is the metaphor of unveiling, identified with the colonization of places like Egypt, Algeria, and Morocco, but also used to describe the British invasion of Tibet. Edmund Candler's account of Tibet is even titled the "unveiling of Lhasa, suggesting how unveiling was used to signify conquest in numerous Oriental landscapes."[12] Commonly, the Orient exists as a tableau of exoticism, visualized in stories and films that display a hodgepodge of imagery that communicates an aesthetic of difference that is *nowhere but everywhere*. This muddled Orientalism characterizes much of modern mysticism. As one example, a "Sufi" practice listed in a meditation app is titled "Kundalini Gong Breath Meditation."[13] It is not Islamic, but in reality, a Hindu/Sikh/Kundalini meditation—a perfect example of muddled Orientalism.[14]

As suggested above, even distinct religious figures like the Buddha and Rumi are often confused. The New Age goddess is another contemporary mystical character that reflects muddled Orientalism. According to her followers, she is the once-powerful universal female, whose importance is negated by thousands of years of patriarchy. She is not culturally specific, but rather, she is a combination of "Celtic, Near Eastern, Greek, Roman, Indian, African, and other indigenous goddesses."[15] The goddess movement, like many modern mystical trends, looks to others for its inspiration—to the Orient, the continent of Africa, and Native American traditions.

The goddess appears at *tribe events* (discussed at length in later chapters) and mystical gatherings, but she is also popular in spiritually centered fitness programs inspired by the East such as belly dancing. This "ethnic dance" borrows from Arab and other dance forms. As it turns out, even the phrase "belly dancing" is an appropriated term, inspired by an Orientalist painting by Jean Léon-Gérôme. Belly dancing also features music that combines elements from around the world and markets it as "global," using hybridized styles of costuming, and adopting names like Gypsy Caravan.[16] As Barbara Sellers-Young notes, "Regardless of the quality of the evidence of a historical link between the goddess and the dance, an entire belief system and related iconography has been constructed within the belly-dance community. It includes images of goddesses from ancient Greece, Egypt and Mesopotamia including Aphrodite,

Athena and Isis."[17] This imagery exists within a larger Orientalist–Islamic iconographic milieu that includes costuming that is reminiscent of the harems of Hollywood films.

Muddled Orientalism is also found at locations rumored to be mystically powerful, which are sometimes referred to as *spiritual centers*. For example, one modern mystic claims that a "karmic cluster" related to King Arthur is located at Glastonbury, in southwest England.[18] This example of the overlaying of Hinduism on British geography only scratches the surface, for the town of Glastonbury features a bazaar of religions from Buddhism to Sufism. Consumers can pick and choose the form of religion or mysticism they want to experience, or they can experience many traditions simultaneously. The marketing behind Glastonbury's many festivals illustrate some of the ways in which modern mysticism sustains numerous businesses.

The creation of products tied to things like *karmic clusters* (centers of karmic power) has not missed the attention of scholars. Faegheh Shirazi introduces the idea of the "clever tool" to describe religious ideas and symbols that may exist as ploys designed to sell products.[19] Although Shirazi's work is focused on the branding of Islam through *halal* products, what she calls "Brand Islam," clever tools can be seen in other markets that use religious symbols as a way to sell products. Other products exploit the appeal of religions like Buddhism, seen, in particular, in the business of mindfulness. As Jon Kabat-Zinn has warned, McMindfulness carries with it the danger of ignoring the foundational teachings of Buddhism.[20] Ironically, some of Kabat-Zinn's critics see his meditation programs as colonizing Asian religion, the very thing he warns against.

In many ways, mysticism is the ideal *clever tool* for the commodification of religion. It promises answers to loneliness, bodily ailments, and life's suffering through a yoga class, Ayurvedic elixir, or a holiday in Bali. This book explores modern mysticism through portable objects—yoga mats, Rumi books, Buddha bumper stickers—and experiential products like fitness programs (goat yoga!) and mystical tourism (also called spiritual tourism).

These products promise the consumer something different, which will alleviate the stresses of modern life. The "spiritual" person often engages in "mystical" practices, from mindfulness exercises to the Dances of Universal Peace, as an escape. There are also courses, vacations, and retreats where individuals can immerse themselves in mystical practices away from home. These holidays offer a more sustained experience through an "inversion of the everyday."[21] As we will learn, mystical tourism offers a respite from the modern world by traveling to the mythical East.

THEORETICAL VOICES

This book relies upon, and expands beyond, the textual and theoretical work I have engaged with in my past three monographs. I have spent many years studying Islam, Hinduism, Buddhism, Orientalism, mysticism, colonialism, and other topics in my field, and pondering the questions, theories, and debates that are discussed in the first three chapters of this book. In some cases, I have seen the business of mysticism in person—in North America, Morocco, Egypt, Syria, Turkey, Iran, Japan, and Indonesia. I am a religious scholar who is intimately familiar with the religions of Hinduism, Buddhism, and Islam, as well as with the field of religious studies more broadly. However, in addition to my own training and expertise, I looked to novel approaches and emerging methodologies that would enrich my study of modern mysticism.

Virtual ethnography is a key part of this project, which I utilized in my study of web-based sources on mysticism, spirituality, and in particular, mystical tourism. For guidance in this area, I turned to Kayla Wheeler, who proposes guidelines for conducting this type of ethnography and treating these communities as "cultural artefacts and sites of culture."[22] I visited the websites of mystical tourism resorts and retreats, studied the public Facebook posts of businesses geared toward mystical seekers, and surveyed products directed at the consumer that featured the Buddha, Rumi, and other so-called "Eastern" mystics. Following Wheeler's ethical parameters, I was conscious of the pitfalls of social media such as the lack of privacy. Mindful of these concerns, I only utilized public posts and content in this book. As Wheeler states, public posts on Facebook and other social media posts of public figures, "constitute a public text."[23] The promotion of businesses on social media through websites and on visual platforms like YouTube is public and thus free of the ethical concerns that private social media posts would bring to my scholarship.

This book is inspired by many important voices from the fields of religious studies, philosophy, critical theory, and anthropology, which I want to acknowledge here. Due to the interdisciplinary nature of this book and of my field, religious studies, I utilize scholars from numerous other fields as well. I would like to begin with *Virtual Orientalism*, the idea proposed by Jane Naomi Iwamura in her 2011 book of the same title. As Iwamura explains, images are powerful influences on the consumer, impacting purchasing trends as well as helping to define religious and pseudo-religious (i.e. spiritual) experiences. This book examines iconic figures from Hinduism, Buddhism, and Islam, including the Mahesh (Maharishi), the Dalai Lama, the Buddha, and Rumi, whose visual representations in contemporary media reinforce "Orientalism's hold on Western imagination."[24]

The power of the social imagination, which Iwamura is so attentive to, was a topic examined in my book *Muslims in the Western Imagination* (Oxford, 2011), but here I am interested not so much in how negative portrayals of the Other are formulated, but rather how positive and romanticized portrayals function in the commodification of religion. The characters that inspire the products of Eastern mysticism—the gentle Buddhist monk, the enlightened Hindu guru, and the wise Sufi master—are male icons fixed in the power of the West's mystical imagination. They are, as Baudrillard would posit, *simulacra*—reproduced images that refer to the original stereotype.[25] These are believed to be more real than reality itself, in part because "the difference between original and copy falls away."[26] This was Said's point as well: that the fictive Orient becomes the real Orient in the minds of the colonizer. The concept of simulacra helps us understand the business of mystical tourism, for what is presented is often a copy of what people desire: an experience that cannot be quantified. For example, there is literally a "staging" of authenticity that takes place in mystical tourism, where the performance of spirituality is part of the commercial exchange at the basis of tourism.[27]

As I note above, religious studies is an interdisciplinary field that is heavily influenced by the discipline of philosophy. Zygmunt Bauman has written extensively on modernity and "liquid modernity." In liquid modernity, individual validation is no longer a matter of "imagined totality," but rather of "life politics" that are focused on meaning-making.[28] The mystical marketplace is focused on creating products and experiences that create meaning. As Bauman puts it:

> This does not mean, of course, that the truths for individual validation and the raw stuff of which individuals would mould their meanings have stopped being socially supplied; but it does mean that they tend to be now media-and-shops supplied, rather than being imposed through communal command; and that they are calculated for *seducing clients* rather than *compelling the subordinates*.[29]

The seductive power of the Orient is seen in the products outlined in this book, which rely on a kind of exotic allure. To be sure, modern mysticism features the seductive qualities through forms of Hinduism, Buddhism, or Islam that are removed, rearticulated, and sold in the religio-spiritual marketplace. It is, using Bauman's words, part of liquid modernity.

Many images and ideas associated with the East, such as yoga, function as powerful symbols in public. Yoga, like many of the religious traditions from the East examined in this book, has become capital—sold and bought like any other product. The late anthropologist Lévi-Strauss called these *floating signifiers*. James Faubion describes a floating signifier as "a meaning-bearing unit that nevertheless has no distinct meaning, and so is capable of bearing any meaning, operating within any given linguistic system as the very possibility of signification."[30] Images of the Buddha, the lotus flower, Rumi, and Shiva function in this way—attached to products as fluid symbols of the exotic and the promise of the East. Floating signifiers sustain certain ideas about the Orient and its religious cultures. Circling back to Iwamura, she argues something along these lines when she writes about the visual forms of Orientalism:

> These forms train the consumer to prefer visual representations and the visual nature of the image lends the representation an immediacy and ontological gravity that words cannot. Thus, the Asian sage is not simply someone we imagine, but his presence materializes in the photograph or moving picture before us. Buttressed by newsprint or a film's story line, the visual representation adds gravitas to the narrative and creates its own scene of virtual encounter.[31]

As Iwamura points out, a large part of the business of mysticism involves the idealization of the Orient, its peoples, and traditions. This involves casting the Hindu, the Buddhist, or the Muslim as a type of pre-modern noble savage who imparts knowledge to the North American or European spiritual seeker.

A critical piece of this process of idealization is the denial of coeval time. The anthropologist Johannes Fabian has written extensively about this problem and more specifically, how the scholar often places the Other in a different time, denying him or her the same space we occupy. "The history of our discipline reveals that such use of Time almost invariably is made for the purpose of distancing those who are observed from the Time of the observer."[32] The denial of coeval time places the mystic Oriental in the past, affecting the way that people and places are conceptualized. This denial is a powerful force in the modern mystical marketplace, casting the traditions of Hinduism, Buddhism, and Islam as ancient pathways for solving modernity's problems. In modern mysticism, the East becomes fetishized, offering a space through gratification—through practices, products, and experiences—that is missing in one's normative existence. The Orient's magic and spirituality is presented as the antithesis to the modern West and its post-Enlightenment commitment to rationality and logic.

While the focus of this book is on three major religious traditions associated with the East, other religions and communities come into the conversation, including Native American, African, African American, and Jewish—most notably, Kabbalah. Christian theology is also an important part of modern mysticism that informs the way some consumers negotiate the marketplace. The identification of mysticism with health and wellness is a key theme in this book. In Western culture, the idea of the *favored* is situated in the theology of the human body as an expression of divine sacredness. As Luke Winslow explains, being overweight is "symbolic of a moral and divine offense."[33] The idea of the *unfavored* is key in Joel Osteen's prosperity gospel, but it is also linked to New Age ideas of self-help and spirituality, which play a critical role in the cohabitation of mysticism and wellness, including the many products, therapies, and practices discussed in the following chapters. The image of the favored also plays a role in mystical tourism, where being healthy, thin, and happy are of utmost importance.

Michel Foucault, who has influenced much of my past work, has a strong voice in this book as well—first, through his notion of the "technologies of the self," the practices "which permit individuals to affect their own means or with the help of others a certain number of operations on their own bodies and souls, thoughts, conduct, and way of being, so as to transform themselves in order to attain a certain state of happiness, purity, wisdom, perfection or immortality."[34] These technologies are central to the business of mysticism, what Wade Clark Roof called the "commodification of the self in modern society."[35]

Foucault's *heterotopias* are also an important part of this study. Heterotopias, or counter-sites, attempt to represent a utopia but are, in fact, marked by their *difference*. As he explains, in addition to utopias:

> There are also, probably in every culture, in every civilization, real places—places that do exist and that are formed in the very founding of the society—which are something like counter-sites, a kind of effectively enacted utopia in which the real sites, all the other real sites that can be found within the culture, are simultaneously represented, contested, and invented.[36]

The business of mysticism, with its spas, health retreats, and mystical destinations, offers numerous heterotopic spaces. Foucault distinguishes between two types of heterotopias—those of crisis (troubled adolescents, the elderly) and those of deviation (countercultural types, hippies)—and modern mysticism contains both of these, for people in existential crisis formulate alternative identities that point to the crisis of modernity.

Chapter One focuses on some of the challenging definitional issues at play in the study of mysticism and spirituality. As we will learn, these challenges are often due to the cohabitation of colonialism, race, and religion in formulations of modern concepts like mysticism. In order to define our subject, I propose we describe this as *modern mystic-spirituality*. This is a way to acknowledge the relationship between these concepts and their entwined histories in the study of religion and production of knowledge. Modern mystic-spirituality is defined as *the search for meaning outside institutionalized religion in modernity that often involves contemplation, the search for meaning, and an end goal that is beneficial to the physical, emotional, or/and psychological health of the individual through the use of religious practices and traditions sourced from numerous places, especially the Orient/East.*

This book covers a lot of ground. The study of mysticism in Western academia, the mystical marketplace, Orientalism, cultural colonialism, Hinduism, Buddhism, Islam, and mystical television and film are the main areas explored. The challenges in organizing this material weighed heavily on me and, in the end, I settled on three chapters focused on the unpacking of historical and definitional questions involving commodification, modernity, religion, mysticism, Orientalism, and colonialism. This foregrounding is necessary to understand the force of mysticism today, how it moves in the world, and what work it does in people's lives. Three chapters then follow that center upon the expression of Orientalism in the marketplace, with a particular focus on Hinduism, Buddhism, and Islam and their expression in products, health regimens, vacations, and entertainment.

SUMMARY OF CHAPTERS

The first chapter takes us on a journey through the history of mysticism. This serves as the foundation for the remainder of the book. As a concept in academia that emerged in an Orientalist milieu, the idea of mysticism was, in many ways, a project about defining the true religion of Protestant Christianity and fitting everything else into that vision of the world. In Western academe, the religions of the East were a product of invention (Hinduism), polemics (Islam), or romanticism (Buddhism) incongruent with the ways in which people lived out their religious lives. These newly defined topics of study were also identified with mysticism, located in the exotic Orient. The exotic still holds a special place in modern mysticism, and it is often connected to the East and its religious traditions. This chapter concludes with a meditation on the ways in which the mystical expresses itself in *tribe events* like Burning Man and the Hanuman Festival, which offer Orientalist adventures for the artist, yoga student, and spiritual seeker.

Chapter Two looks at the ways in which the Orient is assumed by products, practices, and lifestyles by consumers of mysticism. The religious cultures of Hinduism, Buddhism, and Islam are subject to colonization through numerous mechanisms, but this chapter primarily focuses upon three topics: the practice of cultural colonization, whitewashing of mysticism, and the branding of Oriental mysticism in products from priv-lit (like *Eat, Pray, Love*) to the "kid-calming mist" sold on *goop*, Gwyneth Paltrow's hugely successful company.

Chapter Three discusses the business of mysticism. This chapter introduces the idea of mystical capitalism (similar to Kathryn Lofton's "spiritual capitalism") and its role in what I call the *mystical marketplace*, by placing it within a larger discussion about consumers, including the Nones, individuals who claim to be spiritual-but-not-religious. I propose that these spiritual quests, which range from yoga to mystical tourism, are symptoms of the frustration and apathy experienced by people living in modernity. The appeal of mysticism is in part an escape, but it is situated in capitalist practices, and thus involves commodification and cultural colonization, topics taken up in greater detail in the following chapters on Hinduism, Buddhism, Islam, and television and film.

Chapters Four, Five, and Six explore the material expressions of Orientalism and mysticism in specific ways through four specific topics—the mystification of Hinduism, Buddhism, and Islam, and mystical television and cinema. Chapter Four focuses on Hinduism and Buddhism. In many ways, these are intertwined traditions, but in the minds of many modern mystical seekers they become translated into a *generalized* Eastern spirituality. This chapter looks at the history of Buddhism and Hinduism in North American mystical movements. Considerable attention is also given to the mystical tourism attached to these traditions, especially in places such as Bali.

Chapter Five examines Sufism, presented in the mystical marketplace as a multi-religious form of mysticism (a claim I strongly contest). Sufism's appeal is seen in the popularity of its most famous poets Rumi and Hafiz, and in its identification with Orientalist styles, seen in Rumi-themed restaurants. Mystical tourism also focuses on Sufi spirituality, especially in locations such as Tukey and Morocco. Much like Hinduism and Buddhism, modern mysticism whitewashes Sufism. This is a problem of particular concern in North America, where Black Muslim culture—Malcolm X, Muhammad Ali, and hip-hop—is erased from the popular narrative espoused by self-declared Sufis.

In the final chapter, I look at the broad appeal of the mystical Orient in the general public. In particular, I am interested in its expression in television and film. Granted, the presence of Orientalist themes, symbols, and images in entertainment, and the role of mysticism in these cultural expressions, is a topic worthy of a book-length study. Indeed, this is a topic I plan to publish an entire monograph on. For the purposes of this book, however, I focus on one example each of mystic television and mystic cinema—*Lost* and *Star Wars*. While not unique in their adaption of Orientalism and use of mystical narratives, they include particularly strong elements of Hinduism, Buddhism, and Islam.

Lost and *Star Wars*, much like mindfulness retreats and Sufi-themed holidays, promise people an escape from their mundane lives. I am deeply sympathetic to the search for enchantment that is in the minds and hearts of many consumers. I am critical of the colonizing of religious traditions that are part of mystical consumerism, but the problem lies in capitalism's corruption of the foundational teachings and practices of these traditions, not in the search for transcendence. As one teacher confessed about the devaluation of mysticism through profit: "Ultimately, whatever enlightenment points to never increases or decreases in value, but what is lost is an appreciation for the preciousness and precariousness of those possibilities within human consciousness that remain the most sacred."[37]

1

Histories of Religion and Mysticism

The essence of Krishna consciousness, after all, is easy, "Simply chant Hare Krishna … If somebody does not want our rituals, that is not an important thing. We simply recommend that you chant, that's all."

Steven J. Gelberg[1]

Krishna Consciousness, like many other forms of modern mysticism, proposes that the Orient offers an answer to modernity's problems. This chapter looks at the history of mysticism as an idea. How did we arrive at this place, where mysticism is viewed as an easy path and the antithesis to the post-Enlightenment's disenchantment with religion? The bifurcation of the world into West and East, modern and ancient, orthodox and mystical, is strongly Orientalist. Said described this perspective as "a set of structures inherited from the past, secularized, redisposed, and re-formed" situated in a system of classification.[2] These are the structures that help to sustain the mystical marketplace.

This chapter tells the story of how the *idea* of mysticism evolved as a part of colonial history, explores its relationship to the study of Hinduism, Buddhism, and Islam, and explains how these ideas about religion shape the products and lifestyles discussed in this book. Scholars created ideas like Hinduism (a word coined by the

British in India) and formulated visions of other religions of the Orient in a colonial milieu. Modern beliefs about mysticism are products of "a discursive history that is bound up with the power struggles and theological issues of Western Christianity."[3]

These ideas survive today as powerful forces in academia, the wellness industry, entertainment, and social life. The last chapter of this book focuses on mysticism's popularity in television and film, illustrating how other religious traditions are consumed through Hollywood entertainment. Countercultural festivals, also known as tribe events like Burning Man and Hanuman Festival, offer some of the newest spaces for the consumption of Eastern brands of mysticism through the performance of Buddhist rituals and the construction of Orientalist temples, Buddha robots, and Rumi slides. As we will learn, Burning Man shows how Orientalism is often expressed as a gendered, consumable landscape that offers enlightenment, healing, and spiritual renewal. Tribe events are a type of domesticated mystical tourism, offering spaces for spiritual renewal and mystical transformation in places such as Colorado, Nevada, or California.

Mystical tourism, which has a large share in the mystical marketplace, is popular in places identified with Hinduism, Buddhism, and Islam, such as Thailand, Bali, and Turkey. In a 2001 tourist commercial for Thailand, a robot is pictured in a tropical forest, at a nightclub, in a local Buddhist temple, and at the back of a traditional Thai fishing boat that travels "down a misty serene river with the sounds of nature of the dense forest on both sides."[4] At the end of the ad the robot transforms into a young Caucasian man, his body healed and restored by his discovery of a "humanity that makes him more human himself."[5] The Orient, and perhaps an Oriental person, heals his body and soul.

This commercial is an important reminder of the role gender plays in the history of Western ideas about mysticism. Centered around a male spiritual guide such as a Sufi shaykh, Buddhist monk, or Hindu guru, these characters identify religious authority with masculinity. Diverging from the gendered Orientalism of a sensualized East and the display of Muslim female bodies that promises the gratification of the colonizer or tourist, the mysticism of the East offers something else. As I have written elsewhere, this gendered Orientalism remains a powerful force in the world, "The seductive eyes behind the veil and the delights of the harem are but two of many representations of Muslim girls and women found in everything from advertising campaigns to Hollywood film."[6] Modern mysticism features a different kind of gendered Orientalism. Asian sages—the sadhu (holy man), the monk, the Sufi—are men who represent a different kind of gratification, one that is connected to religious experience, rather than sexual conquest.

The Oriental sage makes many appearances in this book. He is often feminized, moving quietly and speaking softly. Unlike other men from the East, such as the aggressive and sexualized Arab, he rarely poses a serious threat to Western power. Only in the cases of the libidinous guru and the threat of miscegenation is he of concern. A departure from such figures as the Japanese samurai and the Muslim despot, the sage is a queered figure—he is *different*. As Iwamura argues:

> Although the Oriental monk has appeared to us through the various media vehicles of American pop culture, we recognize him as the representative of an otherworldly (though perhaps not entirely alien) spirituality that draws from the ancient wellspring of "Eastern" civilization and culture. And as Americans' current love affair with such figures as the Dalai Lama attests, the representation of this icon has only gained in popularity and impact.[7]

The guru is important because he represents Orientalist discourse and the East's powerful and mysterious religious power. Gurus are located in the past—exemplifying Fabian's denial of coeval time. The mystics that popularized meditation, yoga, and Sufism were often viewed as *existing in another time*. As Iwamura points out, Suzuki, who helped to popularize Buddhism in North America, usually donned an American sports jacket and a pair of slacks, but newspapers chose portraits of him in the most "traditional attire."[8] These presentations illustrate one of the ways that mysticism and Orientalism are entangled in powerful ways.

As we embark on this journey through the history of mysticism, it is important to understand how powerful the identification of the Orient and mysticism remain. Consider *Eat, Pray, Love* (2006), Elizabeth Gilbert's popular self-help book. Gilbert tries to find meaning in yoga and meditation instruction in New York City, but it is not enough. So she goes to India to "experience 'the real thing,'" which is where the "source" of prayer and meditation is located.[9] Her language is almost identical to that of early Orientalists like Edward Lane who referred to Egypt as the "source" of all life. As is often the case in mystical tourism, Gilbert is healed through a native; in this case, a Balinese man. She even professes, "You healed me."[10]

What this brief introduction to mysticism shows us is that the East, whether identified in a spiritualist movement like Krishna Consciousness or at a location such as Thailand, India, or Bali, is often presented as the answer to modernity's problems. The Orient plays a critical role in modern mysticism. It is an exotic space one can travel to and from with great frequency, allowing the mystical seeker comfort when they need it. For Gilbert, the romance of poverty also brings with it the promise of mysticism. She literally seeks transformation from a "mystical" girl who "performs menial tasks as a way to achieve a constant meditative state."[11] In the search for transcendence, poverty is romanticized and identified as mystical, but always held at a safe distance.

DEFINITIONAL TRAPS

This chapter argues that mysticism is a category of knowledge that was created and is sustained by the creative force of Orientalism, both in the ivory tower of academia and in the mystical marketplace. As I pointed out in my Introduction, it is critical to understand how the idea of the mystical was constructed before looking at the ways in which it exerts power in the marketplace. Like other modern concepts in the academic study of religion, mysticism has been subject to the influences of history, political power, race, and colonialism. According to François Gauthier:

> The nation was the backdrop and background for the Westphalian and post-Reformation type of congregational Christianity in the West. This model was then disseminated worldwide through European imperialism and colonization. It became the template for the "invention" of religion in non-North Atlantic countries, as it was enforced and/or interiorized with variegated effects in the various cultural, societal, and historical contexts.[12]

As we shall learn, mysticism, like *religion*, is an invention of the Western academic that has been applied to other religious traditions, including Hinduism, Buddhism, and Islam, often in very problematic ways.

In recent years, several scholars have shown how our understanding of other people's religions is shaped by the colonial histories of politics and race. David Chidester's book on the influence of studies on Southern Africa on the comparative study of religion reminds us of this history and its relevance today. "As we have seen, the frontier has been an arena in which definitions of religion have been produced and deployed, tested and contested, in local struggles over power and position in the world. In such power struggles, the term religion has been defined and redefined as a strategic instrument."[13]

Mystical, spiritual, and New Age therapeutic models often utilize, or are inspired by, the East. At times, these models show how mysticism functions as a racial system. In Sandra Segal's Human Dynamics programs, which are very popular in Sweden, participants learn about prefabricated behaviors that are aligned with cultures. In this system, Europeans are "emotional" and Asians "practical."[14] This classification of human behavior relies on Darwinian ideas about race and behavior, illustrating just how powerful Western ideas about religion and mysticism are. The systems of power reflected in these ideas rely on a racialized view of the world. As Neda Maghbouleh reminds us, "race is a master status tied to group oppression and domination."[15]

Our understanding of religion and its related concepts—including mysticism—is shaped by post-Enlightenment ideas about truth, reality, and rationalism, as well as colonial interactions of Europe with the rest of the world. Jonathan Z. Smith famously wrote that religion is "the creation of the scholar's study ... with no independent existence apart from the academy."[16] The idea of religion is embedded in a history that compares "Christianity with itself" and in so doing, defines "corruption" in the practices of the Catholic, who is seen as prone to "superstition" and guilty of "Pagano-papism."[17] Catholicism was deemed suspicious by the scholar because of its mysticism. These are the critiques of religious tradition that worked themselves into Western scholarship. As we will learn, the mystical marketplace is built upon the idea that the Orient offers difference, a difference that sets it apart from the rationalism in Christianity and the modern West.

Religion is not a universal category of knowledge. Talal Asad has written that: "There cannot be a universal definition of religion, not only because its constituent elements and relationships are historically specific, but because that definition is itself the historical product of a discursive product of discursive processes."[18] Asad suggests that religion's "constituent elements," like mysticism, are also ideas created *by* scholars *for* other scholars. Mysticism is a product of this intellectual project and like religion, it is a category of human experience that is not easily worked out.

As the Buddhist scholar Richard Payne explains, ideas embedded in the Protestant Reformation, like mysticism, have real power: "Many of the Protestant reformers argued for a reduction in the number of sacraments—Christian rituals—or even more radically, the complete elimination of ritual from the church. Sacraments were felt to interfere with the individual's relationship to God."[19] How Hinduism, Buddhism, and Islam fit into this narrative of the world's religions was shaped by the interwoven history of colonialism and racism. One consequence of this process is that Christianity's own internal traditions, like Catholicism and Gnosticism, were placed in problematic categories. As April DeConick explains: "'Gnosticism' and 'Gnostic' are no exception to this deconstructive trend. They have been reduced to 'Christian.' This, of course, doesn't solve the problem but instead imposes another grand narrative on the early Christians, which domesticates Gnostic movements and presents them as no-nonsense *alternative* forms of Christianity."[20] If these are the ways Christianity is evaluated, one can quickly see how the study of other people's religions is on shaky ground. Orientalism is intimately involved in these evaluations of religion, which also involve a racially ordered vision of the world's religious traditions. According to George Lipton, "secular Sufism" is "built upon a revival of nineteenth-century Orientalist bifurcation between a Semitic Islam and a supposed Aryan mysticism."[21]

The idea of a rational–mystical dichotomy is very European, based in Kantian philosophy and used to cast the entire Orient as a mystical space.[22] As Lipton puts it, "the anti-Semitic, Protestant scholarship of nineteenth-century Europe mirrored Kant's racial historicism by portraying the divine commandments of Judaism and Islam as a coercive theocratic veneer covering a universal, autonomous spiritual core."[23] Obviously, this reflects racial anxieties when it defines white people as rational and other folks as mystical. This is important and as scholars have shown, both religion and mysticism are racialized categories of knowledge. Kant's evaluation of Judaism as a theocratic and slavish religion was compared to the pure and true religion of Christianity, a superior religion that was viewed as the foundation of a universal faith.[24] This idea of universalism is often at the core of modern mysticism, which often recasts Hindu, Buddhist, and Islamic traditions as forms of a universalized Christianity.

Ted Vial's 2016 book on religion and race opens with the following words: "Race and religion are conjoined twins. They are offspring of the modern world. Because they share a mutual genealogy, the category of religion is always already in a racialized category, even when race is not explicitly under discussion."[25] Race and religion reveal themselves in numerous spaces, including in the study of mysticism, which is often cast as a form of secret, eternal Christianity. "In this essentialized and anti-Semitic conceit, Islam is understood as *inherently* intolerant and incompatible with Western secularism, while Sufism (commonly referred to as Islamic mysticism) is claimed to be profoundly tolerant and secular *because* similar to Christianity."[26] There are elements of dressing up, costuming, adopting, and performing other cultures that constitute a big part of the mystical marketplace. The mystical marketplace often whitewashes traditions, keeping racial differences at a safe distance.

Mysticism is often identified with the East and its traditions, which had great appeal for early scholars and travelers, much like their attraction for consumers today. These more precise histories, focused on the rebranding of Hinduism, Buddhism, and Islam, are taken up in Chapters Four and Five. However, it is important to know that the East had been a tableau for Western fantasies long before the emergence of the mystical marketplace, Oprah's Favorite Things, and Gwyneth Paltrow's company *goop*.

As we will learn in Chapter Four, Tibet is a place on which numerous wishes and desires were imposed, a process which continues to this day. As Dibyesh Anand notes:

> While early Christians sought traces of a forgotten community of Christians here, theosophists looked for the lost brotherhood of wise hermits. In the mid-19th century, Joseph Wolff popularized the idea of a long-lost population of Jews in the Himalayas. On the other hand, the Nazi SS sent an expedition in 1938–39 to ascertain whether Tibet was an abode of true Aryans or not.[27]

Fantasies were imposed on Tibet far earlier than this, in fact. Herodotus (d. 425 B.C.E.) wrote of the "most extreme lands of the earth" where giant ants dug up gold, and thieves had to work fast to escape the monsters before they smelled them.[28] In the 1800s, Tibet was imagined as a lost biblical land, the site of "a remote, but powerful, people on Mount Zion at the end of time" as prophesied by Isaiah.[29] Tibet continues to have a powerful place in Western ideas about mysticism, but it has company in the larger Orient—Morocco, Bali, Egypt, Turkey, and elsewhere. The colonial encounters in these lands, and in particular in India, were where British colonial agents, scholars, and artists invented what we now know as modern mysticism.

INVENTING MYSTICISM

The problems with the definitions of religion outlined above extended their reach into the study of mysticism. Early scholars of religion often described mysticism as the antithesis to a modern, rational, textually based religious life, as if religious mystics had no access to texts. As scholars of religion are well aware, the concepts of mysticism, Hinduism, Buddhism, and Islam are part of a larger system of power. The construction of religion *is* part of the colonial apparatus of knowledge. Western perceptions of Hinduism, Buddhism, and Islam are inventions—constructions of meaning embedded in the power structures of European empire. As Richard King has shown in his work, the traditions of the Orient have been presented in a profoundly Christian language, suggesting that the universalism we see in mysticism has an important genealogy that reveals much about the way world religions were constructed. In one eighteenth-century study of religion, the author claims that the Buddha was a "heavenly spirit" who left "Paradise," and describes the ultimate goal of Buddhism to be "union with God."[30]

Mysticism is closely connected to the idea of a mystic India that inspired the countercultural Eastern spirituality associated with the Beatles and other celebrities. In the 1960s and 1970s, India became popular as part of the hippie trail, featuring middle- and upper-class Americans (and Europeans) drawn to Hinduism and Buddhism. This "spiritual turn to the East" is part of a larger process that sees a rejection of "the cold consumer society of the West" in favor of the "inherent spirituality" located in the East.[31]

Spirituality is a commodified and contemporary form of mysticism that universalizes religious traditions and markets them—often in the service of the wellness industry. Jeremy Carrette and Richard King explain spirituality as a kind of disguise, a clever play on the idea of mysticism that "is a means of colonizing and commodifying Asian wisdom traditions."[32] The East, much like in the age of classical Orientalism, became associated with the promise of "instant enlightenment," which as scholars have pointed out, included the idea of "pleasure."[33] The idea of instant gratification as part of a mystical practice is known as *immediatism* and is seen in the Krishna Consciousness example that opens this chapter. In the words of Arthur Versluis, immediatism is "a perspective emphasizing direct and immediate access to spiritual insight, and does not carry along with it ancillary doctrines that valorize ancient religions and cultures or for that matter, contemporary world religious traditions."[34] Immediatism is at the center of much of modern mysticism, from online mindfulness programs to Sufi retreats promising a profound change in one's life.

During the colonial period, Indian culture was described vis-à-vis European religious sensibilities, casting Asian religions in terms of exoticism, ritual, and emotions, in contrast to the restrained Protestant Christianity of the British. As Iwamura notes: "All around him, the British colonialist found examples of social confusion and spiritual excess that it was his responsibility to contain—if only by literary means."[35] Mysticism was framed as a symptom of this spiritual excess. It also became embedded in both the comparative study of religion and the evolutionary theory of religion. In Ted Vial's study of religion and race, he reminds us that concepts used in religious studies are part of an anthropology, a culture, and an identity that is Christian and white. The ways in which mysticism is deployed—against Catholics as well as Hindus, Buddhists, and Muslims—is part of a larger strategy of self-identification formulated by racial concerns. As Vial puts it:

> Modern religion and race are the offspring of a new theological anthropology. This anthropology recreates race and religion because it reformulates the relationship between the individual and the group. It makes group membership an organic part of personal existence and identity; it shows how an individual is shaped by the group to which the individual belongs. It leads moderns to infer certain expectations about behavior, about moral dispositions, and about intellectual abilities based on group membership.[36]

Hinduism is perhaps the most dramatic case of academic invention in the story of mysticism, and as one would guess, it became a useful academic and colonial tool of the British. In fact, Hinduism did not exist as part of the vernacular before British Orientalists codified it into law, ultimately constituting a mark of identity in modern India. As King writes: "The term 'Hinduism,' which of course derives from the frequency with which 'Hindu' came to be used, is a Western explanatory construct. As such, it reflects the colonial and Judaeo-Christian presuppositions of the Western Orientalists who first coined the term."[37]

The early study of Buddhism involved more creative interpretation than outright invention. Scholars initially identified Buddhism as an African religion, then a cult of Shiva, before it was ultimately cast as an Eastern form of "correct religion" that, like Christianity, "resides in scriptural texts, in formal doctrine."[38] Initially, Buddhism was identified solely with texts—an effort to make it into "an agnostic, rationalist, ethical individualism grounded in philosophical reflection."[39] Later, it went through other transformations, affected by Romantic ideas of the East, the mysticism identified with other traditions, and a particularly Christian understanding of the world. All of this resulted in the idea of Buddhism we see now, "With its reduction to classic texts and avoidance of both practicing monks and a rich ritual life, the western construction of Buddhism seems particularly affected by a Protestant understanding of religion."[40] As Richard Horsley explains, Buddhism is one of several traditions that offer a path back to religious experience:

> Given the reduction of religion to individual faith or spirituality, then, is it any wonder that many Westerners felt that something was seriously lacking in their lives and in their society? The Buddhism constructed and consumed by Westerners is deeply implicated in the imperial relations in which western elites, longing to be more complete and

> whole again, looked to subjected peoples for the sources of their own salvation and healing—to Buddhist wisdom and meditation, to Native American closeness to the earth and sweat lodges, to African American spirit and vitality.[41]

In the United States, the first public efforts aimed at educating the public about Buddhism were seen in the late nineteenth century. The World's Parliament of Religions meeting in 1893 was held as part of the 400th anniversary of Europe's "discovery" of the Americas, an event called the "Columbian Exposition."[42] The fact that this foray into religious studies took place at an event commemorating the colonization of the Americas is a point not lost upon scholars. The exposition took place at a time when affluent Americans were fascinated with the Orient. American Orientalism (discussed at length in the following chapter) influenced architecture, painting, clothing, and décor. It is no surprise that the interest in Buddhism at the exposition was largely focused on the clothing of Buddhists, including a "fascination with their silk robes."[43] In some ways, this fascination remains in force today through the visual culture of Buddhism, which is seen in the visage of the Buddha in popular culture on everything from yoga mats to T-shirts and bumper stickers.

The study of Islam was shaped by a profound Christian anxiety surrounding religion, race, and bodies, which at times involved strong polemical tirades against Islam and the vilification of Muslim men. As I have argued in earlier work, "When we consider Muslim monsters as a corpus—a genealogy of images that are related, at times closely, and at times through several degrees of separation—it is evident that they contribute to the ways in which Muslims are conceptualized today—as interruptions that disturb normative humanity, civilization, and modernity."[44] Sufism was separated from Islam through a process of whitewashing that described the tradition as Christian or universalistic. Today, Sufism is presented in the mystical marketplace as a form of universalistic spirituality. Rumi, a devout Muslim, is often portrayed as a dashing poet, a handsome vision in his robes and mustache.

India helped to define Sufism as an Oriental tradition located firmly outside Islamic circles. In this respect, Islam shares a similar history with Hinduism and Buddhism through the ways that scholars, and later, spiritual seekers and consumers, have rebranded its religious traditions. Beginning in the eighteenth and nineteenth centuries, scholars began to sever Sufism from Islam. "Sufism was presented as a different and esoteric practice mostly based on Neo-Platonic and Neo-Zoroastrian beliefs, rather than Islam."[45] Much like Aryan theories connected to the Hindus and Buddhists, scholars presented numerous theories about Sufism's origins. Among these was the racist proposition that Sufism was a miraculous reaction to Semitism by the Aryan mind.[46]

The erasure of Islam from Sufism is situated in larger Orientalist notions of religion that were discussed earlier in this chapter; in particular, the idea of a *true* religion versus all other religions. Today, modern "non-Muslim" Sufis reject a Muslim identity with great ease, carrying on the tradition established by scholars nearly two hundred years ago. In the nineteenth century, scholars insisted Sufism was a "mystical sect," which they often described in rather fantastic language. As William Rounseville Alger wrote in 1856:

> The Sufis are a sect of meditative devotees, whose absorption in spiritual contemplations and hallowed raptures is unparalleled, whose piety penetrates a depth where the mind gropingly staggers among the bottomless roots of being, in mazes of wonder and delight, and reaches to a height where the soul loses itself among the roofless immensities of glory in a bedazzled and boundless ecstasy.[47]

To some degree, the study of Islam has forged ahead, rejecting parts of Orientalism with great vigor. In other ways, the field remains entrenched in ideas that rely on this old system. Linguistic studies of Islam still reflect Orientalist notions of the golden age of Islam, located in the distant past, which is why Arabic, Persian, and Turkish continue to be the dominant languages of academic study. The field often ignores the largest populations of Muslims living in Southeast Asia. The denial of coeval time cited by Fabian, noted in my Introduction, is often present in these attitudes: "Once other cultures are fenced off as culture gardens or, in the terminology of sociological jargon, as boundary-maintaining systems based on shared values; once each culture is perceived as living in its Time, it becomes possible and indeed necessary to elevate the interstices between cultures to a methodological status."[48]

The universalizing of Sufism is taken up in greater detail in Chapter Five, but it is addressed here because of the part it plays in rebranding Islamic religious traditions as mysticism. Musical expressions of Sufism in North America and Europe often use words such as love, passion, questing, journeying, heart, and soul—keywords of New Age thought.[49] As Amira El-Zein argues, Rumi products are often marketed with the language of spirituality to appeal to an audience of mystical seekers: "It may be argued that Rumi's enormous success in America is due to the fact that Americans find in his work a whole program of spirituality that may be summarized in four points: love; the Sufi universe; illusion versus reality; silence and emptying the self."[50] By subscribing to this vision of Rumi, one can completely erase his Muslim identity. The promotion of sacred music in Morocco is an example of universalizing in the public sphere, where "the phenomenon of the sacred music festival draws on the religious sentiment evoked by sacred music to create a transnational (thus mobile) notion of the 'sacred' that is in many ways a counterpoint to the specificity and ideology of more orthodox forms of religious practice."[51]

In American Sufi movements, we see some of the ways in which Sufism exists—as a contemplative practice identified with Islam, a practice aligned with specific genealogical lineages, and the "essential stuff" of Islam. This last category is where we find the blurring of Sufism and New Age religion, the commodification of Sufi figures like Rumi, and the adoption of his poetry as spiritual teachings. Carl Ernst describes the existence of fake Sufism thus:

> The multiple "translations" of poets like Rumi and Hafiz illustrate a very postmodern concept of the poetic text. Almost none of these are by authors conversant with the original language, and while some like Coleman Barks are professional poets who work closely with translators and standard editions, there are "versions" of the Sufi poets that have no discernible relationship with any original text.[52]

Similar types of translation projects are seen with Hinduism and Buddhism, which become sold as yoga and meditation, Zen style, and mindfulness under the panopticon of modern capitalism.

Closely related to mysticism is the idea of *perennialism.* This once popular approach, identified with scholars like Mircea Eliade, whose writings included ideas such as a "transhuman Reality" and a vision of Sacred Time that offered Transcendence, is now out of fashion in much of academia.[53] Perennialism is the "many paths to one mountain" view of religion, which all have the same essence or in Eliade's phrasing, *Center.*[54] Today, it is viewed as a strongly problematic view that obfuscates the distinctions between different religious traditions while privileging Christian understandings of God, religion, and mystical experience. Aldous Huxley (1894–1963) founded the perennialism movement with his book *The Perennial Philosophy* (1945), an anthology of world mysticism that combines numerous concepts from Hinduism and Buddhism to create a mystical vision of the world.[55] As Douglas Osto points out: "In addition to using the terms

'Dharma-Body' (Sanskrit *dharmakāya*), 'Suchness' (*tathātā*), and 'Void' (*sūnyatā*), Huxley often uses 'Not-self' (for Pāli *anattā*; or Sanskrit *anātman*), and 'Mind at Large.'"[56] He saw psychedelics as a doorway to mystical experience, offering a fast track to what would normally take an individual decades to achieve.

Modern mysticism relies on a similar understanding of transcendence—one that is easy and quick, but also available for the right price. The idealization of mystical experiences—at times, through the use of mescaline or LSD—is problematic for many reasons, including the fact that experiences cannot be qualified. As Zaehner points out (*Mysticism, Sacred and Profane*, 1961), mystics do not experience the same things—mystical experience is not the same from person to person.[57] Religions are different, people are different, and mysticism—like religion—is not a native category. The idea that mystical experience is consistent is powerful, despite evidence to the contrary: "For instance, in Rinzai Zen particular importance is placed on the 'kensho experience,' a sudden flash of awakening; whereas in the modern practice of *vipassanā* as taught by S. N. Goenka, an experience of *bhanga*, or 'dissolution,' is valorized."[58]

Early scholars were challenged by the sophisticated religions of supposed "primitives" whose traditions impacted the idea of mysticism.[59] Mysticism is one of many categories used to describe other people's religious lives. In many cases, mysticism provided a safe category for complex traditions that could not be assigned into categories like "primitive," "animist," or "nature." Hinduism is perhaps the best example of this. It is an idea constructed out of the many religious communities in India by academics. Alternatively described as a way of life, a religion, and a cultural system, Hinduism's complexity defies categorization with its mystical practices through the sadhu (holy man), rituals like seeing God (*darśan*), and tradition of speculative philosophy.

Mysticism, much like other concepts in the academic study of religion, is an idea formulated with one specific religious tradition in mind—Christianity. The imposition of Western mysticism on other people's religions is so strong that Western thinkers have insisted on it, even in cases where it clearly makes no sense. As Richard King points out: "This is an astonishing statement to make—that the notions of God, communion, the soul and themes of a loving relationship between the two can be found in (actually imposed upon) all non-Christian religious experience."[60] While it is astonishing, these assumptions run through much of modern mysticism in ideas like the spiritual self (personal theology) and union with the Divine (the Logos).

Claims about mysticism are not just historically located in past European thought; they are also situated in a profoundly modern way of understanding the contemplative, spiritual, mystical life. These ways of understanding organize the world into "the rational knowledge of scientific empiricism and the inner knowledge of spiritual experience."[61] These ways of understanding are very vague, making it possible to fit all sorts of things under the umbrella of mysticism. Academia doesn't do much better. In one case, a scholar suggested a definition of mysticism as "spiritual practice and its experiential data."[62]

Universalism is one way to explain other people's traditions so that they fit into particular Christian ideas of God, theology, and religion. Statements like "God has many names" and phrases like "the Eternal One" and "integral spirituality" populate contemporary mystical writing.[63] Traditions that are spiritualized often have their own code language. In the case of Sufism, appeals to a "universal Islam" are found in the writings of James Frager and other universalistic Sufis.[64] Buddhism is often talked about in terms of karma, mindfulness, and enlightenment. In one study of Buddhism in Denmark, karma and tantra were used with far less frequency (151 and 32 times) than mindfulness (310 items), and of these 310 only 19 also mentioned Buddhism.[65] This example shows how a religious tradition can be translated into mysticism or spirituality. As we learn in Chapter Three, the erasure of religious traditions, including their sources, texts, and rituals, is part of the cultural colonization that benefits the mystical marketplace. The erasure of religion is one place this is seen, resulting in a silencing of religious communities and their traditions. Megan Sijapati describes the meditation corner of the mystical marketplace in this way: "Meditation and mindfulness practices now proffered in mainstream American culture as secular modalities of the wellness industry have demonstrable historical roots in dharmic religious traditions, particularly Buddhism and Yogic Hindu traditions, but in some cases Islam as well. The task then, for scholars of religion, is to trace the ways this elision of religion takes place and to interrogate what it means for religious institutions and religious communities."[66]

SPIRIT, SPIRITUALISM, SPIRITUALITY

As we have seen, Hinduism, Buddhism, and Islam are often mistranslated in the mystical marketplace. The theology of Rumi becomes a bumper sticker. Zen philosophical teachings become a decorative style. Yoga changes from something "to be achieved only by virtue (*punya*) gathered over many past lives" to an exercise program.[67] Modern yoga functions as a veritable expression of modernity, based on scientific claims and "as such highly rational and instrumental in its approach to explanatory frameworks for 'how it works.'"[68] To yogaphobics, it is posited as a modern threat to Christianity, failing to "search for an authentic form of yoga."[69] In the corporate world, Buddhism has been redefined to fit the capitalist model. As this study notes, Zen is seen as a way to create change in that world:

> Gabi believes that Zen Buddhism is the best source to employ for adapting a new strategy towards "change."

> According to him, Buddhism "relates to the world as something that changes all the time internally and externally. Once you accept it, your reaction to change is much better." In order to develop awareness of the "here and now," Gabi appropriates the Buddhist principle of impermanent reality and the concept of compassion. In his work with teams, he uses Buddhist meditative tools and focuses on topics such as burnout and change.[70]

Mysticism is certainly not limited to North America. In other contexts, syncretism and hybridization are processes that may lead to a turn away from traditional, organized religion. In Thailand, spirit traditions, astrology, and the Hindu flavor of many Buddhist practices reflect the hybrid practice of religion. The urbanization and mobility of Thailand's growing population includes a displacement of people's beliefs: "The sense of displacement, frustration and helplessness among the urban population often leads them to seek spiritual sanctuary through the worship of hybrid deities and their mediums."[71] Popular culture also encourages spiritualism in news stories and television shows that include "commercial biographies of popular magic monks, astrologers or spirit mediums; famous amulets; or tips for winning lottery numbers."[72]

Spirituality is really a *codeword* for mysticism. It is described as "a broad and holistic construct that crosses disciplines and approaches."[73] In one study, spirituality is attached to the following qualities: an urge for personal experience, a desire to see the big picture, letting go of the ego or self, resisting or moving beyond instant gratification, examining the meaning of life, believing in the unity of humans and creation, becoming integrated with others, being on a journey, using ritual, experiencing self-actualization, understanding that anything is possible, living in the present, accepting responsibility for one's own problems, being grateful, undergoing transformation, and understanding suffering as part of life's journey.[74] This list sounds a lot like modern mysticism. Mysticism and spirituality even share the same parasitical nature that feeds off other religions and cultures to sustain itself.

Mysticism has generated its own ancillary systems of meanings including its own set of code words such as *spirituality*. Spiritual seekers often identify as "seekers" of self-transformation:

> In all such instances, the quest culture finds its strongest version in explicit appeals to "seekers" using highly rationalized procedures and techniques at self-transformation. An omnipresent theme in such activities is the promise of greater discovery, experience and connection: participants are encouraged in their pursuits to discover the sacred, archetypal dimensions of life; to experience the divine energy that is within all of us; to discover the inner child; to be reunited with their inner guidance; to discover the joy of personal healing; to experience or at least get close to experiencing one's own underlying perfection; to connect with universal life forces; to experience their own bodies and sensual selves; to discover the infinite love that is within; and to experience more fully the powers of beauty, creativity, life, and joy within each person.[75]

One scholar describes spiritualism as the "old gnosis" that rejects the post-Reformation and post-Enlightenment view of the world and includes a long list of traditions, movements, and belief systems, "the hermetic, magical, alchemical, astrological, and occult traditions; Islamic and Hindu mysticism; Kabbalah; Zen; I Ching; Tarot; Taoism; chakra yoga; Buddhist tantra; and ancient Gnosticism."[76]

Spiritualism has a long history in the United States that has seen a resurgence in recent years in the popularity of mystical products and experiences. Early spiritualism was present in colonial New England among the Quakers, and in healing practices that included prescribing the pharmaceuticals of the day.[77] Nineteenth-century Spiritualist leaders such as Andrew Jackson Davis (1826–1926), while describing God as a "substance" and a kind of matter, did not always look to Eastern religions for their spiritual theologies.[78] At times their ideas were very much situated in post-Reformation Christian thought. Other leaders, for example, Charles W. Leadbeater, were deeply influenced by Hinduism, illustrated in the title (and content) of his 1927 book, *The Chakras*.[79] As is the case with the Nones and New Agers, Leadbeater viewed the *chakras* as an integral part of the mystical path that ultimately brought the individual into union with the Divine.

As I noted earlier, modern spiritualism is popular with Nones, unchurched believers, and followers of New Age religion. Scholars have pointed out that New Agers and evangelicals also have similarities—in particular, in their search for meaning and an immediate and intense connection to the Divine.[80] Immediatism is much like mysticism in that it does not promote specific practices.[81] It has long been popular in the United States, including "Ralph Waldo Emerson in Transcendentalism, William S. Burroughs in the Beats, Robert Anton Wilson in Discordianism, and René Guénon in Traditionalism."[82] Today, figures like Eckhart Tolle and Oprah Winfrey, for example, might be considered popular spiritualists.

The search for wellness is an important part of spiritualism and, as we shall learn, it is often focused on the individual. Networks often exist outside churches and other institutions and rely on mystically based practices and traditions from the East—practicing yoga as part of a spiritual quest, reading Rumi as a meditative strategy, and placing Tibetan Buddhist flags as protective devices are a few of these traditions. Traditions identified with Eastern wisdom—Hinduism, Buddhism, and Islam—are often placed alongside New Age practices that refer to spiritual vortexes, sacred pools and mountains, and energy fields.[83] These New Age places and rituals often borrow from Native American,

Buddha and Moai statues in a stonework shop, Batu Bulan, Bali (courtesy of the author).

African, or other traditions, resulting in places like Sedona, Arizona, which is a spiritual marketplace for the upper middle class and celebrities like Oprah.

In modern mysticism, the concept of God is articulated in numerous ways that depend on one's community. It should be noted that the traditional names for God or gods—Brahma, Allah—are rarely invoked in these cases. Instead, spiritualists use their own special language, which is intentionally non-specific. "Sometimes that which is found within the inner self is called God even though its meaning may be very different from the more orthodox usage of that term; at other times the term God is replaced by any number of possible substitutes, such as Goddess and Sophia in feminist circles, or simply Higher Power or Universal Force."[84] The proliferation of these terms is part of what is available for spiritual consumers in the *divine supermarket*.[85] An entire aisle of this supermarket dedicated to the East, where consumers can buy products inspired by India, Egypt, Morocco, and elsewhere. Scholars have suggested that this *hyper consumerism* is part of modern life, marginalizing some forms of tradition while invading public and private life, including religious life.[86] As Jacqueline Hodder puts it, these "postmodern expressions of religion can be found in New Age or evangelical forms."[87]

As discussed throughout this book, New Age religion has a smaller share in the religious market because mysticism has taken it over, replacing LSD and crystals with green-tea lattes and tree bathing. New Age practitioners are often called "teachers" or "healers" rather than "ministers," making it clear that what they do is different from traditional religion. One such teacher, Barbara Ann Brennan, has claimed that a spirit anatomy of chakras can be "opened" through therapy and cure illnesses that are caused by "energy blocks."[88] In this system of belief, chakras become part of a new vision of the body, illness, and healing that does not involve or credit its Hindu (and Buddhist) origins. The healer, in this case Brennan, "reawakens" the "ancient memory" of the self and, by doing so, "S/he touches the spark of God in each cell of the body and gently reminds it that it is already God and, already being God, it inexorably flows with the Universal Will towards health and wellness."[89]

Another example of New Age religion borrowing from the East is the New Age Judaism found in contemporary Israeli spirituality. One teacher, Gavriel Meir, organizes workshops that tailor mystical practices for the coexistence industry, including Sufi teachings.[90] As one study notes, Meir is typical of New Age spiritualists and mystics in his pan-religious philosophy. "Meir combines new-age spirituality with coexistence initiatives. Among his influential teachers, he mentions Native American Shamans, Buddhist teachers (Thich Nhat Hanh, Joanna Macy) and Sufi sheiks from Africa, Turkey, the Holy Land, and India."[91]

New Age, spiritual, and modern mystical teachers borrow from a seemingly endless number of traditions, but they are quite intentional about their courses, workshops, and retreats. As scholars have pointed out, the programmatic nature of modern mysticism makes it different from traditional modes of religion such as the Roman Catholic Mystical Body of Christ.[92] The New Age groups are small communities that utilize a language of intentionality and healing, wellness and meditation. As one scholar notes: "New Age healers have a program."[93] The radical inclusiveness of New Age religion, spiritualism, and contemporary mysticism results in the muddled Orientalism we see today, discussed in detail in Chapter Two. This should not be confused with the cohabitation of religious traditions, which is a totally different subject. As many scholars have pointed out, Hinduism, Buddhism, and Islam have at times shared territory, rituals, and even entire traditions as they do today. In Kashmir, Rishi saints have incorporated yogic methods in their practices and Baba Rishi (Hazrat Payam-ud-Din) is an important figure for both Muslims and Hindus.[94] Visiting the holy shrine of Baba Rishi is serious business. People visit it with young children for their first haircut and believe that if a fire is seen in its old fireplace (where the saint used to make his meals), it is a bad omen.[95]

One final point needs to be made about religion and mysticism. The descriptive aspects of religion like liturgy, texts, and rituals, are observable and somewhat quantifiable. Mysticism and spirituality are not. This is why academic studies on texts are more respected than those on contemplative theology. It is extremely difficult to work out what mysticism is, which makes it a particularly good product to exploit for profit. As one study of mystical Muslim music puts it, spirituality is not a descriptive act but a language:

> Rather than conceiving of spirituality as located in particular and competing cantons of belief, it is possible to consider

> spirituality as a discourse of subjective belief that cuts across and is shared by a wide range of religious and spiritual traditions. It is this universalizing language of postmodern spirituality and the desire to universalize—or perhaps more accurately translate—subjective experience that emerges most starkly when discussing religious belief and musical practice with Muslim musicians.[96]

In this case, spirituality is nothing and everything, subject to no analytical process, and therefore, able to be assumed by anyone, including the modern mystical seeker.

MYSTICAL UTOPIAS

North American religious history includes traditions of summer camps, religious holidays, and bucolic retreats such as Chautauqua and Spiritualist conventions.[97] Experiencing culture, relaxing, and the contemplation of nature were all part of early American tourism, where festivals and retreats often functioned as domestic versions of overseas travel. Today, festivals like Burning Man and the Hanuman Festival, which are examined at the end of this chapter, function as spaces where religions can be constructed, experienced, and bought and sold—all without leaving continental North America. Like many heterotopias, these tribe events recreate a kind of utopian vision that is marked by difference.

Heterotopias often function as queered spaces or sites of *difference* that provide an escape to the past and a departure from the present; as such, they depend upon Fabian's denial of coeval time. As Foucault reminds us: "Utopias are sites with no real place. They are sites that have a general relation of direct or inverted analogy with the real space of Society. They present society itself in a perfected form, or else society turned upside down, but in any case, these utopias are fundamentally unreal spaces."[98] The Orient is a kind of heterotopia of the mind, an inversion of the West that is created in the imagination. Expressed in many of the practices, products, and spaces that are part of modern mysticism, they reproduce ideas that exist somewhere, perhaps in history, in a far-off land, or in fantasy. The mystical tourist seeks spaces where spirituality and wellness goals can be lived out.

The New Age movement may have passed its apex, but its focus on inner peace, wellness, self-realization, meditation, esoteric teachings, and bodywork live on in mystical utopias, including tourism.[99] These spaces reflect Foucault's technologies of the self, where the body is commodified as a symbol of the mystical path. Hinduism, Buddhism, and Islam inspire many of these products and practices, from mindful cooking instructional CDs to neo-Sufi poetry circles. *New Age Orientalism* is a useful concept that describes these practices, products, and communities: "The emerging rise and growth of ayurvedic 'wellness and spa culture' in the West (Euro-America), and also in the East (India), in recent decades is relevant to the analysis of Orientalism."[100]

New Age Orientalism reflects fantasies about India, Egypt, and Morocco as well as the larger geography of the imagined Orient—places like Indonesia and Thailand. The Australian or American visiting Bali, Thailand, or Vietnam, and the European visiting Egypt, Turkey, or Morocco, is hoping for an exotic experience, even if they live geographically close to their mystical location: "Although Morocco is only separate from Europe by the narrow Strait of Gibraltar, most Europeans view the country as another world: an unknown realm from centuries past, a distant desert kingdom full of adventure and an oriental fairyland as glamorised in the 'Arabian Nights'."[101]

Some places identified as powerful, spiritual, mystical, and special—Glastonbury, Black Rock, Santa Fe—are not even located in the Orient. However, they capitalize on a dizzying number of religious traditions from the Orient, all placed under the umbrella of modern mysticism. Glastonbury is viewed as a mystic center, and it claims ancient Celtic, Hindu, Buddhist, and Islamic/Sufi connections. These are used to sell products and services to the spiritual seeker: "For those seeking accommodation, some Bed and Breakfast establishments offer particular types of healing or meditation to discerning clients to enhance their stay in Avalon."[102] Glastonbury has been called a spiritual vortex, a site of chakras, and a zodiac, and some modern mystics even claim it was the site of King Arthur's Round Table, which may have been built with help "from above"—by aliens.[103]

In other cases, mystical centers are identified with an older, singular tradition. Iona, a small island off the coast of Scotland, with only 105 residents, and 250,000 visitors each year, is called the "cradle of Christianity in Scotland" and is identified with Celtic spirituality.[104] A "thin space," it is viewed as a place where lightness and darkness intermingle and where spirits are present among the living; like Glastonbury, Iona is believed to be a center of mystic power.[105] The hotels, spas, and healers that have businesses in Glastonbury, Iona, and other mystical sites attempt to recreate an extinct location (or locations) where visitors, pilgrims, and tourists can live out their fantasies of the East and its mystical traditions.

THE GLOBAL MARKET

The search for mystical experience is not limited to Burners, the name given to annual pilgrims to Burning Man. Much of this book is focused on North American and European popular mysticism that is rooted in the East and its religious traditions. However, the mystical marketplace is expansive. In India, the guru Sathya

Sai Baba (d. 2011) refers to "world" religions such as Islam, Christianity, and Zoroastrianism as part of his appeal to devotees in South Asia and beyond.[106] An account of Suleyman Dede, a Sufi shaykh from Turkey, describes the fluidity of practices among white, affluent Americans: "One moment we would be whirling like dervishes, then Vipassana Buddhist meditation, then Arica exercises, followed by brain-burning Ibn-Arabi studies, maybe a fling with Scientology, a little map-dowsing, singing vowel sounds with movements, vortex meditations, walking meditation, a green meditation; it never ended."[107] As these examples suggest, modern mysticism is popular globally. In Indonesia, the largest Muslim-majority nation in the world, the emergence of New Age, mystical, and spiritual traditions include Salamullah, the Brahma Kuamris, and Anand Ashram.[108]

The mystical marketplace is global, at times moving in circles around the world. The popularity of modern mystics and gurus reflects the "experiential spirituality and a judicious eclecticism" that are part of the search for meaning in the modern world, popular among the Nones and other spiritual seekers in North America, Europe, and elsewhere.[109] While visiting West Java in 2018 and 2019, I noted that advertisements for Zen healing spas were popular, especially in the fashion capital of Bandung. This is an example of Eastern mysticism circling back to Asia, creating a space for businesses that offer alternative healing models.

The global appeal of mysticism is rooted in its identification with the Orient. As Said and others have pointed out, *essentialism* is a hallmark of Orientalism that can express itself in numerous ways—from the Romantic visions of the Orient to the characterizations of Muslim men as necessarily violent. The Romantic side of this discourse casts Hinduism, Buddhism, and Islam as sources of mystical truth and has broad appeal. As one scholar notes:

> The wisdom and spirituality of the ancient East has rarely been disputed, and in fact has been glorified by adherents

> to a host of movements over the centuries, from the American Transcendentalists, to the German and English romantic poets and scholars, to environmental activists worldwide—not to mention the various representatives of Indian nationalism since the waning of the British empire.[110]

The East has been identified as a center of mystical energy for centuries and today, this belief is used as a marketing tool in modern mysticism. Adopting the practices of the Orient is a way to transform the mind *and* the body. As Wendy Brown argues, this reflects the modern way of thinking about identity as essentialist and rooted in belief:

> These beliefs and this consciousness are presumed to issue from the essence or inner truth of the person or, at minimum, from his or her culture, ethnicity, or sexuality. In this peculiarly modern discourse of the subject, opinions, belief, and practices are cast not as matters of conscience, education, or revelation but of the material of the person of which certain attributes (racial, sexual, gendered, or ethnic) are an index: hence, the notions of "black consciousness," "women's morality," "cultural viewpoint," or "queer sensibility." In each case, one's race, sexuality, culture, or gender is considered the consciousness, beliefs, or practice—the difference—that must be protected or tolerated.[111]

Modern mysticism is linked both with the practices associated with the East and the resurgence of Christian mysticism in North America. This resurgence is seen in everything from the popularity of Celtic spiritual music to the numerous reports of visions of Mary. In recent years, the dedication of American Catholics to Mary has often included venturing on the Internet. As Paolo Apolito points out, a simple Google search for Marian apparitions can result in unexpected and even unwanted results. "You can access sites on 'unexplained mysteries' and the paranormal in many different ways while seeking information and images concerning Catholic miracles. For instance, if you look for sites on the Shroud, you will eventually run into Mysteries, which adds to the 'unsolved mystery' of the Shroud and such other subjects as Stonehenge, prehistoric monuments in Great Britain, the hidden chambers of the pyramids, the giant footprints of the wild men of the woods, UFOs, and other such mysteries."[112] As Apolito explains, these sites are a few examples of the ways that Catholicism is appropriated as part of "a standardized, uniform fabric of all-inclusive spirituality."[113] The exoticism associated with the East, seen in the reference to the pyramids and other mysteries noted above, is also seen in new religious movements, New Age, and traditions that are inspired by new technology. As one scholar observes, "Popular cartoon characters adorn vehicles in Taiwanese funeral processions. Text messaging has been used for Catholic confessional. And Buddhist merit can be accrued over the Internet."[114]

Religious celebrities, who have grown in popularity in recent years, include Oprah, Deepak Chopra, Aa Gym (Abdullah Gymnastiar), and others. In addition to the cult of personality that surrounds some celebrity gurus, indigenous or native mystics are often believed to hold supernatural powers or other magical qualities. Chogyam Trungpa, the founder of the Naropa Institute in Boulder, Colorado, associated with "crazy wisdom," was viewed in this way. One of his students claimed to have been healed by looking in his eyes, and on a later occasion stated, "His body emitted golden rays and wild birds would come and sit on his outstretched arms."[115] I wonder if this student is a lapsed Catholic, for the description of Trungpa reminds me of the beautiful paintings of St. Francis that reflect the visual piety of Renaissance-era Christian visual piety.

MYSTICAL TOURISM

The popularity of mystical places, and the bodies attached to these places, suggests the importance of the senses, emotion, and experience in modern mysticism. The importance of the senses is rooted in late eighteenth- and early nineteenth-century Romantic thought, and includes the "right to feel emotional about the natural world and scenery."[116] The search for experience influenced the emergence of health and curative treatments in the nineteenth century, including sea bathing in Britain, where the ocean was seen as bestowing "health-giving properties" to vacationers.[117] Europeans also searched for more exotic locations where they could experience the world and its mysteries. India has long been a favorite destination for these mystical tourists. As John Urry writes: "The mystique of India's religions, and the enigmatic beauty of its sacred sites, hold exotic appeal for Westerners disenchanted with their own materially rich but spiritually impoverished cultures."[118] India still appeals to many individuals seeking mystical experiences, but today, it is part of a larger field of practices, places, and traditions that make up the mystical marketplace.

Places popular with mystical tourists often exploit both an "idea" of a place and the actual people who live there. These locations are often enclaves, "meta-spaces of in-between."[119] Enclaves are often viewed as desirable, healing, and exotic. The projections, or fantasies, attached to enclaves can come into conflict with the lives of local communities. For example, Balinese tourism publicly professes the principle of *Tat Twam Asi*, whose core ideals are brotherhood, peace, and harmony.[120] This is more of a mirage than reality, however, and does not represent the tensions between the Hindu majority and tourists, Muslims, government officials, and others.

The mystical East is a mirage created by Orientalism and people's need to escape from the stresses of modern life. As one study notes about India: "This mythical India, assumed to be free of the values and ethics of a consumerist capitalist economy, proved to be anything but spiritual. Such versions of India could easily be manufactured and distributed."[121] The mythic India that exists today reflects the kind of individual spirituality we see among mystical seekers. It reflects an interest in Eastern mysticism that doesn't require a teacher, guru, or authority figure. In modern mysticism, it is often the self, or a series of itinerant teachers, who guide the individual in his or her religious quest. The rejection of religious authority is part of what Charles Taylor has called "the narrative of self-authorization."[122]

Scholars studying the history of Indian gurus and other mystical leaders in North America have noted corruption as a serious problem in individualized forms of mysticism. "As such, corruption amongst gurus ran rampant as they extracted money and obedience from their followers who sought the most 'authentic' experiences possible, following in the footsteps of the icons of popular culture that led the way."[123] As the recent scandals involving North American and European Muslim intellectuals like Nouman Ali Khan and Tariq Ramadan have shown us, no religious tradition is safe from allegations of corruption and exploitation.

The mystical marketplace is saturated with products and practices that require a guru, teacher, or guide. One of the most infamous scandals in Buddhist circles involved a student of Chogyam Trungpa, Osel Tendzin, who had HIV and spread it among Buddhists in his community after Trungpa told him he could change his "karma" and suggested he had "some extraordinary means of protection."[124] Of course, not all guru scandals are this tragic, but it illustrates the dangers of mystical and neo-mystical movements. One of the more troubling stories about Trungpa is known as "the Snowmass [Colorado] affair," referring to an occasion that illuminates some of the issues with gurus. "In the fall of 1975, during an exclusive retreat for advanced practitioners, at Trungpa's command, two participants [the poet W. S. Merwin and his female companion], after refusing to attend a party, were taken forcibly from their room and stripped naked in front of the assemblage."[125]

One of the operative beliefs attached to mysticism and, by extension, to mystical tourism, is that the body of the Other is special—a conduit of healing and transcendence. Often this magic takes place when the guru, teacher, or master is alive, but miraculous events can also happen after they die. At Chogyam Trungpa's funeral, his followers claimed to see rainbows, as well as turquoise clouds in the shape of a dragon's tail in the sky.[126] Beliefs about Hindu, Buddhist, and Muslim mysticism may involve the attachment of eroticism to these bodies. In tantric traditions like Tibetan Buddhism, promiscuity and eroticized practices are part of the appeal for some followers. In the case of Vajradhatu, Trungpa's organization that became Shambhala, sexual practices with real partners and "visualized partners" were common practice, so much so that any criticism of these behaviors was silenced.[127]

The linking of sexual intercourse to a blessing, enlightenment, or healing is not limited to the American guru. Mystical tourism often crosses over into sexual tourism through portrayals of beautiful Southeast Asian women, Moroccan boys, and other foreign bodies who hold the promise of a mystical experience. As Deborah Root observes: "One of the most persistent tropes of exoticism is the fascination with the erotic possibilities of the colony, which in effect becomes the eroticization of racial power."[128] The body of the colonized Other, or the host culture, is often viewed as a curative object for the tourist. An ethnography of tourists who visit Thailand states:

> Through his interaction with this woman, Brad has cast himself as his own conception of a masculine, heroic man, with an added pseudo-Buddhist twist. Brad had been poisoned (a diagnosis that, it should be noted, came from a website and not from a doctor) by the rapacity and greed of

> the West, requiring that he flee. Arriving with an idea of the spiritually pure East in mind, Brad can escape his mid-thirties, find his "true" nature, one which has been linked to Thailand all along.[129]

The history of mystical tourism is rooted in conquest and the accumulation of material culture from the East. Initially, the fascination with the Orient and its peoples was located in the objects on display, rather than the actual cultures in which they were situated. As one example, Asian arts, including *noh* costumes, were collected as cultural commodities, at times with no interest in *noh* theater.[130] These and other objects associated with the East often existed in private collections held by the wealthy. Islamic items such as carpets, calligraphic art, and vases adorned with Arabic are also part of the histories of the richest American families like the Vanderbilts and Hearsts. This material culture is discussed more closely in Chapter Three, but a brief discussion of the performance of foreign religions and cultures follows here as an introduction to the ways in which people experienced the Orient before the development of mystical tourism.

Since the emergence of Orientalism in the late eighteenth century (Napoleon occupied Egypt in 1798), the East and its people have been put on public display—in museums, theaters, even circuses—for the amusement of Europeans and North Americans. As the historian John Kuo Wei Tchen has shown, Chinese people were even put on display—including "the Chinese lady" Afong Moy and others.[131] These human displays of culture are early examples of the Orient and its traditions—including its religious traditions—in the marketplace. Japanese, Chinese, Egyptian, Moorish, and other people—were all subject to display, part of the large apparatus of colonial possession. Omai, the Polynesian who toured Europe and was the subject of a famous portrait by Joshua Reynolds, is one famous example. "Omai became the darling of elite society, fêted by celebrities such as

Portrait of Omai by Joshua Reynolds (courtesy of Wikimedia Commons).

Samuel Johnson and the Duchess of Gloucester. He was escorted to Britain's greatest spectacles—theatres, the House of Lords, the University of Cambridge—although it was not always clear who was meant to be entertained during these excursions."[132]

Reynolds's portrait of Omai shows him in Arab dress, complete with flowing robes and a turban—a costume ridiculously out of place in tropical Polynesia. Omai introduces the role clothing plays in the strategy of possession, through allowing the wearer to appropriate the culture he or she is dressing up in. The kimono was popular among European and North American white women in the nineteenth century. Stores specializing in Eastern products like Vantine's featured performances by kimono-clad shop girls and white performances of Asian personas also included photo studios and other types of elaborate staging of Japanese styles.[133] As discussed in a later chapter, the Japanese geisha or lady was one of many personas taken on by affluent Europeans and Americans seeking a temporary escape from their own world. Today, yoga is one of many practices that involves costuming through athletic wear that features Eastern imagery and styles. However, it is whitewashed through the removal of Hindu references in yoga poses, in both CorePower Yoga (designed for caloric burn) and Bikram yoga, which prohibits any chanting.[134]

European and North American voyeurs who observed, collected, and possessed objects from the East in the past two centuries were much like the consumers of modern mysticism. The operative word in marketing these products is "spirituality," which corporatizes religion, and specifically mystical practices, that appeal to the spiritual shopper. Carrette and King call this the "silent takeover of religion," where businesses use "the positive gloss of spirituality to support corporate interests and work practices."[135] Among the many ways this exists is through "spiritual consultants" who often utilize concepts like "an authentic source," "the power within," and the "light and love" within us all.[136] Often used as a codeword for mysticism, spirituality also has a history intimately connected to the Orient.

MYSTICAL WELLNESS

Religion is often a case of cross-pollination involving numerous influences on the development of rituals across traditions. For example, walking meditation is associated with Buddhist mindfulness and especially with the work of contemporary masters like Thich Nhat Hanh. It also exists in the Sufi tradition, where it is encouraged as a way to discern consciousness and be more attuned to the divine in the living world. Here it focuses on the self-awareness that is a necessary part of the religious path. As one Naqshbandi aphorism goes, "Look down and see whose feet are those that walk."[137] Inter-religious influences on walking meditation are different from the colonization and commodification of Eastern religions for profit, seen in the meditation apps that flood the marketplace. As Megan Sijapati notes, "There are mobile apps that offer a variety of meditation techniques guided by a range of instructors of religious or non-religious orientation."[138]

Restraint is a key practice in many of the health, wellness, and spiritual programs inspired by the East. The restrictive diet is modeled upon Ayurvedic practice. North Americans who practice Tibetan Buddhism may elect to take silent retreats where they stay in isolation, with no speaking or communication with the outside world for months. At the same time, the East is viewed as a place of excess. In particular, it is framed as a site of excess with regards to the expression of one's sensuality. As documented in my earlier work, there is a long history of Muslims presented as sexual monsters, rapists, and perverts, starting with the medieval characterizations of Prophet Muhammad and continuing today with hijab porn.[139] The sensuality of the East is seen in other areas. Scholarship on belly dancing cites the "otherness" and "naturalness" often identified with the practice. Statements such as "The Pakistani like big booty" or "In Turkey, they love for the women to have flab" signal both North American attitudes surrounding women's bodies (thin is in, fat is unacceptable) as well as the fetishizing of the Other.[140] As the co-authors of one study of exotic dance note: "Western women's projections onto Middle Eastern women of an autonomous and powerful sexuality reflect their desire to contest what they see as a denial of the female body in their own culture. Aligning themselves with the perceived unselfconscious excesses associated with Middle Eastern dancers, these female dancers distance themselves from Western ideals of self-restraint."[141]

Fetishizing the exotic today is seen in many of the mystical products and practices examined throughout this book, the ways exotic bodies are treated socially, and how they function aesthetically in popular culture. As Graham Huggan notes, "commodity fetishism links up with earlier forms of exoticist representation, arguably becoming the postmodern version of exoticist mystique."[142] Sufism is framed in much of popular New Age discourse through the highlighting of drunk Sufis. They are not literally drunk, but are inebriated by their love of "the Divine." However, for the modern mystic, the wine of Divine love is a Pinot Grigio, and the Beloved that is Allah is a romantic partner.

Although not the focus of this book, religious individuals who identify as Hindu, Buddhist, and Muslim also participate in the commodification of religious symbols, including those identified with mysticism and contemplative practice. In Indonesia, Muslims visit Abdullah Gymnastiar's complex in Bandung called Daarut Tauhid. Here, they can meet him, take his courses, and buy souvenirs, but this is also a place where "spiritual tourists" (*wisata rohani*) purchase mystical products like pilgrims' honey.[143] In North America, numerous examples of spiritual tourism exist, including the Hanuman Festival in Boulder, Colorado and Burning Man, located in the Nevada desert. These events are not solely inspired by the traditions of Hinduism, Buddhism, and Islam, but often they include them in imagery, ritual, performance, and paths of healing. These are all characterized as "event-structured religion," and exist in two forms—intimate circles and mass gatherings.[144] As the following section discusses, both of these community styles are oppositional to traditional religion and exclusive.[145] The following chapters include traditions, commodities, and experiences inspired by Hinduism, Buddhism, and Islam. Two examples of mystical festivals—Hanuman and Burning Man—reflect some of the different ways in which these religious traditions and their symbols appear as part of event-structured religion.

JOIN MY TRIBE

Tribe communities and events often feature mysticism as a key part of their marketing campaigns. These "tribes" are typically identified with a neo-mystical movement or have roots in a New Age community. They tend to consist largely of white, affluent individuals who dabble in numerous forms of Eastern religion—yoga, Sufism, meditation—who describe themselves as counter-cultural, radical, or alternative. For example, the members of Full Circle, in Venice, California, consider themselves part of a tribe.[146] Tribe events often showcase the same people who market new forms of yoga, meditation, or Sufism. Such is the case of John Friend, who developed the Anusara yoga system in 1997 and, in 2011, was invited to lead the closing ceremony at the Wanderlust festival.[147] In this way, tribe communities are part of the fabric of the mystical marketplace.

Event tribalism is a term sociologists use for annual events like the Hanuman Festival and Burning Man, reflecting the *soft tribalism* that is antithetical to anthropological definitions of tribal as "social organisations defined by ascribed traditions of common descent, language, culture and ideology, and reliant on the maintenance of boundaries."[148] The soft tribalism evident at these gatherings is not just descriptive, however; it is seen literally in the costumes, artistic creations, performances, and products that riff on the exotic. The East, especially Hinduism and Buddhism, is often on public display at these events, presented in forms and styles that communicate the *difference* attached to heterotopias.

The Hanuman Festival takes place every year in Boulder, Colorado, a popular center of Buddhist learning in North America. As discussed in Chapter Four, this college town is the home of Naropa University and the Shambhala Center—important centers of Trungpa's "crazy wisdom" branch of Tibetan Buddhism. Hanuman is primarily marketed for white yogis and yoginis, who populate the website and the large crowds of attendees. The soft tribalism evident in many alternative health and spirituality-themed annual gatherings is at the core of Hanuman's messaging. The festival's 2018 website included a link titled "Our Tribe" featuring the sponsoring organizations, foundations, and corporations that included Prana, Bhakti Chai, CorePower Yoga, Yoga Outlet, and Lululemon, and their brand icons, many of which incorporate a lotus flower, Hindu god, mandala, or other Eastern motif.[149] Following these images was the second part of this page, titled Ambassadors, including seventeen yoga-minded individuals—twelve of whom were female, and all of whom were white—who served as the face of the 2018 Hanuman Festival.[150] The teachers at Hanuman were overwhelmingly white as well. Out of fifty teachers, facilitators, and speakers, all but five were white, and included only one African American.[151] The whitewashing of yoga was evident here, as it was on all other parts of the website, where only a few African American participants were shown, and even fewer Asians were featured. A few teachers from India were featured on the Hanuman tour webpage, which advertised yoga retreats for sale—$2,500 for double occupancy (airfare not included)—with promises of "wisdom," visits to temples and shrines, and vegetarian "farm to table" food.[152] These examples of mystical tourism help to illustrate the role Orientalism plays in the wellness industry.

In 2018, Hanuman Festival offered a number of differently priced ticketing options for participants along with music concerts, opening and closing ceremonies, and a busy marketplace (called the Community Village) where yoga gear, wellness products, meditation aids, and other items were sold (in 2018, sellers paid $1,250 for a small tent-booth and $2,350 for the larger size).[153] The commodification of Hinduism and Buddhism and the co-option of Islam through Sufism is also evident throughout the festival. One past teacher at Hanuman cites one of her two mantras as coming from Rumi: "Let the beauty you love, be what you do."[154] This is likely #FakeRumi, as it was translated by Coleman Barks, whose lack of expertise in the language Rumi wrote in has been well documented by scholars.[155] As I learned, one of the founders of the festival featured another Rumi mantra on his website, illustrating the ways in which Hinduism, Buddhism, and Islam are often seamlessly blended together in tribe fests, in products, and through the images that advertise spirituality and sell mystical experience.

Burning Man is a music festival, temporary artist colony, and transitory religious community. There is even an initiation ritual of sorts one must undergo to gain access to information about tickets (which in 2018, were priced up to $1,200 a person), where one has to answer questions about Burning Man's rules. The annual festival takes place in the Nevada desert and is largely made up of white middle-class North Americans. The attendees come from a wide variety of communities, including "ferals, neo-pagans, neo-hippies, spiritual seekers, counter-culture promoters, Goths, hipsters, post-punks, libertarians, backpackers, folk musicians, vegans, Star Trek aficionados and circus artists."[156]

The founder Larry Harvey sees religion as a corruption of the sacred and envisions Burning Man as a "spiritual movement far from the church."[157] He advocates a visionary idea of modern mysticism that includes personal transformation and an "opening of the heart," transcendence, and a "sacred vision of unity."[158] These are the same ideas voiced by many of the self-declared mystics and spiritualists who are discussed throughout the book. Burning Man is definitely a heterotopia of countercultural excess. The strong expressions of sexuality and contemporary art seen at

Burning Man include the display of "ambulatory and automative genitalia," as well as centers of "sacred sexuality."[159]

Interestingly, Harvey has voiced a strong critique of consumerist culture, and while the exchange of money is prohibited during the festival, its founder rakes in huge profits every year. Burning Man attendees must adhere to ten "principles," which are listed under Philosophical Center on the official website (www.burningman.org). Two of these principles, Decommodification and Gifting, are especially relevant to the subject of this book. No monetary exchanges can take place and outside sponsors are prohibited, providing the illusion that Burning Man is an anti-capitalist venture. As Sarah Pike argues, festivals like Burning Man advertise anti-materialism while participating in the market: "Not only do corporate products appear everywhere on the bodies and in the camps of festival-goers, but many festivals are sponsored by large corporations. In 2011, Earthdance, which champions sustainable goods, listed sponsors including Knudsen, Santa Cruz Organics, Frey Vineyards, and Lagunitas Brewing."[160] In fact, most tickets for Burning Man sell for between $425 and $1,200. Based on my calculations (without counting the limited "low income" tickets, which run $160), ticket sales for the 2018 festival were over $17 million dollars. This figure does not include the parking fee, which is $80. Burning Man is not limited to the Nevada site and has several satellite locations around the world.

The isolation—Burning Man's location in the desert—and its penetrable quality, reflect Foucault's First Principle of the heterotopia.[161] Like many heterotopias, Burning Man involves a purification through the desert, which has been described by attendees as having a detoxifying effect. This is a profoundly Orientalist notion, tied to Orientalist musings on the desert as a place of magic, danger, and spiritual power. The exotic allure of the desert takes center stage at Burning Man, seen perhaps most profoundly in changing constructions of The Temple, where huge structures function as veritable shrines.[162]

Burning Man also reflects Bahktin's notion of the carnivalesque as a poly-mystical site with temples, shrines, and altars to existing and newly created gods. Among the rituals performed at Burning Man are meditation, yoga, initiations, prayers, and "monkey chanting."[163] *The Temple of Transition* promises spiritual change as a real possibility, perhaps through an Eastern tradition like yoga or with the help of a psychedelic drug.[164] Among the structures are those dedicated to Hindu and Buddhist figures, often with hefty price tags. While festival-goers make claims about the perils of materialism, the reality is very different. "Burners spend thousands of dollars on elaborate camp decorations, costumes, and art projects to take with them to their utopia."[165] In this way, Burning Man is a microcosm of the mystical marketplace.

Mysticism is a messy colonial business. Tribe events like the music and art festivals discussed here are not solely focused on the traditions of Hinduism, Buddhism, and Islam. They also try to appeal to Native American and pre-Christian (pagan or heathen) communities, offering workshops by Shoshone, Incan, or other individuals.[166] At times, the people running these workshops have contested identities—they may not really be Native or indigenous, for example, but are performing these traditions by wearing costumes with feathers or animal skins. The costuming seen at Burning Man provides a rich space in which to discuss cultural colonialism.

Mysticism is embodied in the clothing and speech of many Burners. However, it is the large-scale art installations where we find the most impressive Hindu, Buddhist, and Sufi themes and imagery. In 2009, a "Sufi Slide" was erected, and other reports from Burners have described Sufi swings in the part of Burning Man called "Swing City." In 2017, a Kickstarter campaign was established to support the building and erection of a huge neon installation focused on Rumi's words (which are, in fact, likely #FakeRumi), "Everything You Need Is Inside You." The Zendo

Project (a riff off "Zen") was a portable meditation site made of 5,000 pounds of recycled cardboard that featured a hodgepodge of Oriental products including Tibetan rugs, Chinese lanterns, and Japanese futons.[167]

Burning Man has numerous camps, several of which advertise Hindu and Buddhist practices. The Monkey Bar Theme Camp is aligned with the group called the Sun Guardians and has offered different programming every year. In 2017, programs included women's nude yoga and meditation; in 2016, men's nude yoga and "no bullshit meditation"; and in 2015, a Feast for All Saints and mud wrestling "in honor of Hanuman."[168] In 2014, an event titled Monk Fetish was advertised with a collage of Buddhist monks and a Losing Your Religion Ritual/Ceremony led by a "shaman and healer" who promised a ritual that would combat "the confining, controlling aspects of religion to live peacefully and harmoniously."[169] This ceremony presented modern mysticism as an alternative to religion, reflecting the appeal of individualized spirituality in the mystical marketplace of Burning Man.

The Buddha Camp is another theme camp which offers a mix of "Buddhism and mayhem," creates a "temporary Buddhist utopia," and creates, among other things, "a series of Buddhist and espresso activities."[170] Activities include Buddhist chanting ("Reveal your inner Buddha"), naked espresso ("unadulterated espresso"), restorative yoga ("Lost your zen at Burning Man?"), Short Term Marriages ("Met someone[s] so special you want to spend the rest of your burn with them … or maybe just the evening?"), and Ask a Buddhist Life Coaching ("Judeo-Christian worldview put a dent in your burn?").[171]

Buddhism is the main tradition being borrowed from in these activities, but there are other strongly Orientalist elements. The group photograph shows forty-two individuals (all white except for one), most in various states of undress, with a couple at the center wearing headscarves. The hijab-ing of this couple at the center of the photograph suggests that the veil has a strong attraction for many, even at an unconscious level. The mystique surrounding the veil contributes to its popularity as a symbol and, in some cases, it is simply seen as a lifestyle brand. In one Oprah show, "modern" Muslim women were introduced as Americans "except with different accessories."[172] This is one example of how exotic symbols become commodified and their meaning reduced to a form of capital. As Kathryn Lofton writes, "Religious difference in Oprah's America is a fashion choice rather than a theological commitment."[173]

Burning Man's camps are relatively small compared to the shrines and temples erected at the festival. These enormous structures showcase the talent of artists who work with a variety of natural materials they must pack in to the site and dismantle at the end of Burning Man. Shrines and temples feature many types of imagery associated with the East, from the lotus tree to the mosque dome. Each year these structures have grown in size and complexity, and while some offer futuristic visions of architecture, others reflect an aesthetic that is particularly tied to the Orient. In 2008, the *Basura Sagrada* built by Shrine On and Tucker Teutsch reflected Hindu and Balinese styles; a temple complete with similes of offerings. Documented in a splendid book of photography by N. K. Guy, this temple is one of many structures evocative of Eastern mysticism.[174] The artist Shrine On, who also goes by the name Shrine, builds shrines, altars, and temples (including the most important structure at Burning Man named The Temple) that incorporate Arabic script, offering plates, chairs, shoes, bottles, Hindu iconography, and African, Hispanic, Mesoamerican, and indigenous motifs.[175] This is the kind of muddled Orientalism that marks much of modern mysticism.

In 2010, Kate Raudenbush created *Futures Past*, a sculpture composed of 7,000 pounds of treated steel and featuring a Bodhi tree.[176] The Bodhi tree is a symbol of the Buddha—the place where he achieved Enlightenment. The search for meaning, which is so central to Burning Man, is represented in this immense artwork, but it is not the only reference to Eastern mysticism. The same artist created *Altered State* in 2008.[177] This metalwork sculpture in white resembled a mosque cupola and reminded me of the tomb of Hafiz, which I visited in 2004 in Iran. David Best and the Temple Crew created *The Temple of Honor*, which looked like a group of stacked genie lamps, in 2003.[178] Decorated with black-and-white designs and human figures, it featured a variety of styles, including geometric designs and Classical and Renaissance columns. In 2011, the International Arts Megacrew erected *The Temple of Transition*, which is perhaps the most Oriental of all of these structures. It featured numerous Moorish arches, domes, and a bridge. As the largest wooden sculpture ever built without a foundation, it was impressive in size.[179] Its Moorish style was arresting—no one would mistake this for anything but architectural Orientalism. Intended to be a contemplative space, the large towers (over 120 feet high) included a Tower of Gratitude, which featured a geometric dome that served as a minimalist recreation of a dome in a great mosque. The recreation of other spaces is one of the hallmarks of the heterotopia, and Burning Man is full of these Orientalist and mystical creations.

Burning Man is countercultural, seen in its explorations of sexuality and drug use, within a space that features radical and monumental architecture. These buildings, of which the temples are the most impressive, feature a dazzling array of Orientalist imagery. In 2002 *The Temple of Joy*, a pagoda-like structure with hanging lanterns, featured a realistic shrine; pilgrims could leave prayers and petitions on its altars.[180] The fact that these temples (and shrines) often function as veritable religious spaces—with offerings, religious paraphernalia, petitions, and prayers—shows how mysticism is not just a product. Mysticism exists as a living and breathing activity.

At Black Rock City, once a year, sacred artwork and religious ritual blend together in Orientalist fashion. As one study remarks,

"Constant exposure to the sky draws reference to its divinity as well. Altars abound. Ancient mythological deities are evoked in sculpture, sound, and dance. Replicas of the Buddha, both monumental and diminutive, are pervasive, as are Hindu icons and imagery."[181] These fantastic creations illustrate the allure of the Orient in its grandest forms. Of course, mysticism is not an activity restricted to the tribe festivals like Burning Man; as we shall see, it is found in more mundane spaces like shopping malls, as well as in exotic locations such as Morocco, Indonesia, and Thailand.

One last example concludes this discussion on tribe communities and the role of white wealth within them. Powder Mountain is different from gatherings like Burning Man and Hanuman Festival, as a real-estate development that caters to the super-rich rather than the moderately affluent. However, it is also fashioned as a spiritual utopia seen in tribe events and mystical tourism. Because of its secrecy, it is difficult to determine what Eastern undertones and imagery it will ultimately include in its marketing, architecture, and activities (although yoga will certainly be featured). This intended community in Utah is still in its early phases, but will cater to the rich and famous, visionaries and corporate millionaires, celebrities and entrepreneurs, who will create "A beacon of inspiration and a light in the world."[182] In 2013, five co-founders bought the mountain for forty million dollars and hatched their plan for a community located between the Utah towns of Eden and Paradise that would cater to elites who would formulate a vision for the future.[183] One of the founders of Powder Mountain built himself a cabin with "a stove suspended from the ceiling" and a ladder that leads to a "cubbyhole" in the ceiling where his visionary thinking takes place. Powder Mountain is not alone, preceded by Further Future in the Nevada desert, the Juniper Networks retreat near Santa Cruz, and Esalen, the countercultural, bohemian institute set on a cliff in Big Sur, California.[184] All of these spaces—Hanuman Festival,

Burning Man, Powder Mountain—involve the themes examined in the following chapters—mysticism, the lure of the East, Buddhist, Hindu, and Sufi language and imagery, and the commodification of these traditions. As we shall see, the ways in which these traditions are placed together, often in chaotic fashion, illustrates how "Orientalized" much of modern mysticism is.

It is important to stop for a moment to remember that modern mysticism has many true mystical seekers—individuals who dedicate their lives to the search for truth and who love other traditions openly. Some of these individuals cautioned against the dabbling in religious traditions that was a sign of their times. Thomas Merton warned against what he called the "secular" life, as "any life imprisoned in the cycle of addiction to the illusion of newness and change, caught in the myriad diversions for anaesthetizing our human anguish."[185] Although Merton was deeply influenced by Buddhists such as the Tibetan teacher Chogyam Trungpa, he did not exploit these traditions for profit, but rather spent years integrating Buddhist practices into his own Christian contemplative tradition.

2

Cultural Colonialism, Muddled Orientalism, and the Mystic Poor

Unlike the energy drink, Kabbalah Water has been sold through the Centres since the late 1990s and is presented as instrumental to the practice of Kabbalah.

Mara Einstein[1]

Although Kabbalah is not a central focus of this book, like yoga, mindfulness, and Rumi reading groups, it utilizes key mystical phrases, such as "global consciousness," "ancient wisdom," and "secrets of the universe" in its product promotion.[2] The Kabbalah Centre markets esoteric mysticism as a universalistic spiritual path, identifying it with Judaism and other ancient traditions that come from the East. Kabbalah also illustrates how celebrity culture, Orientalism, and fitness fads collide in the mystical marketplace. Mara Einstein's study of the Kabbalah Centre documents allegations of exploitation of the sick, the large sums of money given to the Centre by some of its followers, and the Centre's claims that Kabbalah Water is "curative," when it is actually just "spring water bottled in Canada."[3]

The Kabbalah Centre's marketing strategy reflects how cultural colonialism is at the center of the practice of modern mysticism. The religious rules outlined in Jewish mystical texts are not followed. Most members of the Centre do not read or speak Hebrew or Yiddish, and many are not Jewish. As one Kabbalah student noted: "I have no idea what it [the Zohar] says, but it doesn't matter, this is powerful stuff."[4] In modern mysticism, paying large sums of money and wearing a red string allows one to adopt an exotic culture as an identity. In the words of one follower, Kabbalah gives them "the telephone line to God."[5] Kabbalah is perhaps the best-known case of the celebrity spirituality that surrounds several traditions of modern mysticism, with Madonna as its most famous proponent. Reportedly, rabbis have blessed her stage before performances and she has claimed to be a reincarnation of the biblical Queen Esther; other followers include Britney Spears, who tattooed a misspelled version of one of the seventy-two names of God on the back of her neck "in nonsensical Hebrew letters."[6] Demi Moore, Marla Maples, Alex Rodriquez, and Ariana Grande all have been associated with the Kabbalah Centre, a following that has dropped off in recent years as it has fallen out of fashion as the dominant mystical trend in Hollywood, replaced by newer spiritual fads.

Celebrity mysticism is often trendy, illustrating how modern spirituality is often characterized by a kind of casual dilettantism. Mystical movements inspired by Hinduism and Buddhism have their own histories of celebrity, including the Mahesh and the Beatles, TM's popularity with David Lynch and other Hollywood stars, and the Dalai Lama's influence on actors such as Richard Gere. These have often influenced the popularity of mysticism in North America among the general public, who look to celebrities for trends ranging from hairstyles to diets.

Religious figures have warned against the lure of these faddish movements to no avail. Chogyam Trungpa, the controversial Tibetan teacher famous for his pedagogical style called "crazy wisdom," imparted many lessons on egotism and the benefits of meditation. His teachings on the self and spiritual materialism are introduced through the Three Lords of Materialism—the Lord of Form or Body, the Lord of Speech, and the Lord of the Mind.[7] The Lord of the Mind cautions against "spirituality as self-improvement or therapy" and says that things like "Yoga, drugs, prayer, meditation, trances, and psychotherapies all can be used to advance ego's agenda" because they often hold on to the self.[8] According to Trungpa, the Lord of Speech is also implicated in the ego's use of spiritual or religious practice: "The Lord of Speech is involved in spiritual practice as well. In following a spiritual path, we may substitute a new religious ideology for our former beliefs, but continue to use it in the old neurotic way. Regardless of how sublime our ideas may be, if we take them too seriously and use them to maintain our ego, we are still being ruled by the Lord of Speech."[9] Sadly, some of the same dangers Trungpa warned against became issues for him in his own life, a story we will learn about later in this book.

Trungpa's teachings provide a valuable way to think about cultural colonialism. As he points out, spiritual capitalists use religious traditions in problematic ways. Although he doesn't name colonialism in the teaching quoted above, it is often embedded in modern mysticism, resulting in the mimicking of other cultures. Ironically, despite Trungpa's teachings, Tibetan Buddhism is romanticized to such an extent today that many of its Western followers are strongly invested in the charismatic aspects of the tradition.[10] Steven Gelberg calls this "'make-believe,' imitation, exotic role-playing."[11]

CULTURAL COLONIALISM

Many scholars have written on the ethics of cultural colonialism, at times calling it adoption or appropriation.[12] I am most interested in pointing it out where it appears in modern mystical and spiritual movements, and how it reflects a continued fascination with, and seduction by, Western fantasies about the Orient. Hinduism, Buddhism, and Islam are often presented as pathways to physical, psychological, and spiritual freedom, achieved through a removal of religious matter—texts, rituals, and practices that are laborious, or don't fit into the concept of "mysticism." For example, Sufism is cast as a tradition distinct from Islam. "Numerous converts display an enthusiasm for and an attraction towards Sufism which is also found in Westerners converted to other oriental religions (Buddhism, Taoism and so on). Sufism is imagined, idealized, just as an order is, and both are perceived without reference to the Islamic society which gave birth to them."[13] As we will learn in Chapter Five, contemporary Sufism often erases Islam, even claiming it is a mystical movement with Christian origins. In other cases, it is a New Age practice focused on spiritual exercises, thus being identified with both spirituality *and* fitness.

Cultural colonialism encompasses a large number of acts, from dressing in ethnic styles to adopting certain forms of speech. In this book, I am most interested in the adoption of symbols, signs, and practices from other religious traditions and cultures. As a white Muslim scholar, I do not want to minimize the ways in which these colonizing acts may be offensive, harmful, and traumatic. I define cultural colonialism as *borrowing, adopting, or stealing another person's culture, religion, or tradition without giving credit to that tradition or being part of that tradition or identifying with that tradition.* Modern mystical teachers often incorporate parts of religious practices from Hinduism, Buddhism, and Islam into their business models, and in many cases, they claim ownership over them. In doing this, they can profit from other people's religious traditions through an assumption of identity.

The prolific author, Idries Shah, stated that he was part of an "esoteric" lineage of Naqshbandiyya (a Sufi *tariqa*, or order) from Afghanistan, a claim that has never been corroborated by scholars. He was never recognized by Naqshbandiyya leaders such as

Shaykhs Kabbani and Nazim and, according to some, "acted as an independent teacher with no strong connection to organized Sufism."[14] He changed Islamic rituals like *dhikr*, the Sufi ceremony of remembering God, into "spiritual exercises" that take place within study groups.[15] The writer Robert Graves, a follower of Shah, took it a step further, completely severing Sufism from Islam. Graves claimed, "The Sufis are at home in all religions" and sadly, are "commonly mistaken for a Muslim sect."[16] As the previous chapter showed, this sentiment was established much earlier by Orientalist scholars who helped to create the idea of universalistic Sufism.

Not everyone practices cultural colonialism. Efforts to create conversations, networks, and practices that engage multiple traditions often come from Hindus, Buddhists, and Muslims, as well as other religious folks. Hindu products created by Muslims for sale in Bali are not examples of cultural colonization. As argued by Vineeta Sinha in her work, there is not always a "negative impact of commodification."[17] Perhaps one distinction lies in who is using a religious product. Hindus have a religious intent behind the purchase of ritual items that does not change if a Muslim or other non-Hindu produces it. In Sinha's words, when

> religious symbols are transposed to an unrelated context, there is indeed the potential for their misappropriation and abuse. Recent examples involving Hindu symbols come readily to mind: Italian designer Roberto Cavalli's depiction of the deity Rama on designer bikinis, French shoe manufacturer Minelli's shoes with the image of Rama, Lacey's footwear featuring the OM sign on shoes, just to list a few prominent examples.[18]

These are examples of cultural colonialism.

Selection and commodification are two hallmarks of colonial economics. The commodification of mysticism relies heavily on these practices and can include the assumption of new identities. As Andrew Rawlinson points out, in a single century there are examples of North Americans taking on the identities of "Hindu swamis, Zen roshis or Sufi sheikhs."[19] In some cases, religious foundations are severed from contemplative practices, resulting in material goods that express a focus on the self, as opposed to service to others. In the mindfulness industry, these products include instructional books on mindful cooking and driving. This emphasis on the self is different from Buddhism, where "Mindfulness practice is designed to promote well-being in ourselves and others or—in the language of the Buddhist noble truths—to work toward the reduction of the suffering of all living beings."[20] In this case, modern mysticism replaces the repair of the world with a self-improvement project.

The commodification of the body is a key part of these practices. A "healthy" lifestyle is critical to the success of numerous successful spiritual entrepreneurs from Joel Osteen to Oprah Winfrey. The therapeutic industry and the business of religious marketing are linked. Spiritual cosmopolitanism is popular with those cobbling together an amalgamation of spiritualist, mystical, and body-centered identities and practices.[21] In some cases, there is no overt religious messaging but, instead, we find the inclusion of product placement promising a better life. In the March 2018 issue of *The Oprah Magazine*, The O List (Oprah's favorite things that month) features reusable Tiffany & Company coffee cups, billed as an alternative to paper cups that create waste.[22] In other instances, products are tied more directly to living a more intentional, ethical, and spiritual life. Such marketing strategies reflect Baudrillard's idea of identity, where individuals consume what they think signifies their vision of the self through the use of signs, symbols, and motifs—the Om sign, the yoga mat, and the whirling dervish.[23]

The mystical lifestyle and the Oriental aesthetic are seen in many industries, including fashion. Bohemian chic was popularized in the nineteenth century as evidence of the "displacement of class structures."[24] Today, Bohemian is a style that crosses class, available at Wal-Mart and Target as well as on the runways of New York and Paris at high prices. The late Talitha Getty, "avatar of North African style," was an important designer of Bohemian style, whose work was described by one fashion scholar here: "It was an orgy of orientalism: flowers, feathers, paisley and curlicues were the order of the day, an aggressive hedonism."[25]

The Bohemian style is often subsumed by ethnic or global styles. Julieta Tello, who refers to herself as a "curator" of "boho, ethnic and travel-inspired treasures from around the world" mixes pieces from Zimbabwe, Morocco, Ghana, Thailand, and India to create her "personal sanctuary."[26] The curatorship of a sanctuary patterned upon cultural artifacts is hardly new; this is exactly what Orientalists did in the past. Tello follows the traditions of earlier *cultural collectors* that include fashion designers, interior decorators, and expatriates. Foreign residents of Morocco are known to adopt the "Riad style," "Self style," "Homo style," or another public presentation of their new life that is often modeled on Orientalists of the past, complete with neocolonial behaviors like having service staff, even thinking of themselves as "a pasha, like a king."[27]

Religion is a form of modern capital that goes beyond design and fashion. The existence of "the market as a logical extension of God's natural law" in Osteen's ministry, discussed earlier, is seen in the marketing of Eastern religions as mysticism and spirituality.[28] Examples of this sentiment abound, from the success of Elizabeth Gilbert's *Eat, Pray, Love* (discussed in more detail in later chapters) to the $14-billion self-help book industry that includes the books of Marianne Williamson and Oprah Winfrey.[29] Gilbert's spiritual journey takes her to India and later Bali; she finds scrubbing floors in an ashram in India a "mystical" experience that, in her words, results in her feeling "a holy radiance of silence" and ultimately is healed by a local "medicine doctor" in

Bali.[30] As Diyah Larasati notes, this temporary experience of poverty is "a sign of the attainment of true otherness."[31] It is safe because the mystical dabbler can return to her home culture (white society) at any time.

India and Bali, featured in Gilbert's travelogue of spiritual experiences, are part of an expansive list of exotic places associated with the East that are imbued with magical, mystical powers. Morocco, Egypt, Thailand, Tibet, and other places have long been colonized by writers, artists, and, more recently, the entrepreneurs at the center of the business of mysticism. Contemporary spiritual seekers look to these places as curatives for the ills of modern life. Such is the case of Tibet, viewed by many as "a sacred land in which the paranormal is commonplace."[32] Today, Bali is a popular destination for mystical seekers.

Cultural colonization is also seen in academic circles. As noted in the last chapter, Sufism has been described as an amalgamation of different traditions that is distinct from so-called *normative* Islam. One author claims that "Muslim mysticism is entirely derivative."[33] These efforts to redefine Sufism as something non-Islamic are common, part of the larger colonial project that religious studies is implicated in. As Vincent Cornell puts it, these efforts lead to the impression of Sufism as "a separate sect or even a de facto alternative religion."[34] The work that these colonial adventures do in the world brings up important questions about the popularity of Eastern traditions of mysticism and the efforts to articulate it in ways that make it clear who "owns" it.

Many contemporary examples of the colonization of Sufism are found in Britain. One of these is the Blaketashi Darwish, a Sufi "order" that revolves around the poetry of William Blake and other Romantic writers. The secretive order, focused on the commonalities between British and Islamic mysticism, is rumored to read poetry in the nude as one of its central practices.[35] Their name—Blaketashi—is likely adopted from the Bektashi, a Sufi order popular in Turkey and elsewhere. Later on we will learn about other colonized forms of Sufism; for membership, one does not even need a passing knowledge of Islam. Seyyed Hossein Nasr (who is not without his own critics) calls this "New Age Sufism," and sees it as futile, for in his view, without the spiritual "sap" these unstable traditions will not survive.[36]

Cultural colonization is also found in popular literature. In *Eat, Pray, Love*, exotic religion—Hinduism, Buddhism, local Balinese tradition—is constructed as a panegyric for white, privileged isolation. Hinduism and Buddhism are parlayed into a self-help, white feminist anthem, available for the price of a divorce and a plane ticket to Bali.[37]

FROM THEOSOPHY TO TANTRIC SEX

The Orient has inspired numerous religious and philosophical movements, including those identified with mysticism. Theosophy, a spiritualist movement of the mid-nineteenth century, sought a direct apprehension of the divine, often through an ecstatic or mystical experience. Madame Blavatsky, co-founder of the Theosophical Society in New York, first identified Egypt as the source of wisdom, then India, and eventually Tibet—a place she barely set foot in (being turned back sixteen miles in).[38] She self-identified as a Spiritualist, then a Theosophist, and claimed Lord Gautama fit into an idea of Occultism that challenged old religion, or what was called "theological" Christianity.[39] Madame Blavatsky, like many who adopted or borrowed from religions associated with the East, was also a diehard Orientalist, as one description of her apartment suggests:

> Shelves and tables overflowed with exotic bric-a-brac: a mechanical bird, a wooden Buddha, Chinese fans, ivory cigarette holders. A mural of a jungle scene, complete with

> dried leaves and a mounted, snarling lion's head, covered one wall, while a bat spread its leathery wings over the doorway, and a stuffed monkey, wearing a dickey and grasping a page from Darwin's recently published *Descent of the Species* in one paw (this last being "a comment on materialistic scientists") stood in the center of the room.[40]

Theosophy is part of the history of the West's embrace of Eastern traditions. Along with other such movements, it often subsumed other people's religions into European, and later American, Christian-flavored spirituality. These movements often involve a fair degree of factual revisionism. One early example is found in theories surrounding the origins of Sufism. Claims that these Islamic devotional traditions, which date back to the tenth century (or perhaps earlier), are actually Hindu, Buddhist, or primordial are well known. In 1851, Edward Palmer argued that Sufism was the "primordial religion of the Aryan race."[41]

Theosophy has connections with Orientalism as well, much like the mysticism of today. As Paul Pedersen explains, the longing for the East is one of two central themes that led to the identification of Buddhism with psychology: "One is the sense of loss, the idea that the East is in possession of a truth or wisdom the West has lost and can regain only be learning from the East. Another is the fundamental assumption that man's nature is spiritual."[42] This is called spiritual psychology, and much of it is seen today in presentations of Buddhism, India, "wisdom traditions," and Sufism as forms of therapy.

A particularly interesting case of modern mysticism is found in Los Angeles at the center called Full Circle, which I introduced earlier. This community borrows extensively from Hinduism and Buddhism. Founded by actor Andrew Keegan, Full Circle is located in Venice Beach, California, at a "111-year-old temple," and features a dazzling array of mystical and spiritual practices featuring Eastern imagery, language, and religion.[43] Full Circle is New Age church meets California hippie chic with music, meditation, healing, dance, and various classes. Its minister is Reverend Alexander Polinsky, who founded something called Avatarism (the Hindu idea of avatar gives it its name), which is billed as a kind of game, philosophy, and spiritual practice. According to the movement's website, "Avatarism shows you how to transform yourself very rapidly" and sees this change as "the ultimate freedom."[44] This comes at a price, of course—but for a paid session in Avatarism you can instantaneously transform your life—instant mysticism!

Polinsky is a self-declared mystic who claims to have had his first spiritual experience when he was seven years old, after which he discovered shamanism, inspired by books in his family's library on Africa that reported people becoming "enlightened" through ecstatic ceremonies, which ultimately led him to studies of "Alchemy, Buddhism, Cosmology, the science of brain change, Shamanism, Egyptian lore, world religions and sects, bio feedback, hypnosis, and transcendental meditation."[45] As is the case with many North American mystics, indigenous culture is also part of his life story. At twenty-three, he had his second key mystical experience on an (unnamed) Indian reservation.[46] His third mystical experience took place in 2006 at, where else, Burning Man, after which he became the leader of Avatarism (inspired in part by Dan Gordon-Levitt, the brother of the famous actor), culminating in his current identity, which he described as a "spiritual entertainer in the lineage of Alan Watts, influenced by Ram Dass, Robert Anton Wilson, and Han Solo, with a little Jim Morrison and Kermit the Frog mixed in."[47]

Polinsky is not the only Full Circle member to borrow from Hinduism, Buddhism, and other religious traditions from the Orient. Meditation, sonic alchemy (i.e. music), sound healings, reiki healing circles, yoga, kirtans, and tribal dance are all offered at the center, which is called the Rose Temple.[48] The space includes Persian and Turkish carpets with paintings of Hindu deities on the walls.[49] Full Circle is also a tribe community, much like the Burners profiled earlier. Under the *Community* link on the organization's website, it reads "Join Our Tribe," followed with a description of some of Full Circle's offerings, which are accompanied by code words such as "spiritually" and "healing," "inspirational" and "full potential."[50]

The practitioners of Eastern religious traditions have, at times, capitalized on muddled Orientalism. Such is the case with yogimania. Yoga is so popular that a variety of figures have been able to interject themselves into the market. Hamid Bey, a self-proclaimed "miracle man and magnetic healer" from Egypt who toured the clubs of Los Angeles with Yogananda in the early twentieth century, promoted himself as a kind of general healer.[51] Through capitalizing on both the popularity of yoga and the fascination with the Orient, Bey was able to parlay a career for himself as a mystical teacher and healer of ailments.

The adoption of Hinduism, Buddhism, and Islam into new mystical communities is made easy due to the amorphous, fluid nature of modern mysticism. Concepts like *mysticism* and *spirituality* are, in a sense, meaningless. As Carrette and King point out: "The desire to attribute a universal essence to the meaning of spirituality also ignores the historical and cultural traces and differences in the uses of the term."[52] When used in North America, spirituality can serve to both colonize other people's religious traditions while assuming a Christian language. This seems especially true of Asian religions. "'Spirituality' is a means of colonizing and commodifying Asian wisdom traditions."[53]

As previously discussed, immediatism plays a large role in modern mysticism. People who colonize other religions for scholarly or commercial purposes often get them wrong. Religious traditions are complicated and esoteric, mystical, and contemplative practices are undertaken with a teacher or master for years, not as a multi-week course or instructional DVD. The business of mystic-spirituality has its own celebrities whose quick-fix programs in places such as Bali, Glastonbury, Boulder, and Santa Fe promise rather swift physical and spiritual transformations. Consider Sedona, Arizona, for example:

> In this New Age Vatican City, spiritual seekers will not find a pope or a singular St. Peter's Basilica. Instead, they will find a marketplace of spiritual goods and services—from Reiki healers to aura photographers, vortex tour companies to spiritual retreat centers. They will find spiritualist churches, and they will find venues hosting New Age rock stars like Deepak Chopra, J. Z. Knight, and Michael Beckwith.[54]

Contemporary celebrity guides and healers use mysticism to appeal to people who are uncomfortable with more traditional forms of religion, such as American churches whose pews often sit half empty unless, like Osteen, they appeal to a modern value like materialism.

Hinduism, Buddhism, and Islam have long been a part of mystical, spiritualist, and New Age movements. As I have pointed out, western appropriations of eastern traditions have a long history. The British mystic Alice Bailey (1880–1949) claimed to receive messages from someone named "the Tibetan," also known as "D. K.," and she was not alone, for others claimed to be reincarnations of a lama.[55] Cyril Hoskin, a British man who claimed to have been Tibetan in an earlier life, wrote, "my lonely Tibetan body [lay] safely stored in a stone coffin, under the unceasing care of three monks."[56] As Donald Lopez argues, these were people who mystified Tibet and then mystified the reading public.[57]

In these cases, it is often the "ideas" about the East that dominate the symbolic landscape. As one scholar observes: "For we can never be sure how much of western Buddhism is the real thing and how much is merely a western projection."[58] Typically, Hindus, Buddhists, and Muslims do not practice their traditions in some of the ways they exist in North American mysticism. Instead, we see the imagination, the idea, a nugget—of what takes place in the religious lives of Hindus, Buddhists, and Muslims.

Mystical communities like Full Circle are hardly alone in these productions of the East. As one study of exotic dance notes, the scholarship on belly dance shows that "Western belly dance practices conform more to Western women's conception of Middle Eastern culture than to any actual Middle Eastern practice."[59] As another example, Tantric Hinduism is an extremely secretive practice that has become something completely different in its repackaging as a form of bodily or/and sexual healing. As Sthaneshwar Timalsina writes:

> Tantra in the West functions not in its ability to remain "secret," but in its ability to reveal. In my personal meeting with one Western Tantric guru, he reported that when Sakti flows through his eyes, dzzz ... the flash of light comes out, and sometimes it is so powerful that his eyes start bleeding. In my meeting with another guru, he persuaded me to touch my shoulder and told me that the physical pain I had was now gone. In yet another encounter, one guru claimed that he belongs to twenty-seven members of the chosen beings coming from different galaxies to rescue humankind. These claims are the means to enter into the market: the bigger the claim, the bigger the market.[60]

In this case, only a tangential or fleeting reference to the original tradition is present. There are also exercise programs, some of them extraordinarily popular, that also utilize the Orient as a marketing strategy.

North American fitness programs have successfully incorporated a number of "exotic" practices—karate, yoga, and most recently zumba (which includes exercises based on salsa and belly dance moves as well as Afro-Cuban, merengue, cha-cha, hip-hop, and Brazilian dance). These borrowed practices are refigured to such a degree that participants from the donor cultures may find them unrecognizable.[61] As I discuss in Chapter Four, yoga is perhaps the best case of the Orientalism at play in North American fitness programs.

More troubling cases of cultural colonialism include the sexual workshops described as "native" or "exotic." These namings represent a marketing strategy based on the idea of the colonized or foreign as sexually potent and are invested in colonial images of power. In her study of cultural colonialism, Deborah Root describes an adult HBO documentary series that includes a Cherokee sex workshop that teaches couples how to have sex with the earth.[62]

The East inspires all sorts of capitalist ventures. One finds these types of businesses, which are often linked with yoga, meditation, or some other Eastern practice, on Facebook and other social media platforms. In one example, a sexual yogic feminist teacher named Ronya Sebastian dons yoga pants and a bindi while she simulates an orgasm. The bindi is a mystic symbol, as scholars have noted. "Primarily associated with the third eye of the Hindu god Shiva, the *bindi* represents the corresponding mystic third eye among mortals."[63] By wearing it, Sebastian both identifies herself with Hindu mysticism and corrupts it. Sebastian also uses Eastern keywords to market her business through methods such as "yoni egg," practice, meditation, goddess visualization, "orgasmic breathwork," and "Taoist breast massage."[64] She advertises through Facebook and on her own website, and includes at least one teaser video that shows her simulating sexual pleasure, specifically masturbation, on camera.

The colonizing of religion is not only an issue of commodification. Individuals who practice their religious and cultural traditions—African American, Native American, Hindu, Buddhist,

Muslim—are concerned with spiritual harm. In the case of Tibetan Buddhism, there is considerable debate regarding whether its popularity is compromising to the religion. As Dagyab Kyabgön Rinpoche writes, the "superstition, sectarianism, and dogmatism" caused by Tibet's popularity results in a serious problem. "Inner development, as Buddhism teaches, is impossible under these conditions, and stagnation, delusion, and defensive rigidity stand in their place."[65] In other words, dabbling in other people's religions can cause real damage.

Cultural colonialism involves difficult conversations surrounding the appreciation of another culture and whether capitalizing on it, whether for personal or financial benefit, is ethical. The appreciation of Buddhism might include the serious study of the tradition and the purchase of items that benefit their makers. In Thailand, the production of Buddhist amulets benefits the craftspeople who make them as well as some of the monasteries they are associated with: "For example, the proceeds from the sale of the Maechee Boonruean amulets above are for the repair of the Samphanthawong monastery and a museum dedicated to this nun (maybe the first museum dedicated specifically to a professional Buddhist woman in Thailand)."[66] However, a line is often crossed.

Popular music is an industry where we find mysticism, with the British band Coldplay offering one example. They used a Coleman Barks translation of a Rumi poem titled "The Guest House" on their seventh album, inspired by the lead singer Chris Martin's declaration that the poem changed his life and offered comfort in a time of heartbreak.[67] At a Coldplay concert, audience members waved "digital bracelets that synchronously changed color to Rumi's couplets."[68] In this case, Rumi functioned as a spiritual guide for Chris Martin as well as an artistic inspiration who is simultaneously presented as a spiritual guide for the entire audience. In this example of modern mysticism,

Islam disappears completely. More broadly in the music industry, terms like "Sufi" or "world" music are used to market artists. This illustrates the appeal of universalism in advertising products associated with mysticism: "As recording companies repackage Sufi music as world music, they often undertake a gradual resacralization of the music as a prelude to spiritualizing it for more general consumption."[69]

The commodification of Buddhist or Islamic imagery can also result in the creation of a fad, style, or product that has little to do with its religious source. Zen is an example of hypersignification—a semiotic metamorphosis into a sign with an "explosion of meanings and usages."[70] Zen is used to market music devices that suggest the customer "Find Your Zen," a breakfast cereal called Nature's Path Optimum Zen that promises "inner harmony," and a face cream by L'Oreal that claims to "combat the effects of stress" and make the "skin look relaxed."[71] Rumi and more broadly, Sufism, also suffers from hypersignification, seen in the countless images of whirling dervishes, Rumi quotes, and fake quotes that are attributed to Hafiz and other Muslim poets. A coffee shop in Atlanta features a "whirling dervish" on the menu sourced from Ethiopia, even though whirling dervishes come from Turkey.[72]

The ways in which society displays and incorporates Hinduism, Buddhism, and Islam into social life are not always exploitive. Some of the therapies that emerge from mysticism include efforts to create healthy communities or engage in practices that are beneficial to numerous individuals seeking therapeutic care. A. Reza Arasteh, for instance, was an Iranian psychologist (1927–92) who attempted to integrate different therapeutic models into an integrative psychology, what he saw as "the dialogue between psychology and religion."[73] However, there is a profound difference between making money and creating good in the world. Modern mysticism seems to be much more invested in the former.

WHITE MYSTICISM

Individuals who identify with religion also market themselves. Christian celebrity evangelists like Joel Osteen have an entire corporation built around them; in his case, his is focused on the prosperity gospel—a way to bind Christianity and materialism together into a personal theology. Muslim preachers also *perform* Islam as televangelists, preachers, and spokespeople for a particular community. Abdullah Gymniastiar, a popular Muslim Indonesian preacher, uses his popularity to preach a Muslim brand of Osteen's prosperity gospel. As Marcia Hermansen argues, American Muslim converts perform Islam in ways that may mimic or play the role of a devout Muslim: "Also, in a performance one creates and transforms an imaginary space, and therefore non-verbal elements such as costume and gesture function as much to persuade as do actual verbal utterances."[74]

The performance of Islam in North America is one place where we see cultural colonialism become a complex issue, especially in the context of converts. Consider Hamza Yusuf, a white convert Muslim whose scholarship, role in the first North American Islamic university Zaytuna College, and popularity as a public intellectual are all dependent on his persona, perfect Arabic diction, and the Islamic clothing he wears. As Mahdi Tourage points out in his study of Islamic revivals and the place of white converts in it, these individuals play a role that has supporting characters (Black imams like Imam Zaid Shakir) and other accouterments like "pious gestures," "Islamic items of clothing," "brown" wives, "having many children," and correct Islamic speech (dropping phrases like "Alhamdulillah" and "Mash Allah").[75]

Shaykh Hamza Yusuf's performance of Islam raises interesting questions about the consumptive practices of Muslims. When does religion cross over to a fetish? According to Marx, the "fetishism of the commodity" is a part of modernity in which experiences are sold as products. As Karim Douglas Crow puts it: "Aesthetic value is dictated by financialized value" and "people view the whole being as a marketable commodity."[76] I am not suggesting that Hamza Yusuf views Muslims, or anyone else, as a commodity. In fact, Hamza is against usury and warns of the ill effects capitalism has on the soul. However, the performance of religion can unconsciously involve the mimicking of culture—in this case, Arab culture. Crow articulates this point: "Unpretentious simplicity in Islamic clothing and moderate contentment with minimal possessions may today be 'imaged' as a highly desirable feature of the sought-after 'Lifestyle.'"[77] Hamza Yusuf is authentically Muslim; however, this authenticity is predicated on a certain view of Arab culture. As such, his public persona raises interesting questions regarding racial politics and cultural appropriation. While he does not represent an overt case of capitalizing on a religious tradition as we see in the commodification of Rumi, he walks the line.

By all appearances, Shaykh Hamza is a believing Muslim. However, Islam is commodified and performed in different ways. New York fashion's use of Rumi on the runway (specifically in Donna Karan's show) was described by the *New York Times* in this way: "Cloud-color satins, storm-color cashmeres, glimpses of shoulders and shinbones, and Rumi."[78] Arabic has also been used as a form of exotic style. In an episode of *Sex and the City*, the main character Carrie Bradshaw wore a necklace with a large pendant of *Allah* spelled out in Arabic letters.[79]

Zygmunt Bauman suggests that it is not just individuals like Osteen and Yusuf who function as commodities, but also consumers who are commodified.[80] This includes religious consumers. The commodified consumer fits into a vision of a society that is predicated on capitalism. The commodification of desirable symbols and objects—wellness, beauty, wisdom, the mystical—is an example of this consumerism, which is based on pleasing oneself. "Consumer culture utilizes spectacular images and symbolic products that conjure up fantasies and desires, which suggests that romantic authenticity and emotional fulfillment can be attained by narcissistically and selfishly pleasing oneself."[81] The commodification of religion has even entered the workplace, where "spirituality" is domesticated, integrated into corporate practices, and used to increase production and consumption.[82] Consumers play a role, much like Hamza Yusuf's performance of "traditional" Islam. These performances often use symbols that refer to a recognizable reality. As Jacques Derrida explains, the performance repeats a "coded or iterable utterance" that is "identifiable in some way as a citation."[83]

As discussed earlier, belly dance is one of many practices that was introduced to North America (first at the 1893 Chicago World's Fair), gained popularity, and now exists in different forms, including its assumption of a "tribal" identity.[84] Today, belly dance is part of a larger field of exercise programs and dance styles that offer feminist messaging, featured at festivals like California's Tribal Fest.[85] Wildly more popular than belly dance, yoga is the Eastern tradition that has perhaps suffered the most exploitation at the hands of mystical capitalists. It is a multi-billion-dollar business that includes countless iterations of yoga, most of them having no relationship with Hinduism or foundational yogic practice, and certainly not with yoga as a philosophical system. As one study notes, these versions of yoga include "AIDS yoga, yoga for fertility, pre- and postnatal yoga, yoga for kids, yoga with dogs, aqua yoga, disco yoga, naked yoga, and laughter yoga, as well as trademarked niche brands like Slim Calm Sexy, Goddess Yoga, Yoga Booty Ballet, AntiGravity Yoga, Acro Yoga, Revita-Yoga (to resist wrinkles), Yoga for Golfers, and Taxi Yoga (for people who spend their days driving)."[86] Many practices, including meditation and so-called "Sufi music," include no reference to the religious tradition they come from. They are what I would call *mystical translations*. One example is MBSR (Mindfulness Based Stress Reduction), introduced by

Kabat-Zinn in 1990, which is essentially Buddhist meditation translated into a language for a secular audience.[87]

Another example of this translation project is the use of the *ney*, the Turkish reed-flute associated with Rumi (and the Mevlevi order), in "world" and New Age music. This instrument is branded as a mystical product. In one study of the *ney*, the author notes:

> The processes briefly delineated here, including the touristification, commercialization and nationalization of Mevlevi practices, have all fed into the current revitalization of the *ney*, in a way that simplifies the public life of the *ney* to an instrument of Sufi music only. This has also shaped the instrument in material ways, evident in the marketing and circulating of *neys* branded under the names "mystic *ney*" or the "Sufi flute," occasionally complimented with *ney*-training DVDs.[88]

Islam is also adopted in ways that do not signal commodification, but represent other kinds of rebranding. One example is the use of Muslim imagery, vocabulary, and liturgy by North American non-Muslims. This is seen in the use of "Mecca" as a descriptor for places and the popularity of Muslim names such as Muhammad, Ali, and Fatima by African Americans who may not be Muslim, but have Muslim relatives. The *shahada*, the Islamic profession of faith, is known to be used by the urban gang the Vice Lords, who chant it before beating someone up, an example of both "Islamizing English" and Islam "as a symbol of rebellion and minority identification."[89]

African Americans and Muslims of African descent compose the largest groups of Muslims in America. However, large numbers of non-African American converts to Islam follow white or immigrant Muslim preachers and intellectuals, ignoring African Americans such as Amina Wadud, Zaid Shakir, and others. This is even more apparent in non-Muslim "mystical Sufis," whose fascination with Rumi and Hafiz reveal their Orientalist proclivities. American Muslim history relies on African and African American foundations, but mystical Sufis do not typically cite Malcolm X as a leader. There are numerous examples of how Sufism is whitewashed. For example, Deepak Chopra has described his interpretations as *moods*.[90] There are no references to the great Sufi masters of Africa, and certainly not to Malcolm X or Muhammad Ali, who became aligned with Sufism in his later years.

While white Americans—Nones, spiritualists, and mystical Sufis—ignore the place of African Americans in Islam, they capitalize on their music by adopting the vocabulary, dress, and music of hip-hop. As Su'ad Abdul Khabeer points out, much of this music—hip-hop—is Muslim:

> Since hip hop's beginnings in New York City's South Bronx, Islamicate theologies, such as the Five Percent Nation and the Nation of Islam, have contributed to shaping its current form. Thus, from artists who are more well-known for their secular pursuits, such as the Notorious B.I.G. to a religiously observant Muslim like Mos Def, rappers commonly integrate Islamicate terminology or ideologies in their rhymes. For example, phrases like "dropping science" and addressing women as "earth" and men as "son" and "god" are examples of references from Five Percenter theology that are replete in hip hop music and vernacular.[91]

Capitalism is a powerful force that influences the production of cultural commodities, but also determines who benefits from them. "The story of whites co-opting black cultural forms, and then enjoying more profit than those whose creative powers initially produced them, is nothing new. Hip-hop faces the same fate as jazz and blues, for example, as a sizeable portion of record sales are made to whites, and white record executives are at the top of the billion-dollar industry."[92]

The practices associated with New Age Sufism, New Sufism, Rumimania, and Neo-Sufism are situated in North American racial politics. As El-Zein points out, it is not the scholarly translations of Rumi that sell thousands of copies, but the interpretations of Rumi—glossed from English versions of the poem—by a white New Age author (Coleman Barks).[93] The expertise ascribed to whiteness is apparent in much of modern mysticism—through the whitewashing of religious traditions, the Anglicizing of mystical figures, and in the success of white celebrity teachers like Marianne Williamson, one of the bestselling authors in the self-help book industry, where Americans spend $600 million each year.[94]

Products tied to Eastern mysticism are not the only place that cultural colonialism takes place. African American scholars have written extensively on the cannibalization of Black culture by white Americans as a form of contemporary colonialism. As Baruti Kopano points out:

> To be clear, colonial masters are committed to preserving a role for colonized people as dominated, controlled, and exploited subjects. Although the culture of black America is the foundation for much of American popular culture, black art forms are offered in the popular imagination to marginalize blacks and other nonwhites and to reaffirm white supremacy. Popular culture and the media that are used to disseminate its messages are arsenals of the hegemonic class.[95]

The colonial master often consumes and conquers culture through literature, fashion, and other public pursuits. Rudyard Kipling's *Kim* is one example, where the author addresses racial difference while disavowing it. Ultimately the whiteness is exposed underneath the costume Kim wears.[96] However, what happens in societies where white is the operative identity? Gail Ching-Liang Low suggests that in these cases, "White operates as the invisible norm in racist cultures and exnominates itself as a colour by positioning itself outside of the self/Other dialectic."[97]

The whitewashing of mysticism allows white individuals to adopt a dress, language, or practice as a style, therapeutic model, or form of spirituality. Historically, Europeans and Americans have conquered the East through role-playing. In earlier centuries, Orientalism often took hold of people's imaginations, including some of the greatest writers of Romantic Orientalism who dressed like sultans. William Beckford famously referred to himself as the caliph and named his estate Bagdad.[98] Copious examples of this cultural cross-dressing exist in the historical record. The fashion designer Paul Poiret threw parties that simulated harem life, complete with slavery, liberation, and ornate Oriental costumes and sets.[99] Today, yoginis wear tunics, harem pants, and caftans from companies ranging from Prana (literally, "life principle") to Nordstrom.

Cultural colonization often involves the universalization of religious traditions. In modern mysticism, Rumi becomes a teacher of "moods" and Zen is a fashion and home-decorating style. As William Rasch points out, other people's religions are brought into a universalistic Christianity that is "acknowledged as legitimate."[100] These religions are relativized to fit into a notion of secularism that is, at its core, very Christian. The Catholic liberation theologian Las Casas fell prey to this. In his view, "Religiousness is a seemingly universal category; it defines what is common to all religions—sacrifice. Thus we have competing universalities, namely, a category of Christianity and also the truth of a universal medium, namely, a category of religiousness that serves as a ground for comparing the sacrifice of God's 'only begotten Son' and the human sacrifices conducted by Aztec priests."[101]

CULTURAL CONSUMPTION

In the West, culture challenges the idea of a secular state where religion is privatized. Culture is viewed as a negotiable aspect of modern society. "In liberal societies, culture is positioned as 'background' of the subject, as something one may opt in or out of and also deliberate about. (This is what makes rational choice theory intellectually coherent as a form of social theory for liberal societies, but only for liberal societies)."[102] Because it is negotiable and can be opted out of, it can also be opted into—and sold as a commodity.

In many religious communities, the religious marketplace is not separated into the sacred and the profane. Hindu items in American food markets often include a range of items that offer a convenient shopping experience for everyday consumers as well as those celebrating numerous Hindu festivals and other occasions. "Such grocery stores deal with food items, utensils, appliances, cosmetics, fresh fruits and vegetables, and also religious items. The religious items and statues/idols of Gods share the shelves with shampoo, toothpaste, soap, cosmetics, jewelry, and spices just to name a few."[103] The religious market is not guided by concerns about mixing the religious and the profane. As Vineeta Sinha argues, "marking boundaries between 'sacred' and 'secular' objects is not the primary concern."[104]

Religious items produced by religious folks are common. In Mecca, pilgrims can buy souvenirs and bottles of holy water, and there is no problem with this. What we are concerned with here is something different—products that are made for consumers who deny they are being religious and insist they are practicing mysticism or spirituality. The stuff they are practicing (remember, mysticism and spirituality are empty referents) is constructed from other people's religions. Tantra is one example. In its original Hindu form, it is a distinct and controversial aspect of Hinduism. In North America, it becomes a sexual practice.

"Tantra in the Western mindset differs somewhat from the above depictions and stands for the exotic and orgasmic practices coming from India and Tibet that blend sex and meditation … Tantra has been transformed to a 'Cult of Ecstasy' and the process of romanticisation has been binary."[105]

Religious people have often borrowed from other cultures. One only needs to visit a mosque that was a church, or a church that was a Roman temple, to see an example of this history. The cultural colonialism I am interested in discussing in this and the following chapters is fixated on the East and has been transformed into all sorts of businesses—from courses on the Kama Sutra and its sexual secrets to the "hugging" and "emission of power" marketed by individuals who sell touching and companionship.[106]

The cultural commodification focused on the East is also part of a modern religious marketplace that did not exist in the past. The introduction of choice, buttressed by wealth and mobility and supported by secular ideology, allows individuals to create their own religion. As Michaela Pfadenhauer explains: "Nowadays, religions find themselves in a competitive situation that forces them to make their respective meaning offerings appear attractive. This gives lay people the opportunity to choose between different religious purveyors of meaning and to put together their own eclectic packages of spiritual meaning."[107] Discussed in the Introduction, choice is an aspect of modernity that represents the rejection of the old authoritarian model of religious life.

Dressing up in clothing inspired by the Orient is a transitory process that affluent white people can move effortlessly in and out of. As scholars have noted, dressing in exotic costumes denotes a colonial act where territory, which is mapped on the body, is taken at will. As Gail Low has written: "The primary attraction of cross-cultural dress is, then, the promise of 'transgressive' pleasure without the penalties of actual change. Such metamorphosis does little to subvert existing power hierarchies, since the cross-dresser may always reveal or revert to the white identity underneath the native clothes."[108]

Sacred music, often marketed as "spiritual" or "world" music, is another product where a culture is often consumed; in this case, specific religious and cultural practices are blurred together as a marketing strategy. The music festival held in Fes every year is one example; the "sacred" is reconstituted from colonized or neocolonized territories. "By employing sounds iconically linked to particular sacred traditions and recontextualizing them in contexts of heterodoxy, festival organizers self-consciously create a sort of doxa of their own, one that downplays national and religious differences to emphasize 'spiritual' or 'sacred' homogeneity (Bourdieu, 1977). The sacred is extracted from these traditions like essence is extracted from flowers."[109] The result is a music festival that casts "modern" religion as necessarily authoritarian and dangerous, and "mysticism" as emancipatory and safe.

MUDDLED ORIENTALISM

> *Often, similar types of jewelry would be worn, such as lotus flower, an ohm sign, or a Hindu or Buddhist symbol. In addition, a shawl is often wrapped around their shoulders and worn along with brown leather sandals.*[110]
>
> Description of white migrant female fashion in Bali

Orientalism has generated a catalogue of images that figures prominently in modern mysticism. Through the adoption of particular symbols and images, corporate interests are able to appeal to numerous consumer audiences, from the fashionable hipster to the older wellness-seeker. The end result is often "muddled," seen in the collection of Orientalist symbols one might find at a department store that sells necklaces with the Hand of Fatima alongside Buddha T-shirts. Hence the title of this book, which speaks to the anachronistic nature of mystical consumerism in which material objects symbolizing religious traditions betray their non-materialist teachings. Quoting a fellow scholar, "The Other is an amalgamation of everything that is not part of a secular, white, European-American identity."[111]

In the context of Orientalism, this binary takes on the tension between repulsion and desire for the foreign body. "Orientalism must invoke and inscribe the very pleasure and unpleasure contingent on that difference. Hence Orientalist discourse delivers an Other which is both an object of knowledge and surveillance and an object of libidinous impulses."[112] One way this difference is resolved is by adopting Eastern dress, language, and practices—a symbolic assumption of Hindu, Buddhist, and Muslim bodies—while retaining the power inherent in white identity.

Religious traditions are often confused in Orientalism, whether presented as New Age religions that borrow from Hinduism, Buddhism, and Islam, or in their public expression through material products and mystical tourism. Hinduism and Buddhism are often blurred into an amorphous Indian spirituality and co-opted by Christian contemplatives and others marketing new mysticisms and spiritualities. Bernadette Roberts's use of *atman* as self, and ideas such as "the Great Passageway," are examples of this co-optive strategy.[113] As Arthur Versluis notes, she provides few specifics and instead opts for no "specific directions," just her own experiences as a self-proclaimed mystic.[114] Roberts marketed herself using Hindu and Buddhist ideas, which she essentially rejected in favor of something indefinable and psychological.[115]

Products that emerge out of the Orientalist milieu often include images and symbols from the East—paisley patterns, an image of the Buddha, a Moorish arch. There is also a fair amount of creative license in the interpretation of these images and their manipulation into new products. In fashion, for example, we see this in a wide variety of styles and conventions. "Thus we have Chinese sleeves, Egyptian girdles, Turkish jackets, Russian touquets."[116] We also see the conflation of these styles, both in fashion and other products that are influenced by the arts, cultures, and religions of the Orient. In the last chapter of this book, I discuss how Orientalist style is used in the *Star Wars* films, through both architectural motifs and the use of different forms of veiling, from Princess Leia to more recent characters like Rey.

Orientalism was, at the outset, both an intellectual and colonial project. As Said writes: "The relation between the Orientalist and Orient was essentially hermeneutical: standing before a distant, barely intelligible civilization or cultural monument, the Orientalist scholar reduced the obscurity by translating, sympathetically portraying, inwardly grasping the hard-to-reach object."[117] As such, it evolved alongside and in cooperation with religious studies, anthropology, historical analysis, and linguistics, organizing the East into categories of knowledge, some of which remain influential today. Classification is apparent in this history. As John Urry explains: "The visual sense of possession developed across nineteenth-century Europe."[118] The ways in which the gaze became part of European, and later, North American culture, is important. These persist in society at large, in portable objects related to the East and in mystical tourism. In the nineteenth century, "New Technologies of the gaze began to be produced and circulated, including postcards, guidebooks, photographs, commodities, arcades, cafes, dioramas, mirrors, plate-glass windows," and much more.[119] Today, the gaze can be seen in Rumi postcards and bumper stickers, guidebooks to Buddhist sites, photographs and memes (often with fake quotes) of the Buddha, and other products.

Muddled Orientalism features a collection of images from Japan, India, Egypt, Persia, and elsewhere that are used to represent the exoticism of the East. Some of the greatest works of

Orientalist literature feature these images. In Kipling's *Kim* (1901), a shop in the text is described as including "emblematic totems of the east, there are ghost-daggers, Tibetan prayer wheels, precious stones and jewelry, gilt Buddhas, ivory, friezes of fantastic details, and lacquer altars reeking of incense."[120] The Orient is often the inspiration for fantastic styles. This is certainly the case in fashion. The designer Mariano Fortuny, for example, "called upon a stockpile of Eastern motifs," which resulted in suggestions of Ali Baba or a North African pattern in his clothing.[121] Like many European and American designers, "Fortuny's Orient was as magical and as definite as Delacroix's, hovering between a pilgrim's specificity and a romantic's allure."[122]

In North America, muddled Orientalism has been part of public space since the post-WWI period, when Middle Eastern restaurants and clubs began to emerge in large numbers due to the popularity of Orientalism and, in particular, the interest in Egyptology. These spaces often reflected a lack of refinement: "Orientalist décor reminiscent of a Hollywood film set," with a "fantasy version of the orient to appeal to a diverse clientele."[123] Many of us have been in "Middle Eastern" restaurants with Persian carpets, Moroccan lanterns, Rajastani pillows, and Egyptian tapestries.

In the case of contemporary mysticism, the Orient is one of many places that is used as part of a kind of collective smorgasbord of spirituality. In a 2018 interview, Oprah described her daily spiritual practices. She began with an online Sufi reading and, "Then I meditate. This morning, I observed 20 minutes of silence sitting in my breakfast chair. If it were warmer, I would go outside. My house is surrounded by over 3,000 trees; it feels like I live in a park. When I want to meditate, I can go to a special rock that is carved into the shape of a seat. Or I can sit underneath the 12 live oak trees that I call 'the Apostles.'"[124]

Oprah's brand of spirituality exemplifies the muddled Orientalism that characterizes much of modern mysticism. She

A Middle Eastern restaurant in the American South (courtesy of Matthew Pierce).

begins with some Sufi readings (perhaps sourced from an Islamic text), follows it with meditation (likely based in Hindu or Buddhist practice), moves on to silent meditation (Quaker?), and ends with a reference to Christianity through trees named after the twelve apostles of Jesus. Oprah is an easy study of the appeal of modern mysticism—fabulously wealthy, beautiful, famous, and a self-branding genius—but she is in no way alone in her use of muddled Orientalism.

Muddled Orientalism is an established part of Western mysticism. In the nineteenth century, Madame Blavatsky and The Colonel (Henry Steel Olcott) claimed that Tibetans, Indians, and Egyptians had all identified her brand of Theosophy as the new spiritual movement, and they produced a letter from the Brotherhood of Luxor as proof. "Brother Neophyte, we greet

Thee. He who seeks us finds us. TRY. Rest thy mind—banish all foul doubt. We keep watch over our faithful soldiers. Sister Helen is a valiant, trustworthy servant. Open thy spirit to a conviction, have faith and she will lead thee to the Golden Gate of Truth."[125]

The mystical marketplace has an extensive catalogue of products that features the confused imagery of the East. Christians can practice PraiseMoves or Holy Yoga, and Jews have options like Shabbat Yoga, representing the commodification of one religion for another.[126] The Orient exists as a mythical tableau from which the individual can plug in his or her desires and formulate an identity as mystical, spiritual, exotic, or Bohemian. As one scholar notes, this imagined identity "is invented through translation in different locations, and keeps proliferating because it is repeatedly reproduced (granted in newer versions) through the distribution of modern and current popular globalized culture seen in the depictions made for mass media."[127] These messy translations are the focus of this chapter.

Muddled Orientalism is an example of the tendency to force the world into binary categories. For a long time, people living in North America and Europe have thought of themselves as modern humans, and everyone else as different, or un-modern. These *others* include the people of the Orient as well as those living in other regions, such as the continent of Africa. As Achille Mbembe reminds us: "But it is in relation to Africa that the notion of 'absolute otherness' has been taken farthest. It is now widely acknowledged that Africa as an idea, a concept, has historically served, and continues to serve, as a polemical argument for the West's desperate desire to assert its difference from the rest of the world."[128] The details of Africa are also muddled in the minds of the West—its numerous histories, civilizations, cultures, languages, and communities a blur of exotic words, symbols, and images.

Orientalism is often thought of as a problem that only affects the Middle East. Said focused much of his work on Orientalism dispatched against Arabs, and others have followed suit, producing studies of Orientalism as it relates to the study of Islam. However, its reach goes farther: Orientalism also implicates East Asia. The way that Japanese, Chinese, Thai, and other East Asians (and Southeast Asians) are framed in Orientalist discourse is, of course, different than in Muslim-majority cultures, but it is still harmful. The exotic is still apparent in these representations, which are characterized by a smorgasbord of imagery. As one scholar of Orientalist fashion reminds us:

> By the first half of the eighteenth century, the clichés that had begun to take shape in the baroque period had become well and truly entrenched: long-necked birds; magnificent insects; monkeys; Chinamen with long, droopy moustaches and wide sleeves; arbitrary outcropping rock formations; spiky trees; splayed-roof pagodas (feasibly sharing the landscape with classical ruins)—all assembling in a rambling riot of decorative excess.[129]

In mystical, spiritualist, and New Age movements, this messiness is often apparent. The Orient, Africa, and Native American cultures also are often thrown into a grab bag of mysticism and reconstituted as a new tradition. In one example, Pilangi Dasa (alias Herman Vetterling) produced *Swedenborg the Buddhist*, described as "an astrally projected dialogue between Swedenborg, a Brahmin, a Buddhist monk, a Parsee, an Aztec Indian, an Icelander, an anonymous woman, and himself."[130] This fictionalized theosophy and spiritual text illustrates the influence of Orientalism in modern mysticism.

The ways in which the Orient was collected, displayed, and performed by Europeans and North Americans is part of muddled Orientalism. Bringing together Japanese art, Persian carpets, Turkish silks, Hindu icons, and other objects is all part of the process of collection and possession that Yoshihara and other scholars have highlighted in their work. In some cases, these collecting strategies were distinct and quite focused in the cultural artifacts organized into museum collections around Europe. In other cases, collecting Oriental products was haphazard, including objects like kimonos from Japan, ceramics from Turkey, and carpets from Persia. The Aesthetic Movement played an important role in this eclectic aestheticism, making a large variety of objects available to the public, and not just the wealthy upper class.[131] As the art historian Roger Stein has argued, these collections were a form of cultural appropriation that focused on the East, and in the late nineteenth century, we find a "pastiche of unrelated, exotic formats"—which I have named muddled Orientalism.[132]

Materialism is a consequence of this desire to control, subjugate, and police the subject. Anthropology's self-critical turn has examined this in detail, especially in reference to museums and other projects of cataloguing culture. As documented in Sónia Silva's work on the National Ethnography Museum in Portugal's efforts to decolonize, the presentation of African religious objects as "fetishes" represents the larger colonial project of mystifying Africa and characterizing the culture of the African as "unqualified."[133] Museums, by their very nature, are exercises in voyeurism in which entire civilizations, many that have been brutally colonized, are subject to the colonial gaze.

The harem is another site where the male colonial gaze is particularly intense. The image of the harem as a site of wanton sexual behavior has left an indelible mark on the Western imagination that has influenced the accumulation of objects identified with the East. As one scholar writes, "The harem, in Western discourse, is the archetypal expression not only of orientalism, but of male authority over its greatest rival, the fractious female. The desire to collect is certainly a desire to master things that promise pleasure."[134] The accumulation of these items is tantamount to a symbolic ownership of the Orient.

Sites of mystical tourism include new harems, spaces viewed as mysterious, powerful, and often dangerous. Priv-lit focused on the mystic-spiritual journey often includes a recycling of the tropes associated with the harem. Larasati connects them here: "In this context, Tomė Pires' colonial report, Portuguese paintings depicting Asian peoples published in *Imagens do Oriente no sėculo XVI* (de Matos), and Elizabeth Gilbert's travel narrative culminate in Julia Roberts' retelling of India and Indonesia. Such a simulacrum splashed over time and across continents interchanges the invisibility and the visibility of the female body through spatial appropriation."[135]

One of the hallmarks of Orientalism has always been sloppiness, resulting in a general idea about the East painted with broad strokes. India, Bali, or Morocco are all exotic, antithetical to the "West," and hold the promise of personal transformation. Muddled Orientalism is a part of America's history. The yogi was often interchanged with the fakir (*faqir*) and even taken on as a character on the American stage. "Unlike the yoga ascetics, who for most Westerners appeared only as distant 'natives' accessible via narrative or, at best, photographic media, yogi magicians brought the Orient alive on Western stages. Though often billed as 'fakirs,' they frequently appeared dressed in elaborate robes and turbans, bedecked with jewels and feathers to play up the allure of Oriental luxe."[136] In fact, these entertainers were typically Englishmen or Americans.

The production of Orientalist-themed products is also a muddled process, often having a complicated, wayward path to the consumer. The Moroccan-style "Arabian Nights" lanterns with colored glass are not typically made in Morocco, but India. At times, there is a "manipulation" of symbols in the production of religious paraphernalia. This is certainly true of Hindu religious items. "This sentiment of being connected to the roots has been manipulated by entrepreneurs. As any religious item from India is considered authentic, the items do come from India but are sometimes mass-produced in China from where these are then supplied to India and from India to the rest of the world."[137]

Mystical tourism is examined in more detail in Chapters Four and Five, which focus on sites that are marketed based on their offerings of an Eastern mysticism. Other places feature the Orient, but as part of a larger collection of cultures, from the West and the East. Glastonbury, in southwest England, is visited by tourists who seek healing, knowledge, and personal growth along with ample consumer opportunities that feature a wide array of goods ranging from T-shirts to paintings of chakras and goddess figures. As one study notes, the list of spiritual experiences and products available is a confused amalgamation of sourcing from ancient Britain, the East, and beyond:

> Thousands visit Glastonbury for the Anglican and Catholic pilgrimages; for courses at the Isle of Avalon Foundation (which sees itself as the successor to the Druidic university); for the array of healing on offer; for the annual Goddess Conference or the Glastonbury Symposium on Cereology (Crop Circles); for ritual activity at various times on the eightfold calendar widely observed by "free range" pagans, Druids, and Wiccans; to visit Britain's first officially registered Goddess Temple; and as individual pilgrims, spiritual seekers and tourists. In addition to groups already mentioned, Glastonbury has attracted devotees of Sai Baba, members of ISKCON, Baha'is, Sufis of various sorts, and at least three people claiming either to be, to channel or to represent Buddha Maitreya in recent years.[138]

MUDDLED IDENTITIES

Muddled Orientalism also blurs symbols, styles, and imagery that differentiate white consumerist culture from brown and black women. Beauty products are powerful sites of muddled Orientalism, portraying a kind of pan-Eastern style that scholars have called "exotic cool." OPI nail-polish colors such as "Royal Rajah Ruby" and "Curry Up Don't Be Late" offer a play on words that reflects the cachet of the East.[139] Advertisement campaigns also utilize Eastern imagery, functioning as illustrations of the ways in which Orientalist imagery, words, and symbols are arranged in nonsensical ways. Racially ambiguous "ethnic" models are often used for such campaigns to portray the East. One example is a 2004 CoverGirl ad with the Mexican model Elsa Benitez, who is dressed as an Indian or other South Asian woman, "Dressed in bright pink, with a swath of orange fabric gracing one shoulder (thereby referencing a *dupatta*, a long scarf), Benitez also wears chandelier-style earrings that serve as a prize in the 'Exotic Luxury Sweepstakes.'"[140]

The CoverGirl ad demonstrates the ways in which the exoticized and eroticized bodies of women of color are used to sell products. In the ad, the model exists as part of a larger system of commodification, replacing one brown body with another. "Benitez becomes enfolded within a vision of Indianness as if to signal no latent differences between the two racial groupings: here, the familiar adage, all people of color look the same, is more applicable than other more progressive articulations of coalitional racial politics."[141] Benitez is an example of what Dean MacCannell calls "reconstructed ethnicity," which incorporates a generalized Other race that makes ethnicities into "commodities to be bought and sold," and interchanged, dependent on the market's needs.[142] As MacCannell explains, "Reconstructed ethnicity is the maintenance and preservation of ethnic forms for the persuasion of entertainment not of specific others as occurs with constructed ethnicity, but of a 'generalized other' within a white cultural frame."[143] Muddled Orientalism can be seen as a subset of a larger muddled representational tableau.

White bodies capitalize on these reconstructed identities. Gwen Stefani, during her years as the lead singer of No Doubt

(1986–2004), adopted the bindi, supposedly inspired by her Indian-American then-boyfriend and bandmate Tony Kanal. Media reports called it her "trademark," despite its sacred importance for Hindus as a mark of fertility and "sexual potential."[144] In the late 1990s the bindi, and Hindu fashion in general, was a popular fashion trend seen in characters on television (specifically, on the show *Xena, Warrior Princess*), in *Seventeen* and *Cosmopolitan* magazines, and on the runway in the fashion of Giorgio Armani and Issey Miyake.[145] As John Hutnyk observes: "The bindi becomes a free-floating universal fashion item, and is recruited as an icon of display signifying experience, otherness and understanding at the very moment when it is none of these things (is it ever just a fashion item?)."[146]

The wearing of the bindi by white celebrities was not limited to Stefani. Madonna took it a step further, donning *Vaishnava tilak* facial markings (indicating devotion to Vishnu) and a *salwar kameez* (a traditional style of Asian clothing) to the ire of some Hindus.[147] Once the bindi lost its cachet, celebrities moved on to other forms of exotica. After leaving the bindi behind (and ending her relationship with her Hindu bandmate), Stefani featured the Harajuku Girls as part of her concert performances and fashion and perfume branding. One reading of the Harajuku Girls is that their subsidiary role as backup singers and dancers reinforced the idea of white dominance and Asian subservience. It can be also argued that they represent street fashion in their punk-ish style, which fits well with Stefani's own glam-punk personal style.

The success of Gwyneth Paltrow's *goop* is largely built upon exotic products, including many with an Oriental flair. Paltrow's brand envisions the minimalist body (often called long and lean instead of thin) as part of a larger aesthetic lifestyle that includes "sensations of pain and loss."[148] Sensations of scarcity are expressed through the image of a modern ascetic—Paltrow—who "comes into an awkward juxtaposition with poverty."[149] Seen as well in mystical priv-lit that centers the mystical tourist, this poverty is often linked to products from the East that are "metaphysical, ancient, and foreign."[150] Among these are yoni stones used to cleanse the vagina, which seem to be part of an effort to market products to women who see their bodies as imperfect and that includes the idea that "perfect" genitalia lead to empowerment in an age of post-feminism.[151]

Typographic imagery offers confused (and confusing) presentations of religious traditions associated with the East. At Disneyland, there are abstracted forms that appear to be written in Arabic or Persian script, but mean nothing. This gibberish follows a long history of products that sell exoticism but do so at the cost of factual detail. As Shohat and Stam point out, Arabic is presented as an "indecipherable murmur" and other languages as pure gibberish because English is the language of civilization and humanity.[152] There are numerous examples outside Disneyland and cinema. China markets Shangri-La on the idea of Tibetan religious mysticism and uses Chinese language to do so. As one study notes: "A decree compels all businesses in town to have the signs both in Chinese and Tibetan, which has led to a number of nonsense translations that literate Tibetans cannot understand."[153]

The appropriation of religious traditions—and in particular, mysticism—is at the heart of modern popular spirituality. Oprah's appeal as a spiritual teacher is, in part, predicated upon her interest in and use of different religions in the creation of a kind of pan-mystical ideology. This is an easy spirituality, one that does not require an adherence to ritual, prayer, or other scheduled activities. Carrette and King note that New Age thinkers seem to advise "that we do what we want, albeit with the occasional recommendation that we should reflect upon whether we really want all of these things."[154]

Oprah is not alone in her use of Eastern images, symbols, and ideas. Barbara Ann Brennan, a New Age healer referred to earlier, claims that she is a conduit for five spirit guides and has been a channel for "a being called the Goddess and then the holy spirit."[155] Her use of the goddess and the holy spirit reflects appeals to nature religions and old, mystical forms of Christianity. As others have argued, the return to Catholic beliefs has been a large part of Protestant spirituality in recent years, seen in the popularity of "Celtic" spirituality. The Iliff School of Theology, a small seminary in Denver, Colorado aligned with the United Methodist Church, recently featured the author of works on popular Celtic spirituality John Newell in a visiting professorship, and offers weekly meditation sessions in its one-building campus. In the Iliff case, mysticism is presented as part of a new vision of Methodism in North America.

Brennan also incorporates other religions, including those from the East, in her theology. In *Hands of Light*, her follow-up to *Light Emerging*, she writes about the "haric" level that is located below the navel, a play on the Hindu and Buddhist *hara*, which for Brennan becomes the seat of "intentionality."[156] Hara is used by Brennan to appeal to those consumers (and clients for her healing lectures and workshops) who love the East. Under the guise of muddled Orientalism, hara is not specifically Hindu or Buddhist—it is each and every tradition. This is muddled Orientalism.

THE MYSTIC POOR

Muddled Orientalism paves the way for the Eastern characters, including the mystic poor, whom we see in priv-lit and the movies this genre inspires. Sometimes these come together in one text, as in Elizabeth Gilbert's *Eat, Pray, Love*. As Ruth Williams notes:

> Thus, her interactions with the "natives," especially those in India and Bali, are generally framed within the context of Gilbert's spiritual search. For example, in India, at an

> ashram which Gilbert describes as sitting inside a walled compound, outside of which "it is all dust and poverty," she meets an Indian boy whose "aura" is "incredibly compelling" (126–127). Although he wears the same clothes every day, a fact that marks him as obviously poor in Gilbert's eyes, he seems to possess a "face drenched in luminescence" that moves Gilbert every time she sees it.[157]

Eat, Pray, Love, published in 2006, is not just a book—it is a capitalist enterprise with numerous products. Like other examples of contemporary mystic spirituality, Gilbert draws from the East, in particular India and Bali, and capitalizes on them to sell her brand of white, feminist spirituality, which included product tie-ins with the Home Shopping Network via "three days of on-air branded content" like perfume, tea, yoga gear, prayer beads, and jewelry.[158] There were also tours featuring yoga, meditation, spa treatments, and other spiritual activities.[159]

The mystic poor often play a prominent role in the mystical and spiritual traditions associated with the Orient, seen in the products, practices, and therapies examined throughout this book. The Indian guru, the Buddhist master, and the Sufi shaykh are all examples of "native wisdom," which is seen as an elixir to modernity's "modern" problems. These characters are similar to those of the indigenous peoples of the Americas, whose medicine and religious rituals are also sold as curatives for modern life. The mystic poor often appear in narratives by white authors, some of whom find salvation through relationships with an indigenous teacher or healer. In *Eat, Pray, Love*, all of Gilbert's mystical focus is on men—Mario, Yudi, Richard, Felipe, and Ketut the "medicine man."[160] As is often the case with mystical tourism, the bodies of the Other are salvific.

For the modern mystical consumer, salvific spirituality exoticizes, and at times, eroticizes, the bodies of the Other. Poverty and mysticism are often intertwined. The mystical marketplace features many products and practices that rely on this mythology. Mystical tourism is especially noteworthy for using the local population, often conceived as poor by the tourist, as a marketing technique. Tours that advertise mystical tourism using words like exotic, native, traditional, and authentic are found from Morocco to Bali. In the case of Bali, one company boasts: "Travel like a local on your full day Eco Cycling tour through towns, villages to rice fields with an invitation to a traditional house compound and temple included."[161] This generically spiritual tour could be in Thailand, India, or a host of other locations. Such adventures often involve contact with a spiritual guide, a native of the exotic environment whose mystic qualities can heal, transform, and enlighten the tourist.

The search for wellness, security, and happiness is a worldwide phenomenon with a growing market. One sees yoga and meditation advertisements in Indonesia; yoga is popular in Iran; and Buddhist retreats are found from Colorado to villages in France. In China, the longevity village of Bama is popular with Chinese tourists from other regions of the nation, and like the cases discussed elsewhere in this book, both the landscape and the native healer may play an important role in the commodification of religious practices, foods, and locales.[162] In Bama, the 127-year-old Luo Meizhan was invited to become the brand ambassador for a local water company, thus identifying old age, wellness, and Yao culture with bottled water.[163] The marketing of this product relies on the belief that the land and its people have mystical powers that can be bought for the price of a bottle of water.

Mystical tourism often vocalizes strong colonial overtones that exploit the idea of the exoticized Other. Peru has benefited from the notion of the Meso-American Indian as an exotic and powerful body of mystic energy and wisdom. Much like the branding of other mystical products, mystical tourism brands a place. The branding often includes more typical attributes of tourist sites such as image components (an island or exotic country), natural surroundings (volcanoes, seacoasts), culture (the East), climate (the tropics), and tourist facilities (hotels, an airport).[164] Mystical tourist sites also include a local culture that is thought to have mystical power, expertise, secrets, or energy. *Primitivity* is often marketed at these places, "The Westerners' quest for authenticity is not only expected in pristine landscapes but also in unblemished communities."[165] This authenticity is often rooted in the mystic poor, as discussed earlier.

The mystic poor are not only featured in mystical tourism; they are found in other forms of modern spiritual capitalism, including wellness and exercise programs where the healing powers of the mystic poor are highlighted. Consider the products one finds on the *goop* website, which draw on the curative power of the magical Orient. The elixirs featured on this and other websites provide fascinating examples of the profit-making inspired by the East's mystical power. The Sun Potion "Transformational Foods" line includes products such as the Ashwagandha Ayurvedic Antioxidant, a powder comprised of root and cold-water extract—its brand symbol is the Farvahar, the sign of Zoroastrianism.[166] Billed as "wisdom in a jar," the founder of *goop*, Gwyneth Paltrow, drinks it every morning, "whether or not she is detoxing."[167] In this smoothie, one can ingest the mystical power of both Indian and Persian worlds—through Ayurveda and the ancient wisdom of the Zoroastrians.

The following chapters include examples of these modern mystical products as well as the sites where they are featured—health spas, fitness centers and, in particular, vacation destinations. This mystic power is a kind of cognitive mapping of the world and its people that is dependent on the binary of Western modernity and Eastern mysticism. Muddled Orientalism confuses these spaces in interesting and important ways. In the following chapters, I provide examples from Bali, viewed as a kind of

Mystical Neverland by tourists who may not even know that Indonesia's history is dominated by successive long-gone Hindu empires, or that Bali is located in the most populous Muslim country on the planet.

3

Mysticism, Incorporated

I have no qualms about being a millionaire and I want everyone else to know that they can do it too. People who have achieved an enormous amount of success are inherently very spiritual.

Deepak Chopra[1]

The seductive power of mysticism appeals to individuals who have rejected, in whole or part, the constructions of modern religion. "In general, they are liberally minded and have sought out Eastern religious traditions to supplement or replace religion in the name of an ecumenical form of spirituality."[2] These consumers are heterogeneous, with differing degrees of religiosity, ranging from secular to religious.[3] They also include the "unchurched believers."[4] These individuals have grown disenchanted with the mainline Protestant churches but ex-Christians (or lapsed Christians) are not the only group who participate in the mystical marketplace. Others have a defined religious or cultural identity, such as Jewish or Norwegian, and are consumers of mystical products. At times, these individuals are forced by community or family pressures to maintain a religious identity that they do not embrace.[5]

Religious folks, including those trafficking in the business of authentic *religion*, also sell Hindu, Buddhist, and Islamic products, from portable goods to wellness programs that promise a better life.

One example of this is found in Islam, in Hamza Yusuf's writings, which are identified as "traditional" yet cater to a Muslim audience interested in contemporary spirituality. In his book on spiritual sickness, Yusuf uses language similar to a New Age healer, including words like "spiritual" and "purification," for example stating, "the knowledgeable scholars of spiritual purification have given us this treatment, as they have gleaned it from the teachings of the Quran and the exemplary model of the Prophet."[6]

Mysticism, Incorporated, offers its customers endless choices. The products associated with meditation, for example, include not just one type of item; an entire industry is built around the search for enlightenment. One company sells a meditation pillow that is marketed as the *zafu* associated with Zen sitting meditation.[7] It comes in seven colors; there are styles such as those from the Stillness and Light Collection and the Tibetan Splendor Meditation Collection.[8] It doesn't stop there. One can get a matching or complementary bench, which helps to properly align the body while wearing a prayer shawl, or a hooded meditation cloak.[9] Of course, you need incense—and a CD of meditation music in a room accented by Buddha statues—all available at the same website![10]

ORIENTAL PRODUCTIONS

The identification of the Orient with personal beauty, wellness, and knowledge has a long history. Selling products of the East as curatives is an old business model. Over one hundred years ago, products from Japan were being peddled on the market:

> For example, in the early 1900s, the *Ladies' Home Journal*—widely read by middle-class women at the time—ran a series of advertisements for "Jap Rose Soap" distributed by

> Chicago's James S. Kirk & Co. These advertisements show images of kimono-clad Japanese women in various settings, with a picture of a soap with "JAP ROSE" carved in it. Words such as "transparent," "healing," "natural," and "pure" used in the text suggest the qualities attributed to Japanese femininity.[11]

Today, instead of Jap Rose soap, there is beer yoga, Rumi spiritual tours to Turkey, and mindfulness seminars for corporate executives.

The commodification of the East often involves a process in which religious traditions are reconstituted into new forms. Often a new religion is created for affluent individuals who find the East fashionable. As Thierry Zarcone writes: "It should finally be observed that reading Sufi authors has not always led, as a result, to the great majority of Western converts reading and meditating upon the Quran and the other traditional Islamic texts."[12] This is the appeal of mysticism—it is a concept that takes on what its practitioner wants.

Many of the products that capitalize on Eastern forms of mysticism do not reflect the ways that Hindus, Buddhists, and Muslims practice their religion. Tibetan medicinal products may or may not rely on actual Tibetan medicine; however, they promise that the East provides an answer to modernity's problems, such as alienation, stress, and weight management. In many cases, the fantastic, mystical, and even erotic qualities of the East are at play in these products and therapies. Like many of the cases detailed in this book, the mystical marketplace traffics in Orientalist sentiments. As a powerful example, Tibet exists in the imagination as much as it does in the real world.

> On the one hand, as an authentic "alternative" system, Tibetan medicine may offer up new, effective drugs for some diseases and psychosocial conditions, particularly in

> the context of the epidemiologic and demographic transition. On the other, Tibetan medicine represents holistic, spiritual wisdom that may fulfill that sense that we moderns have that we lack something crucial to our well-being. In this telling, Tibetan medicine in the West emerges as a form of enlightened self-care, in which the pursuit of techniques to maintain health merges with Western ideas about Eastern spirituality.[13]

These misappropriations of Hinduism, Buddhism, and Islam are variously sold as mysticism, spirituality, or New Age. Scholars of secularism, such as the philosopher Charles Taylor, suggest that modernity includes a kind of disenchantment. As Taylor writes: "The Reformation as Reform is central to the story I want to tell—that of the abolition of the enchanted cosmos, and the eventual creation of a humanist alternative to faith. The first consequence seems evident enough; the Reformation is known as an engine of disenchantment."[14] The popularity of mysticism in the world today tells us that people are not ready to let go of enchantment. The search for a sense of wonder is so popular, in fact, that it inspires much of Hollywood's most successful cinematic adventures—the focus of the last chapter of this book. Mystical products represent a kind of pushback—an effort to have some enchantment, or magic, in our lives.

There is cachet in the exotic imagery associated with the East. The 2018 Nike Dusk to Dawn running shoes designed by artist Ali Cha'aban were limited to thirty pairs, using the exotic allure of Arabic lettering (which read "No Parking," an allusion to "Don't Stop") to create a luxury item that could only be won through a contest that promoted the Nike brand. The luxury Nike shoes sell good old-fashioned Orientalism, featuring Arabic script that its buyers probably cannot even read.

A region treated with both revulsion and desire by Europeans and North Americans, the Orient has suffered from colonialism's exploitation for centuries, including the theft of its religious cultures. As Anya Foxen writes: "On the one hand, it served as a receptacle of Western fear and disgust at its purported uncivilized backwardness and depravity. On the other, it was a place of a kind of magic, mystery, and spiritual enchantment that had long faded from the rationalist landscape of Western culture."[15] Commodifying Hinduism, Buddhism, and Islam allows for the selection of the exotic, mystical parts that hold the greatest appeal. This corporatization has in some ways taken over where colonialism left off. When New Age, mystical, and therapeutic models borrow from the East, they secularize their product to make it palatable to the consumer. Sweden is one of the most secular nations in the world—New Age is seen as "mumbo-jumbo," while Asian sources of "inner growth" practices are marketed as mysticism: "Brahman, Atman, Chi or other traditional concepts are transformed into a unified, spiritual force, the 'inner potential.'"[16]

The commodification of the Orient often reconstructs new products and services that are then assumed by whiteness. The muddled Orientalism discussed in the previous chapter is often seen in the mystical products and services discussed in this book: Hindu, Buddhist, and other Orientalist imagery mixed together to sell yoga gear; the Rumi of Deepak Chopra is identified with New Age practices; and a Coldplay concert becomes a Sufi revival. Through the erasure of religious identities, a new "generally Asian" or "casually Orientalized" mysticism emerges, subject to adoption.

In the eighteenth and nineteenth centuries, theosophy, immediatism, and perennialism played a role in these adoptions. As Anya Foxen reminds us: "In a similar dynamic, on American soil, Orientalism combined with the ideologies of a universal religion allowed the West to claim India's holy men as its own. The superhuman potential of the Yogi becomes the latent birthright of all humanity."[17] The opening-up of these traditions, which provided comfort to some, also resulted in the assumption of religions and communities by the marketplace. Today, cultures are for sale in an open market, available for purchase by any consumer with an Internet connection and credit card. The fabricated Shangri-La in Zhongdian, China, features all sorts of products that "sell" Tibetan spirituality. "Tibetan Buddhist ornaments like Dharma Wheels adorn the main façade of hotels, souvenir stands, and restaurants while Tibetan *thangkas*, brass prayer wheels, and *chortens* are part of the 'sacred' décor of the new airport."[18] In other cases, the Orient is all mixed up in the muddled Orientalism we are now familiar with—an image of the Buddha, a Rumi meditation CD, the yoga mat with Ganesha imprinted on it. As we will learn, these forms of mystical capitalism are a consequence directly tied to the condition of modernity.

ESCAPING DISENCHANTMENT

This transition from old forms of religion to mysticism and spirituality is often explained as a consequence of the secular turn, brought about in the West by the Reformation, the critique of the Catholic Church, and the growth of the religious marketplace. Scholars have suggested that decline theory may help to explain the emergence of the Nones:

> According to this individualization framework, in the modern era individuals move progressively away from churches and religious groups for a variety of reasons, including a dislike of the political involvement and undertones as well as the authoritarianism found in many Churches, a disagreement with the Church's stance on certain social issues (homosexuality, pre-marital sex, abortion, etc.) or simply a lack of time and/or will to participate.[19]

However, decline theory has its detractors. For one thing, it does not explain religious resurgences like those seen among American evangelicals, Muslims, and other communities. More importantly, the popularity of mysticism may in fact signal an interest in religion, which has simply been renamed New Age, mysticism, or spirituality. The new naming allows one to profess a secular and spiritualist lifestyle without adhering to a religion in the classical sense. It is apparent that modernity includes, for some, a falling out of love with institutionalized religion, what Max Weber called "the disenchantment of the world." Weber predicted that economic rationality would eventually replace religion, resulting in the elimination of the mystical from the human world. Thus far, that hasn't really happened, and many people seem to want more transcendence, not less. They find this in modern mysticism.

As noted in the Introduction, I am sympathetic to this desire for enchantment. Clearly, many people are seeking some magic in their lives. Charles Taylor has written extensively about the alienation attached to modernity, which he sees as involving a radical change in people's thinking. This change includes the introduction of choice. Whereas in the medieval and early-modern world people believed in their appointed religion, now there is a religious marketplace that offers endless options. One can be a Jewish Wiccan, a Muslim Buddhist, or a Christian Sufi, or all of these things, at different points in life. Taylor sees the transition to modernity not as an outright rejection of God, but a choice in how the mystery of the world is worked out in the minds of individuals.

> On another dimension, the gamut of beliefs in something beyond widens, fewer declaring belief in a personal God, while more hold on to something like an impersonal force; in other words a wider range of people express religious beliefs which move outside Christian orthodoxy. Following

> in this line is the growth of non-Christian religions, particularly those originating in the Orient, and the proliferation of New Age modes of practice, *of views which bridge the humanist/spiritual boundary, of practices which link spirituality and therapy* [my emphasis].[20]

Thus, we can understand the turn to secularism as a rejection of strict religious adherence and a movement toward choice—the kind of intellectual freedom not seen in the medieval world. Peter Berger says something similar, suggesting there has been a shift from religion that is "highly institutionalized" to the "de-institutionalized."[21] Today, religious decisions are not an unquestionable assumption.[22] Institutionalized religion is often critiqued for its patriarchy, corruption, and harsh rules. De-institutionalized religion, as we shall see, carries its own costs, seen in the scandals attached to gurus, the philandering of televangelists, and lack of structure.

Rejecting the thesis that he once promoted, Berger proposes that secularism and religion is not an either/or dichotomy, but rather an entwined relationship. This is helpful in understanding mysticism and its relationship to religion because such a view accounts for pluralism, which often includes the adoption of religious practices from the East. As Berger points out, "often without being deliberately identified with specific religious traditions, cultural practices rooted in Asian spirituality have become widespread both in the United States and Europe."[23] Spiritual shoppers have a wide range of religious, spiritual, and mystical choices, from Native American to Sufism, from Jewish Renewal to Celtic Christianity. New Religious Movements (NRMs), some of which only have a few members and others that number in the tens of thousands, also emerge out of this cohabitation of the secular and the religious.[24]

Freedom is not just seen in choosing one's religion, but in *how* one practices the religion one identifies with. This is not only true for the spiritual seeker, but for those who follow a so-called *organized* religion such as Christianity or Islam. Some contemporary Catholics ignore prohibitions on birth control, abortion, or divorce. Often referred to as "cafeteria Catholics," they make choices in how they constitute their religious lives. In Islam, the element of choice is seen as well, such as in Muslims who drink alcohol. As one study points out:

> In their everyday life situations, they may deliberately sacralize the profane in order to actualize their own ideal individual selves. No wonder that they may take Hafez's symbolic adornment of wine ("The face of my Beloved is reflected in my cup; Little you know why with wine, I always myself align.") into a common cultural practice that liberates them from the influence of traditional religious institutions and empowers them to practice a different form of Islam. This does not, however, mean the loss of faith in religion.[25]

The religious marketplace illustrates the dizzying number of choices available to people in the modern world. The marketplace capitalizes everything, even religion, making all practices and products susceptible to commodification. As one study on mindfulness programs in the corporate world notes: "Workplace and commercial applications of mindfulness are concerned only with specific strategic outcomes linked to productivity and persuasion. Moreover, many of the techniques employed at this level clearly fail to meet the autonomy criterion since they are directed at controlling and manipulating hearts and minds for ulterior purposes."[26]

The religious marketplace is a symptom of the cohabitation of religion and the public spheres. Marx and Engels believed that religious solidarity would be replaced with secularist solidarity, while Durkheim's view of religion is as a socially constructed entity, in balance with other forces, including the market.[27] Polani sees decommodification as a part of the defense against the erosion of human relationships.[28] Modern mysticism can offer the intimacy that is missing elsewhere. Zygmunt Bauman is also attentive to this problem of intimacy. He proposes that values generated by the market are essentially false in the sense that they are based on unsatisfactory objects of consumption. In religion there are many options, but a "scarcity of reliable signposts and authoritative guides."[29] His view helps to explain why the commodification of religion for profit is so popular. Religious consumption is offered in an almost endless number of forms, but leaves people empty. As Bauman has written, liquid modernity entails a kind of unsatisfactory mouse wheel where "each form of social design has been proved to produce as much misery as happiness if not more."[30] The yoga class, Rumi CD, and mindfulness holiday offer fleeting moments of intimacy and an escape from the shackles of modernity. Mystical products, including wellness retreats and holidays, provide the illusion that we are escaping modernity, when we are really just participating it in a different, and often expensive, way.

CONSUMING RELIGION

Religious voices have provided some sound critiques of these consumptive practices, urging followers to return to what they call *tradition*. However, many of these same people just push more products on the consumer in the name of religion. The halal lifestyle—living in accordance with Islamic rules for behavior, eating, praying properly, and so on—often requires consumption—of the prayer rug, the halal lamb, and the Proud To Be Muslim T-shirt. As Karim Douglas Crow argues: "Consumers should be nudged toward acquiring the external trappings, while (hopefully) relying on their widespread shallow comprehension of veritable Islamic values. Thereby, consumers may naively fancy they have possessions of the whole and achieve a counterfeit contentment through external trappings, while remaining heedless of its inner depths."[31]

Like Islam, Buddhism can also function as a lifestyle. For those who post Buddha memes on Facebook, quote the Buddha (often times with fake Buddhist mantras), and paste Free Tibet stickers on their cars, Buddhism may be about amassing products with trendy imagery. In Slavoj Žižek's words: "Western Buddhism, this pop-cultural phenomenon preaching inner distance and indifference toward the frantic pace of market competition, is arguably the most efficient way for us to fully participate in capitalist dynamics while maintaining the appearance of mental sanity—in short, the paradigmatic ideology of late capitalism."[32] This is the illusion of modern mysticism; through the consumption of the appropriate objects, one can *be Buddhist* in one's own way.

Mysticism includes new and alternative ways of being in the world that entail the "suspicion of clarity, precision, analysis, and rationality" in favor of "Romantic themes of the vague, the complex, the irrational, the anarchic, the chaotic, the wild, the Dionysian, the exotic, the esoteric, the heretical, the ancient and primitive, the apophatic, the holistic, the mystical, and the divine darkness."[33] As I have mentioned before, New Age religion often borrows from older traditions. At the same time, it is important to understand that New Agers are different from the Nones in several respects. For one, New Agers typically exist in religious communities with teachers, often called healers or guides, and Nones tend to be more independent, moving from one teacher to another. The followers of New Age religion also have a particular set of ideas that is fairly common, focused on energy, its manipulation, and its potential for healing psychological, emotional, and physical ailments. "As a discourse community, New Agers are preoccupied with issues about energy and its transmutation into matter. Intellectually dominated by their vision of the new physics, they have seized commonly held notions of Albert Einstein's dicta on matter and energy and used them to formulate a cosmology that articulates their basic religious and philosophical vision."[34] Energy is less important for the Nones, who rely more on emerging and changing understandings of the self.

These two subsets of spiritual seekers also have much in common. As we have seen, New Age religion often borrows from the East, incorporating Hindu or Buddhist icons and invoking Rumi and other Sufi figures. Ted Andrews is a New Ager who has written about the promise of modern science to heal the individual, but he also believes in "subtle bodies" that form aura energies and can be manipulated through metaphysical states that include *pranayama* (breath control).[35] The *chakra*, another Sanskrit word, is a popular idea in New Age religion, often connected to the auras that healers can see but that are invisible to others. Auras are often described as a kind of chakra, and are an important part of Tibetan Buddhism. This idea of aura is taken from the classical meaning of *aura*, a Greek word meaning breath or breeze that in religion, refers to the presence of God in an object like a painting (not a person).[36] Focused on esoteric teachings, Tibetan Buddhism is often focused on *Vajrayana*, which uses the visualization of the Buddha in its rituals. In the chapters focused on Hinduism and Buddhism, I discuss how some of these ideas are translated into symbols and then sold as products in the form of visualization guides and books, T-shirts, and more. Modern mystics also refer to chakras, Sufi enneagrams, and other Eastern systems of knowledge.

As I have stated earlier, the main focus of this book is the refashioning of religious language and symbols identified with Eastern mysticism into new traditions, practices, and products. Symbols are often articulated as the *essence* of religion. In the West, this is a powerful idea that assumes religion is an "interior" experience, a particularly Protestant Christian notion. The anthropologist Clifford Geertz made the claim that religion is a state of the mind—that it is separate from the rest of social life—politics, economics, power. He defines religion as "(1) a system of symbols which acts to (2) establish powerful, pervasive, and long-lasting moods and motivations in men by (3) formulating conceptions of a general order of existence and (4) clothing these conceptions with such an area of factuality that (5) the moods and motivations seem uniquely realistic."[37] However, religion as a category of human experience resists strict definitional parameters. As David Chidester writes: "Religion is a difficult term to define, because everyone already 'knows' what it means."[38] When scholars attempt to define it, the end result is either situated in locative understandings of religion situated in views of Protestant theology or binaries that argue that *true* religion is opposed to *fake* religion. Other people's religions are often subject to these analyses; hence, Sunnis are true Orthodox Muslims, Sufis are "mystics," and other self-identifying Muslims are *something else*.

Religion participates in power relations, capitalism, and other systems of domination. The products associated with Eastern mysticism are often valued, gifted, and surrounded by ritual, all signifying the "fetishism of commodities" that Chidester points to in his work.[39] As he has argued, "the commodity is an object of religious regard."[40] What this ultimately means is that people are doing religion even while rejecting it. This turn to mysticism is evident not only among Nones but is seen among many Protestants, whose interest in mystical forms of Christianity has grown exponentially in recent decades. The popularity of the desert fathers, medieval mystics, and Celtic spirituality are three examples of mysticism's popularity in this population. Celtic "spirituality" refers to the pre-Christian Celtic religion, the Celtic Church, and the mysticism inspired by the "Celtic spirit." As one study notes, mystic Christianity "is often predicated upon the image of the 'spiritual Celt,' inherently spiritual and intuitive, in touch with nature and the hidden realms, epitomizing in many ways that which is lost but longed for in contemporary society."[41] The popularity of Celtic spirituality relies on the idea that modern Christians are located in the current time, but true Christianity is located in the past, once again introducing the past as a powerful and mystic era.

At times, popular Christianity relies on muddled Orientalism. Eckhart Tolle's synthesis of Hinduism, Buddhism, and Islam, alongside many other religions, packages spirituality in a digestible perennialist form.[42] Such interest in Christian spirituality and mysticism allows a space for non-Christians and those who resist identifying as "traditional" Christians, functioning as a conversion tool to the unwitting mystical seeker. From the viewpoint of the self-declared Christian, "This is a disturbing situation: it is as if the reading of a Christian mystic such as Meister Eckhart resulted in a non-Christian adopting Christianity without ever bringing him to a reading of the Gospels."[43]

The Nones incorporate practices that are Buddhist, Hindu, or Islamic in origin, but they are presented differently. Often seen as tools for improvement—yoga classes, meditation retreats, reading Rumi—they are marketed by obscuring or erasing their ethnic or cultural foundations. Yoga is a prime example. This Hindu religious practice is now identified with the starlets of Hollywood who grace the covers of magazines advertising diet and exercise programs. "Women's magazines and daytime TV have done much to promote yoga by profiling latter-day equivalents of Gloria Swanson (e.g., Ali MacGraw, Jane Fonda, Christy Turlington, Jennifer Aniston, Gwyneth Paltrow, Madonna) who have embraced Hatha for health, stress relief, spirituality, toned abs, postnatal slimming, or some combination of the above."[44]

White feminism and the environmental movement also consume the Orient and its religions. At times, Hinduism, Buddhism, and Islam are subsumed in North American (and to some degree, European) spiritualities such as "feminist spirituality" and "eco-spirituality."[45] Rumi—one of the most important Muslims to have ever taken pen to paper—is often cast as a perennialist thinker whose focus on love is taken to such an extreme he is de-Islamicized. The great scholar of Islam Annemarie Schimmel "has criticized the vulgarization of Rumi's concept of love and the emphasis on his role as the timeless, spaceless, ecstatic, the master of Love, especially in the social circles where love of Rumi has become almost fashionable in recent decades."[46]

RELICS AND OTHER COMMODITIES

The commodification of religion is not new. I recently published a book that included numerous discussions on the products attached to Islamic pilgrimage. In the Middle Ages, Christian pilgrims often collected tokens, water bottles, oils, and of course relics, including pieces of wood said to have come from the Holy Cross. Sacred spaces such as Jerusalem and Mecca often serve as inspiration for large numbers of products. In her book on the commodification of Jerusalem, Annabel Jane Wharton explores the many ways in which religion and materialism intersect. Her documentation of these products includes relics, souvenirs, replicas, pilgrimages, and theme parks such as The Holy Land Experience. As Wharton writes: "Jerusalem first circulated in the West in the form of its physical fragments—pieces of stone, drops of oil, bits of bone, particles of wood. The city proved a productive source of sacred debris by which the divine might be possessed."[47] In the Middle Ages, relics were big business, with workers, clients, and serious competition for products to buy and sell. As Patrick Geary notes, different styles of relics were preferred by diverse consumer groups, illustrating how extensive the production and dissemination of religious commodities was.

> Shifting tastes in relics were accurately reflected in the varieties offered by these thieves. In the ninth century, Carolingians wanted Roman and Italian martyrs. Thus Deusdona provided Roman saints, while other Frankish thieves operating in Italy dealt in saints not only from Rome but from as far away as Ravenna. Anglo-Saxon kings were interested in continental saints from Brittany and Normandy. In order to supply them, relic-mongers acted as agents, buying them from desperate and unscrupulous clerics or simply stealing them from poorly guarded churches.[48]

Relics continue to be popular among Catholics, but Protestants have invented their own material objects. This is in spite of the Reformation's harsh attitude toward pilgrimage and its religious accoutrements, the "Early Modern Protestant animosity towards traditional Christianities' *sacra*."[49] Scholars have argued that these function as modern relics and, as in the medieval period, even generate relic trafficking. In one historical case, the minister, evangelist, archaeologist, and missionary Selah Merrill (1837–1909) was accused of trafficking in stuffed animals and relics.[50] Today, one can go to a pilgrimage site like Borobudur, a Buddhist monument in central Java, and find everything from T-shirts to key chains with miniature images of Borobudur. Pilgrims to Mecca may collect holy water or other items as proof of their pilgrimage or gifts for relatives and friends. Religious people are not exempt from participating in their own brand of commodification.

This discussion of relics may seem like a digression, but it shows how commodification has been transformed from smaller, religion-specific relic markets to global markets that offer Rumi pillows and Buddha sex toys. In the United States, where much of this book is focused, commodification is big business. Even the rituals, commemorations, and economics tied to Americana are intertwined in "commerce and religion, celebration and consumption," seen in holidays from Christmas and Easter to Valentine's Day and Father's Day.[51] In fact, these holidays include old histories of consumptive patterns that were often modeled upon the "courtly model of consumption," which was then emulated by the masses.[52] Today, the public take yoga classes, buy Rumi meditation CDs, and practice mindfulness—reflections of the allure of the East in the religious marketplace.

Graham Huggan has posed the question: "Is it possible to account for cultural difference without at the same time mystifying it? To locate and praise the other without also privileging the self?"[53] It seems that the answer is no, but it is complicated. Often times the search for a better life through the East is reflected back onto the individual in claims about finding one's self, discovering what was hidden, or some other kind of knowledge. In one study of Middle Eastern and salsa dance, a belly-dance teacher remarked, "It is a folk dance, but it's very rooted in what comes naturally to the body, for the most part. It's relaxed, it's knowing your body and if you take the time to learn Middle Eastern dance, you're gonna learn more about yourself."[54] Self-improvement is a good, but there are ethical questions at play when one assumes another culture, or if one makes money off it. A friend of mine—also a religious scholar—has lamented the success of Bhakti Chai, asking, can white people just leave our chai alone? Another fellow scholar points out the caftans sold online for hundreds of dollars, asking why everything in her culture seems to exist as a business opportunity for someone in Boulder, Santa Fe, or Berkeley.

MYSTICAL CAPITALISM

Kathryn Lofton calls the branding of mysticism "charismatic capitalism" or "spiritual capitalism," apt descriptors for the marketing of religion as both a lifestyle and a commodity.[55] I call it *mystical capitalism*. The products detailed in this book are often inspired by the Orient and identified as new spiritual or mystical practices. In some cases, they are part of a marketing strategy that is geared toward one's "domestic and relational wellness."[56] Buddha lamps, Rumi calendars, and yoga "meditation" music are all examples of the ways in which the East is marketed and sold as a lifestyle brand. Oprah's monthly magazine includes a section in each issue dedicated to her "favorite things," which are often directed toward the mystic quest. References to the East include such products as Cocokind Golden Elixir and an organic face mask with turmeric, a spice from Indonesia.[57] These products promise to help in "sidestepping the doldrums" of winter—this is self-help through beauty and wellness products.[58]

Mystical capitalism involves the historical movements we have learned about in earlier chapters, including spirituality. The word *spirit* comes from the Latin *spiritus*, meaning breath or wind.[59] In new traditions, the spirit may refer to anything from an awareness of one's breath to the essence of the self. Another illustration of the universalistic expression of spirituality is found in music. In some cases, artists use mystical code words, and in other cases, they invent a new vocabulary. Sami Yusuf, the British Muslim singer whose music reflects Islamic themes as well as universal ones, calls his style "Spiritique," which he describes thus: "It incorporates and utilizes Middle Eastern and Western harmonics, underpinned by spirituality. It's all-encompassing, all-inclusive … It will utilize music as a facilitator for spiritual appreciation, regardless of race and religion."[60]

Like spirituality, New Age religion includes anything and everything under the mystical umbrella. As Mara Einstein notes, New Age is not only "virtually impossible to define," it is an expansive category that includes aliens and UFOs, mental and spiritual healing, sacred places, spiritualism, and mysticism.[61]

Like Foucault's panopticon, it is a huge eye that surveys and takes everything in. Anne McClintock wrote that: "The Panopticon thus embodied the bureaucratic principle of dispersed, hegemonic power."[62] New Age, Orientalism, and mysticism simultaneously resemble each other and work together in the commodification of the East and its religious traditions.

New Age religion capitalizes on the appeal of mysticism, which is aided by capitalist structures that exploit the exotic appeal of difference. "Generally speaking, the New Age movement has a blind spot about money, and people involved in these practices tend to see no problem with buying and selling spirituality. This may make life easier for the would-be shaman, but not everyone can afford $335 for a Kilaut drum from Maryland, advertised as the 'only source' for such an item."[63] Its appeal to earth-based spirituality and profession of a back-to-basics lifestyle including health food, gardening, and products like homemade kombucha is admirable, but New Age fails to critique the capitalist structures and cultural commodities that underpin its success.

Mara Einstein argues that New Age is in decline, seen in the reduction of New Age conferences, bookstores, and publications.[64] Mysticism has taken over, seen in the popularity of Kabbalah, Sufism, yoga, Neo-Buddhism, and the numerous practices that have emerged in recent years geared toward spiritual healing. If we accept Einstein's argument that New Age is an expression of marketing, the mystical marketplace has adopted this strategy with great success. Mind/Body/Spirit has taken over the mantle of New Age in numerous products, seen in such places as the renaming of *New Age* magazine as *Body + Soul*.[65] The focus on profit is extremely powerful—and a critical part of the story told in this book. "There are no free churches to go to; there are paid-for lectures. There are no free Bibles to read; there are books to buy."[66] The Mind/Body/Spirit industry uses mysticism to sell lectures and books, spa vacations, meditation retreats, and spiritual seminars.

Mysticism, like New Age, is often presented as a resurgence of lost or suppressed mystical power. This is seen in the characterization of Tibet as a special place that needs to be "saved"; the goddess, who is cast as a powerful figure in new religious movements; and the popularity of Gnostic and Celtic Christianity. In her study of Gnostic religion, April DeConick compares it to New Age religion: "While modern New Agers feel themselves to be part of a spiritual transformation of humanity with the beginning of the Age of Aquarius, the Gnostics believed that their initiations set in motion the transformative process of universal spiritual renewal, finally enabling human spirits to rejoin the great transcendent aeon and regenerate God's fullness in the last age of the world."[67] This may be true, but today's mystics are also radically different than the Gnostics of the past. New Agers, spiritualists, and modern-day mystics use other religions and cultures in their quest for transformation, often with little regard for the sanctity of these traditions. Gnostics worked more closely within the confines of their own religion—Christianity.

Mystical capitalism is a profit-driven industry that reflects a style of commodification that is, "not necessarily created with the objective of honoring religious practice and sentiment."[68] Many of its products are aesthetically pleasing and fashionable, like meditation aids with an image of the Buddha or yoga mats with an abstract form of a Hindu figure like Ganesha. These are not religious aids that help one escape *samsara*, but products that look good. Hindu and Buddhist symbols are often featured in the world of fashion. As one study argues, the use of Indian and South Asian imagery allows Americans to adopt an exotic style temporarily while remaining white and affluent. A 2004 CoverGirl ad replete with Eastern imagery is but one example. "Here Indianness becomes associated with a Bohemian aesthetic, closely aligned with the kind of cultural capital that enables a departure from the seemingly dull and ordinary trappings of life, without compromising the all-Americanness of Cover Girl cosmetics."[69] These are the places where we see muddled Orientalism, mysticism, and cultural colonialism collide.

The impulse to accumulate such items can be explained in part by Thing Theory. The disenchantment with organized religion noted by Weber, Taylor, and others brings with it the need for something else. As one scholar notes, "things act as an alternative to theory; they have a particular appeal for those jaded by texts, ideas, and theories."[70] There is something about *things* that is particularly powerful about the West—people collect material objects because they are the very element that makes them anxious, suggesting a "primal Protestant anxiety" about things.[71] The enchantment promised by mysticism, the sacred, and spirituality is often presented as an alternative to secular rationalism. In the case of sacred, or "world," music, it represents "the promise of reenchantment through belief in the universality (translatability) of sonic devotion."[72]

The supremacy of capitalism in the world economic system plays an important role in these strategies of production, as previously noted. An additional ethical problem that is often raised by these products, such as South Asian fashion and yoga wear, is that these products are often made by the poor. By assuming them as part of their lives, consumers benefit from the outward signs of these communities. As one study notes, in the case of hip-hop, these practices "give further motivation to those who also see the potential rewards of the cultural capital of blackness, and who are eager to assume everything but its burdens."[73]

American individualism is an important catalyst when it comes to religious and cultural products. Products are advertised everywhere—on billboards, television ads, in movies, and social media. As Mara Einstein argues: "Advertising and marketing have taken hold of the American psyche and co-opted the American dream ... to distort individuality into a perversion. Individuality is no longer about making the world a better place ... it's about how much you can buy and create your identity through these purchases."[74] This is an example of Talal Asad's "conscripts of modernity," which he sees as an inescapable part of today's world. Individuals are trapped in a web of technology, advertising, and product placement.

As we know, the Orient is a product of the imagination that provides rich inspiration for the modern capitalist entrepreneur. A cognitive space with a vast imaginative territory, it gives us the yoga mat with Buddha imprinted on it, the Rumi mindfulness CD, and wellness retreats in India, Morocco, Bali, and Turkey. These products have historical antecedents such as the "Christian yoga" promoted by A. K. Mozumdar on his arrival in Seattle from India in 1906, which culminated in the publication of a periodical titled *Christian Yoga Monthly*.[75] As examples of commodified Orientalist mysticism, they center the East as a source of mystical knowledge, enlightenment, healing, and self-improvement.

As I noted earlier, the Avatarism found at the Los Angeles New Age center called the Rose Temple takes its language and imagery from Hinduism. Borrowing, stealing, repackaging, and bastardizing other people's religions is part and parcel of the game of conquest that allows the colonizer to assume a culture, religion, or practice while avoiding the danger of racial contamination. Anne McClintock describes this fear as "the degeneration into which humanity could fall."[76] The assumption of Eastern mysticisms and their associated symbols often involves a whitewashing of Hinduism, Buddhism, and Islam through paths like yoga, Transcendental Meditation®, and New Age Sufism. This project takes place through a capitalist system that includes the clever branding and marketing of mystical products.

BRANDING MYSTICISM

Mysticism is a concept connected to the idea of the Divine—understanding what it is, communing with it through meditation, prayer, and other rituals, and benefiting from it through receiving a blessing, attaining enlightenment, or taming the ego. For the Hindu, the divine may be realized through *darśan*, the "seeing" of gods that marks the rituals of millions of people every day from India to Bali. Hindus also visit the *tirthas* that are found across India, which are essentially crossing places where individuals seek a transcendent relationship. "Every *tirtha*'s tale is of hierophany, the residents of heaven breaking in upon the earth."[77] This is obviously quite different from the Christian notion of God that is focused on a personal relationship with Jesus. For many moderns, the way that people define God is internal and individualistic, as the "self" or "ultimate reality," the "reality" or the "truth."

The description of religious experience has not only changed; it has been altered in radical ways. The questioning of religious authority and the focus on the individual, which were both brought about by the Reformation, in part explain this change. As noted earlier, moving from an age of enchantment to one of disenchantment may be dissatisfying. New Age religion, spiritualism, and mysticism are all reactions to this disenchantment for individuals who feel empty, alienated, or who have a sense that something is missing from their lives.[78] This sense of alienation is exploited in the mystical marketplace, which has taken over where the New Age marketplace left off.

As discussed earlier, New Age is often identified with the countercultural movements of the last half of the twentieth century when the hippie trail, Krishna Consciousness, universalistic Sufism, and other spiritualist traditions became popular with affluent North Americans and Europeans. However, New Age is older than many assume, situated not in the 1960s, but in the British Utopian Movements of the late nineteenth century. First used by utopians at Alcott House, Ham Common, Surrey, England in 1843, New Age later became the name of a periodical founded by A. R. Orage, who was a disciple of Gurdjieff.[79] Like others embedded in the New Age, Eclectic Church, and theosophy movements, he dabbled in many religious traditions and was a committed spiritualist. Orage was one of many early countercultural figures whose independent thought had diverse inspirations—the occult, the East, and utopian movements, among others. Not restricting itself to Sufism, theosophy also had an affinity with Hinduism and Buddhism. The founder of "Christian Yoga," A. K. Mozumdar worked closely with the local branch of the Theosophical Society in Seattle along with the Unity Church and the New Thought group.[80] These are early example of the *rebranding* of religions for European and North American consumption.

Today, the rebranding of religions identified with the East uses Hinduism, Buddhism, and Islam as source material for New Age, spiritual, and mystical products. Hindus, Buddhists, and Muslims are often active participants in this process. According to scholar Ashok Kumar Malhotra, "Hindu spiritual invaders of the nineteen sixties started an unusual business partnership with the people of the West in the garb of spirituality."[81] Perhaps one of the differences between the New Age of the 1960s and the mysticism of today is that the former looked more seriously to gurus and other teachers from the East.

Modern mysticism entails a wholesale assumption of tradition that was not as evident in the 1960s countercultural and emerging New Age movements. In the words of one author, Buddhism is "a practical set of ideas and approaches toward understanding the workings of life."[82] Such characterizations are deeply problematic, ignoring religious aspects of Buddhism such as texts, oral hagiographies, ritual, gendered authority, pilgrimage, and eschatology. The transformation of Buddhism into a trendy identity also allows Americans to co-opt the religion and remake it into an American form of spirituality—a hipster lifestyle modeled upon green-tea lattes and vacations in Bali.

Modern mysticism often involves the reconstitution of Hinduism, Buddhism, and Islam into new forms that result in an astounding number of products, from Rumi restaurants to Buddhist sex toys. These are discussed in detail in the following chapters. In crafting personal spirituality, self-identified mystics utilize a colonial language to explain their personal theology. As one shopkeeper in Glastonbury puts it, "I am Christian, I am Buddhist, I am Hindu—of course I am not really all of these things, but I can *take* [my emphasis] the best, the essence from those traditions."[83]

Religious imagery is part of many religious traditions, including those focused on visual piety. For example, the Mourides of Senegal focus on the saint Amadou Bamba and include a visual repertoire that features public paintings that essentially function as icons. As one study notes: "Like the icons of Byzantium, images of Amadou Bamba and his family are active sources of potency and power. It is common to see Mourides touch Bamba's image to their foreheads or kiss wall murals to receive his blessing."[84] In other Muslim communities, pilgrims press their foreheads to the metalwork of shrines to receive blessings or have an image of Prophet Muhammad or his cousin Ali in their homes. These are all ways that religious imagery is employed in belief and ritual, encoded into the lives of a religion's followers.

Religious imagery is also an important part of Mysticism, Incorporated. Visual imagery can be adopted from other religions and then reproduced as goods that have been desacralized or re-sacralized as part of a "new" religion or form of mysticism. The repackaging and marketing of these symbols often relies on cultures identified as wellsprings of truth and enlightenment—Native American, African, Mesoamerican, Islamic, Buddhist, and Hindu. Religious products that advertise the mystical East also use the language of modern religion: "They recognize the fluidity of the self and the popularity of current psychological motifs like 'personal growth,' 'womenspirit,' and 'holistic spirituality,' and by means of definitions and labels claim on this more subjective space, thereby legitimizing it and enhancing their own market shares."[85] The body may be subject to the disciplinary practices of religion, such as in the ways in which gender is constructed, but it also is an active participant in the formation of new traditions.

New and emerging mystical and spiritual practices and products are often marketed as paths to better health and wellness. These pathways exist outside psychiatry and Western medicine, but often utilize their language. Gwyneth Paltrow's company *goop* is an example I return to; it sells a lifestyle of "ascetic accumulation" seen in everything from the "Zen monkhood" practiced by Silicon Valley men (who drink Soylent protein shakes to boost their job performance) to the juice cleanses, colonics, and elimination treatments sold by Paltrow's company.[86] The Orient inspires many of these new religious/spiritual/mystical practices, offering promises of bodily wellness and spiritual truth. These promises rely on a utopian ideal. "Orientalism is not a picture of the East or the East. It represents longing, option, and faraway perfection. It is, like Utopia, a picture everywhere and nowhere, save in the imagination."[87] This is the world we find in the mystical marketplace.

MARKETING MYSTICISM

Hinduism is repackaged as a product and sold in numerous forms, the most prominent of which is yoga. Buddhism also exists in many new forms, commodified for the modern marketplace. The popularity of meditation, the usage of words like karma and nirvana, and Zen style are three examples. Corporations continue to plunder religious symbols and make money, creating fads: "For example, the media circus surrounding the Dalai Lama turned Buddhism into a fashion, known as 'Buddhist chic,' which involved little more than considering the Dalai Lama as 'cute.'"[88]

Much like Hinduism and Buddhism, Islam suffers under the translation project of modern mysticism. Western Sufi orders often privilege Christian religious themes; in particular, initiation. Guénon, whose brand of Sufism is profiled in the chapter on Sufism, is one example. As Zarcone notes, initiation was a foundation of Guénon's Sufism. "It referred to a ceremony which put into play the notions of the secret, of selection, of spiritual death and rebirth which the nineteenth-century esotericism drew from Alexandrian philosophy and Christianity and the transmission of which has always been made orally."[89] When Oprah described Sufism as a "Middle Eastern" tradition, she was signaling the power of modern mysticism.

Islam is erased in many European and North American Sufi communities. The followers of Idries Shah, for example, do "spiritual exercises" and refer to the "Tradition," eat pork, and drink liquor. Western Sufi orders may be indistinguishable from other new spiritual movements. "With the cross-fertilization of thought, modern Western culture, Christian esotericism and these diverse forms of Sufism are in constant development and promote, in the absence of any control brought by an Eastern or Western master concerned for orthodox teaching and practice, transformations which carry the group onto the periphery and often outside Islam towards new forms of religion."[90]

A great irony in the commodification of Hinduism, Buddhism, and Islam is that, at their core, these are religions that see an ethical life as taking precedence over materialism. Although Buddhism teaches detachment from material possessions, the aesthetic appeal of the East is so powerful that people collect the accouterments that reflect its culture. There is a false sense of security in the turn to these traditions because people remain embedded in modern, capitalist systems. The philosopher Slavoj Žižek argues that Buddhism is the prime example of this. As Møllgaard remarks: "There is some truth in Zikek's claim that western Buddhism is the perfect ideology for late capitalism. For western

Buddhism provides us, beings living in the realm of turbulent risk societies, the pleasant illusion that we are detached from the capitalist spectacle and can enjoy it with that combination of hedonism and asceticism that characterizes our nihilistic culture."[91] As discussed in the first chapter, the prosperity gospel is one way in which money and the *true religion* of evangelical Christianity are co-identified. However, Christianity is not alone in identifying social capital as religious capital. The Nones, the spiritual but not religious crowd, also make the connection between different types of capital, for instance in the claim that "money is just spiritual energy."[92] Mindfulness trainings can include the visualization of financial success, which is no surprise because mysticism has become a form of moveable capital.

To return to a point raised earlier, mystical seekers do not usually admit they are *doing* religion, even though "Belief in God is a central religious tenet in Western culture."[93] Today, these beliefs are tethered to economic systems that result in the products and practices we see in this book. This allows people to participate in capitalism through the accumulation of products. Historically, this has also been the case. In the post-War period (late 1940s), Buddhism's aesthetic appealed to American shoppers. "Within this setting, Zen became a convenient import, unassuming and enchanting—supplemented by an interest in Oriental things, and supplementing that interest."[94]

The universalizing of religions is one part of this project that we need to be especially attentive to. As William Rory Dickson and Meena Sharify-Funk argue, the interest in Buddhism, Hinduism, and Islam is part of a larger interest in "all things 'mystical,' 'esoteric,' 'transcendental,' and 'Eastern.'"[95] In some cases, these religions were subsumed into a transcendental, New Age, or spiritualist movement, and in other cases, distinct communities translated the religious content into a universalistic language. In Krishna Consciousness, devotees rose at 4 a.m., studied scriptures, organized festivals, disseminated texts, and recruited new members, while cultural expatriation took place among others, resulting in the Hindu scriptures becoming "utterances of enlightened sages" and the god Krishna transformed into "the divine author of the Eternal Religion."[96] In modern mysticism, the teachings of Buddhist monks, Hindu sadhus, and Muslim shaykhs are often universalized and made palatable to North Americans who can fit these traditions into their own worldview, making them culture-less and erasing their religious and racial appendages. As one scholar writes: "Swami Vivekananda (d. 1902), for instance, presented Vedanta as the mystical essence of Hinduism, something North Americans could engage in regardless of their religious backgrounds."[97] These reductive moves transform complex religions into a few sound bites.

In modern mysticism, Hinduism's complex system of speculative philosophy becomes a mystical essence, Buddhism's numerous sub-traditions and texts become compassion and non-harm, and Sufism becomes a Middle Eastern sect with no Islamic reference point. Reductionism is popular with perennialists, mystics, and spiritualists who make impressive claims about the world in which we all live. One claim is found here: "In this view, the phenomenal world emerges continually from a single source, an Absolute, which is variously referred to as Godhead, Brahman, Allah, Tao, Buddha Nature, Original Mind, or Emptiness (Sunyata). Hence, all matter, all beings, all of the universe is an incarnation/reflection/child of this one consciousness, this one ocean of being, in diverse forms and aggregates."[98] Contemporary mysticism is often, at its core, Christian universalism. There is a racialized component to this project that is impossible to ignore. In North American Buddhism, in the late nineteenth and early twentieth centuries, there was profound anxiety about "occult Buddhists."[99] This was code for non-whites.

European and American formulations of Sufism have at times involved colonization. Idries Shah was a self-proclaimed Sufi teacher whose mysterious lineage and universalistic writings often borrow from Sufi teaching stories, especially those of the comic character Mullah Nasruddin, a popular figure in Turkey and elsewhere. Shah, whose work is examined in more detail in Chapter Five, was a prolific writer and popular teacher, especially with the generation of North Americans who came of age in the 1960s. Like Swami Vivekananda, he made Sufism palatable for non-Muslims—going further than other "mystical" teachers in claiming Sufism was located outside Islam. In 1964, the preface of his book *The Sufis* describes Sufism as "an ancient spiritual freemasonry whose origins have never been traced or dated."[100] Shah was not alone in framing Sufism as a mystical form that exists outside Islam. An 1867 text describes Sufism in this way: "Steering a mid-course between the pantheism of India on one hand and the deism of the Coran on the other, the Sufis' cult is the religion of beauty … Sufism is really the development of the Primaeval Religion of the Aryan race."[101] More recently, Sufism has been reframed as a form of therapy, through such descriptions as "meditation" for prayer and worship. Rumi is the most popular Muslim figure of contemporary mysticism, where rituals like *dhikr* (the remembrance of Allah) and *sema* (auditioning for Allah, often in the form of devotional music) are reframed as meditation or a set of spiritual exercises.[102]

Some mystical practitioners have been fairly vague about their religious identities, thus helping to increase their share of the market. However, individuals who self-identify as the follower of a particular religion—Hindu, Buddhist, Muslim—also capitalize on the popularity of mysticism. These individuals also function in a system of capitalism, consumerism, and commodities. The sociologist Zygmunt Bauman calls this the "society of consumers." He describes it thus:

> The "society of consumers," in other words, stands for the kind of society that promotes, encourages or enforces the

> choice of a consumerist lifestyle and life strategy and dislikes all alternative cultural options; a society in which adapting to the precepts of consumer culture and following them strictly is, to all practical intents and purposes, the sole unquestionably approved choice; a feasible, and so also a plausible choice—and a condition of membership.[103]

Bauman's vision of a consumer society blends with Asad's conscripts of modernity, which argues that all people living in modernity are, in fact, part of modernity—conscripts, for better or worse. This includes people who are identified as "traditional" or "religious." In the case of Thailand, for example, the Buddhist monk utilizes the practice of *dāna*, or donation, in the administration of meditation centers.[104] This allows the tourist to experience Buddhism while permitting practitioners to stay within the ethical lines of their tradition. Bauman has also coined the term "liquid modernity" to describe the blurring of consumerism, religion, politics, and aesthetics, something we certainly see in contemporary engagement with mysticism through the constantly emerging therapies, practices, and products that flood the market.[105]

Indeed, something about modernity is deeply unsatisfying. Pope Benedict XVI famously argued that the West denies its religious and moral heritage, and thus people search elsewhere for what is missing—for enchantment.[106] It is likely he was referring to mysticism, erased as part of the Reformation's project of redefining Christianity as a move away from what were viewed as the superstitions of the Catholic Church.

MYSTICAL FASHION

Clothing is one of the most popular ways to distribute the portable Orient, whether it be through *Japonisme* that mimics the

Buddhist monk and Japanese court dress, couture fashion that displays forms and motifs from the East, or the mass production of "ethnic" style seen today in the popularity of the tunic and caftan. The element of fantasy in Orientalism is important, for it doesn't require exactness or even a distinct cultural referent. "Orientalism is never a narrow-gauge or scholastic enterprise in fashion. Rather, it is a fantasy, often a composite and customarily syncretized."[107]

Clothing is political; in the case of the Orient, it is often tied to histories of European expansion and colonialism. Sartorial choices are powerful: "Clothes trap the essence of the east; they objectify it. Like souvenir curios which represent fetishized totems, they present the oriental world for consumption. It should come as no surprise then that their later circulation as signs in a capitalist economy ensured their commodification as luxury, opulence, consumption and spectacle."[108] The luxurious textiles and ornate patterns of Japan, China, India, Morocco, and numerous other countries are seen in fashion houses ranging from Ralph Lauren to Yves Saint Laurent (who was born in Morocco). Long before New York Fashion week, the East has been part of the West's repertoire of influences: "World's fairs, expositions, and commercial displays have consistently sought to bring the East to the West in one of its most portable and persuasive forms, clothing."[109]

India, which was so important in the formation of the concept of mysticism in the West, continues to play a powerful role in the mystical marketplace. The adoption of Indian dress and food often represents an idealized vision of how people in India—especially Hindus and Buddhists—live. Historically, clothing from India has often influenced fashion in Europe and the United States. The banyan, sari, and shawl were dominant examples of this in earlier centuries. At times, these forms were combined with Turkish and other styles, seen in the case of the Indian house gown, which today are seen in the "Indian references and paisley textiles [that] abound in men's dressing gowns and robes."[110]

Today, other Indian influences are seen in the popularity of the tunic, which is at times confused with the caftan—an example of the muddled Orientalism discussed in the following chapter. These styles are also found in yoga and fitness clothing produced by Prana and other companies.

In the 1960s, these adopted practices included clothing choices and dietary rules that were intended to express a rejection of American (and European) materialism. For example: "For the countercultural youth engaged in these forms of consumption, wearing peasant skirts or eating lentil soup became a means of expressing discontent with the bankruptcy of the capitalist West and aligning with the morally superior edicts and philosophies of the East."[111] Dressing in Eastern garb means something quite different today. Rather than a rejection of the materialism associated with the West, there is a commodification of the very symbols typically identified with anti-materialist ideology. In the CoverGirl ad campaign discussed in the previous chapter, an Eastern aesthetic is employed as a selling point. The "exotic cool" theme is a form of dress-up. "Women who purchase these cosmetics can be part of this commodified exchange: they can dress up and take on this 'new' look, but they are still purchasing Cover Girl cosmetics, thus ensuring that they are not in any way foreign but resolutely all-American."[112]

Economic and racial privilege play an important part in the role playing of exotic cultures from the East. They allow white consumers to purchase fashionable, fun, and experimental products. Pretending to be Hindu, Muslim, or Buddhist is first seen in the eighteenth and nineteenth centuries as part of consumable Orientalism. Popular with both North Americans and Europeans, products that showcased Oriental styles included household items and clothing. North American women often played the role of women from China, Japan, and Korea—all sites of Buddhism. For example, the practice of dressing in kimonos was not simply wearing different clothing. It was a performance that involved the possession of a foreign culture. As Mari Yoshihara explains: "For the white women in these enactments, Asia was no longer an object that they gazed at or purchased; Asia was now a performance that the women were themselves part of. Rather than being owners or caretakers of Asian objects, or artists capturing the spirit of Asia, women now *embodied* Asian-ness."[113]

Japan has exerted some of the most powerful influences on European and American design and fashion. The reasons for this are complicated, but involve the fascination with Zen, popularity of the kimono, and the modernist aesthetic found in much of Japanese art. As Richard Martin and Harold Koda argue:

> The West's ebullient enthusiasm for Japan is unlike any other Orientalism. More impassioned than its embrace of the Near East, more comprehending than its knowledge of China, and more engaged than with Kiplingesque India, the decisive Japonisme of the nineteenth and twentieth centuries created philosophical and cultural involvements with Zen spiritualism, haiku reductivism, Kabuki grandiloquence, and a pantheistic communion with nature that Frank Lloyd Wright, among many other artists and thinkers, saw so clearly and paradigmatically as Japanese.[114]

Japanese style and its influence on the West are also seen in the popularity of Zen as both a design style and lifestyle. In contemporary religion, Buddhism exists as both an influence on fashion and a lifestyle. Scholars of fashion have largely focused on the female form. However, men also participated in this role-playing. In some cases, colonial men dressed up in drag in order to gain access to forbidden spaces. Perhaps most famously, Richard Burton disguised himself as an Arab so that he could sneak into Mecca and observe the hajj. Less dramatic are the examples of upper-class men in Europe and North America pretending to be Muslim. Men also dressed up as "would-be sultans" in other ways, modeling their life on a sultan or pasha when they retired to a smoking room, and at times, "a fez with a tassel was sometimes worn by men in this supposedly salubrious, exotically-interpreted activity."[115]

GOOP AND THE SEARCH FOR ENCHANTED BEAUTY

This milieu also accounts for the success of the wellness industry and often relies on Eastern tropes. Their aesthetic appeal is linked to the materialist goals of a thin body, glowing skin, and a healthy soul. Self-proclaimed mystical and spiritual teachers like Deepak Chopra also promote the prosperity gospel in their work. Chopra's books include the following: *Creating Affluence—Wealth Consciousness in the Field of All Possibilities* (1993) and in an earlier book, *Unconditional Life—Discovering the Power to Fulfill Your Dreams* (1992). Chopra argues that the material world (like finances) can be altered through inner work.[116] This is Chopra's version of Osteen's prosperity gospel, packaged in an exotic parcel.

Mystical products are part of a larger system of adoption, commodification, and branding that exploits the appeal of the East as a site of exoticism linked to healing, wellness, and spiritual enlightenment. This is apparent in the products and lifestyles attached to them. When white migrants in Bali describe their adopted new homeland as chaotic, they are signaling the ways in which the Orient is thought of as the antithesis to Western modernity, which is characterized as "too neat and tidy."[117] Yoga is another example of this cultural framing, seen as valuable in part because of its origins. As a fellow scholar notes: "Not only is yoga hybridized and 'westernized' through the appropriation and marketization processes, but as a consequence of globalization, it also becomes easternized through juxtaposition with other Asian bodily practices. In this way, yoga becomes part of an eastern package of technologies of the self."[118] Many people who wear fashionable yoga T-shirts with images of the Buddha and Ganesha participate in the commodification of culture, perhaps not cognizant of their part in the colonization of tradition they are implicating themselves in.

The idea that outer appearances and inner spiritual work are connected is evident in the marketing of products featuring Eastern mysticisms. Mike Featherstone and others have illustrated how this is a part of the modern market: "Within consumer culture, the inner and outer body become conjoined: the prime purpose of the maintenance of the inner body becomes the enhancement of the appearance of the outer body."[119] The Dragontree Spa chain, with two locations in Portland, Oregon, and one in Boulder, Colorado, has both wellness and food products that carry the promise of Eastern wellness. Products include the Live Pain Free Meditation Collection and a line of Ayurvedic Body Oils that includes four versions—Vata, Kapha, Pitta, and Tri-Doshic.[120]

Often a "performing self" is at play in modern mysticism that "places greater emphasis upon appearance, display and the management of impressions."[121] Among white migrants in Bali, the adoption of vegetarianism—even though Balinese Hindus who aren't in the priestly class regularly eat meat (and in general, Hindus eat meat)—is very popular. So is the adoption of a particular tropical-hippie fashion style. As one study notes: "Furthermore, the migrants are easily recognized by the way they dress from wearing baggy, naturally coloured pants made from linen, hemp or cotton."[122] This is the costume of Balinese white migrant mysticism.

The industries and products that help people achieve this performing self include Ayurvedic food products, Chinese teas, yoga teachers, and Sufi meditation experts—all reflecting the East as a place that offers therapies, spiritualities, and fashions for the individual seeking a mystical, transformative, and spiritual experience. Dragontree Spa features a "Peace" herbal tea with ingredients identified with Eastern mystic healing such as rose petals, used in "Asian medicine to promote a peaceful and positive state of mind."[123]

Roland Barthes noted that food serves as an identity marker representing community.[124] Food products identified with the East are often found outside the health spa. A large selection of these items can be found at any local Whole Foods or Trader Joe's, from coconut beauty products to tamarind juice. There are other items in the realm of "exotic" and "ethnic" foods, or those deemed physically healing and integral to the mystical path. Mindfulness is marketed, for instance, by the Boulder-based company Earth Balance, which includes "Mindful Mayo Dressings and Sandwich Spreads."[125]

Foucault's technologies of the body come into play when we look at the mystical health programs and wellness practices that rely on Hinduism, Buddhism, and Islam. Feminist scholars have voiced concern over the pressures on women to link economic success to wellness. The neoliberalism of the wellness industry often conceives of a body in ways that are unreachable for most women, who do not have the luxury of "balancing" work and pleasure/wellness.[126] Corporate cultures often highlight a "positive mindset" and good attitude as the responsibility of the individual, values that are more about capitalist production than concern for the wellbeing of workers.[127]

Arianna Huffington has remarked that inadequate sleep (which women are constantly told to get more of, even if they have young children) results in less production.[128] These pressures lead workers, who are also consumers, to seek out paths to health, wellness, and balance, such as yoga, meditation, and other spiritual practices. Through these practices, the business of mysticism and spirituality serves the corporatization of bodies. There are numerous examples of this. American yoga typically negates its Hindu and Jain origins, but refers to it as Eastern, or part of a wisdom tradition. The avoidance of Hindu practices is one of the ways in which yoga is rearticulated as a Western practice and sanitized for a white customers. As one yoga studio owner puts it: "We don't do chanting because people are not comfortable with it ... We never use the word 'God.' We talk about energy, we talk about peace, we talk about mindfulness. We use those New-Agey kind of words."[129]

Today, the technologies of the body that Foucault warned us about influence even the most politically conservative forms of religion, including evangelical Christianity. One of the key ways that the old models of authority are bucked is through the cult of materialism, where individual prosperity and health—including thinness—has overtaken the old forms of religion. As Luke Winslow illustrates, one of the appeals of Joel Osteen's ministry is its appeal to aesthetics.[130] He writes: "By repeatedly and consistently referencing aesthetic dimensions like physical attractiveness, body shape, and hygiene habits, Osteen discursively constructs an aesthetic separation between what he calls God's *favored* and *unfavored*."[131] The incredible success of his ministry is due to his understanding of "the larger social and cultural milieu he operates within."[132] This milieu is populated with products that promise blessings, an improved life, and happiness, often through meditation and self-actualization. The Joel Osteen Ministries website features many of these products, with books such as, *Think Better, Live Better*, *You Can, You Will*, and *Our Best Life Together*; a "Hope" drink tumbler; "I Am" bookends; and an "Anchored to Hope" canvas bag.[133] The mystical marketplace often uses the "clever tools" noted by Shirazi to sell products to the masses.

MYSTICAL TOURISM

North Americans and Europeans participate in colonialism in numerous ways. One way is through experiencing or purchasing the cultural capital of other religious communities. In a sense, this functions as a type of tourism where one can visit a culture, experience a religious tradition, or engage in a momentary practice. I can read Rumi, wear an Indian tunic, sit in a coffee bar with Orientalist décor while drinking a soy latte after a yoga class—a kind of transitory experience that crosses many cultures. This has great appeal. As scholars have pointed out: "Particularly for members of dominant racial groups who have felt a lack of ethnic community, identity, or pride, the global New Age movement and marketplace can provide an alternative type of symbolic, holistic (but nonspecific) ethnicity that also certainly marks a position of privilege relative to those who cannot 'choose' their ethnic ascription so easily."[134]

In the case of mystical tourism, performance is involved with issues surrounding tourist relations with the host culture. As John Frow notes: "It is tourism that destroys (in the very process by which it constructs) the authenticity of the tourist object; and every tourist thus at some level denies belonging to the class of tourists."[135] Mystical tourists do this through claims that they aren't tourists but *students* or *participants* in a spiritual practice. This is a distancing move, as Frow explains: "Hence a certain fantasized disassociation from the others, from the rituals of tourism, is built into almost every discourse and almost every practice of tourism."[136] The very act of denial is colonialism—by creating the illusion that one is not a tourist consumer, the mystical tourist denies all of the colonial attributes of the industry—the gaze, the inequitable relationships, and the stealing of culture, which is often renamed, repackaged, and distributed for the consumer.

The white individual often claims they know more about the practice or ritual than the indigenous person whose life and community are rooted in these very traditions. This claim of expertise, including white "healers" who insist they know more about Lakota ceremonies, is a widespread problem Native scholars and activists call "white shamanism" and "plastic medicine men."[137] *Plastic* medicine men (and women) who claim expertise in the secrets of Oriental wisdom exist as well, and as we shall see in the following chapters, the claim of expertise is part of a clever marketing strategy that has widespread success.

The clients who purchase a mystical tour of India, Bali, or Morocco are, in a sense, "buying" a culture as a form of entertainment. As discussed in the first chapter, tourism often entails a kind of voyeuristic enjoyment of the Other—including the mystic whose spirituality is dependent in some ways on poverty. Migrants that live in mystical locations like Bali often practice colonialism in profound ways that move beyond a symbolic assumption of Hinduism, Buddhism, or Sufism. European and North American female migrants to Bali often adopt a lifestyle that mirrors the colonial adventures of earlier eras. These include an escape from labor seen in the use of a laundry service and cook, which interestingly, was described by one migrant as a way of "giving back" to the Balinese.[138] The adoption of a leisurely life is made possible by the wealth of these migrants and the poverty of most Balinese. In Bali, the spiritual migrant's life includes things like sleeping late, going to yoga, and trying out classes offered by white teachers such as a Femininity and Tantric Sexuality Workshop and others that commodify Bali's Hindu culture.[139]

Priv-lit is a genre of self-help, wellness, and mysticism books "whose expressed goal is one of spiritual, existential, or philosophical enlightenment contingent upon women's hard work and patience, but whose actual barriers are primarily financial."[140] As mentioned earlier, Elizabeth Gilbert's *Eat, Pray, Love* is the best known of these books, "an international safari of self-actualization" that includes visits to India and Bali—two of the places discussed extensively in this study.[141] Oftentimes such places are seen as therapeutic, as are their native inhabitants. Gilbert attributes her healing to a Balinese person. As in other cases of mystical tourism, the body of the Oriental native becomes a site of healing. For the European or North American, the landscape of the Orient has power to transform, heal, and enlighten them. As discussed earlier, this relies in part on the denial of coeval time that Fabian warns us about—where the tourist escapes modernity and *tours* the mystical, powerful Orient, located in a different spatial universe.

Religious conflict also offers products for the mystical marketplace. In Israel, an entire "coexistence industry" involves Jews and Arabs, as well as visiting Americans and Europeans, exploiting Islamic Sufism as a way to "get along."[142] The complete disregard for colonial histories—and the colonial present—is not restricted to the Middle East. Colonized peoples are also exploited in Peru, where "white and mestizo New Age practitioners and tourists fashion ideologies emphasizing the spiritual energy which supposedly resides in Quecha bodies, even as they freely appropriate Quechua cosmology and ritual for a hybridized New Age

A dress shirt featuring a Native American portrait, Santa Fe, New Mexico (courtesy of the author).

spirituality."[143] In mystical tourism, the land and body of the native or indigenous person is often viewed as having healing powers.

Tourism often involves the consumption of other cultures.[144] Wellness tourism is an emerging topic of study. Many scholars focus on descriptive studies instead of the results of these health programs.[145] Mystical tourism involves the consumption of culture, but also the goods produced by the host culture. In many cases, the foreign European or North American sells the knowledge or expertise of a host culture. Many European and American spiritual teachers in Bali combine yoga with some other therapy. The importance of location is also key, for the "therapeutic landscape" is marketed in mystical retreats, journeys, and wellness programs. These are landscapes that are deemed "extraordinary," have a long reputation for healing, and often are far away or geographically isolated.[146] When self-declared healers move to exotic locations, they are able to capitalize on the extraordinary qualities of the place, whether it be the Moroccan desert or the Balinese jungle.

As scholars have noted, mystical tourism, also called spiritual tourism, is similar to religious pilgrimage in its search for meaning. Erik Cohen has famously argued that tourism and pilgrimage often mirror each other. The reward for religious pilgrims often takes place at the end of a journey and involves a transition, what Hindus and Buddhists call a *tirtha* (a crossing), and what for Muslims is constituted by visiting cities such as Mecca, Medina, Jerusalem, and Karbala. For mystical tourists, the focus is less on proper "religious" sites (although certainly, this may be included) and more on the journey itself. As one study notes: "Using the term 'spiritual tourism,' is to deliberately and from the beginning, place the focus of intention upon the experience and the intentions of the tourists themselves."[147] Like the colonial adventures of the past, mystical vacations and holidays cast the foreign location in the role of healer.

Mystical tourists are often focused on a personal transformation through being in a particular place with certain people (indigenous healers who can help them) and specific practices (yoga, local herbal remedies). This subset of the travel industry is geared toward self-improvement through engagement with traditional, indigenous, or New Age therapies. As one scholar notes, as a "type of highly mobile subculture, independent travel constantly generates collective narratives of selfhood and self-transformation as part of an encounter with 'Other' peoples and places."[148] The experience of travel is predicated upon the exotic location and its host culture, which are different than one's home life, denying coeval time.

Bali is viewed as a special island embodied with mystical, religious power. As well, the Balinese are sometimes described as "special," a quality that may rub off on the lucky visitor. Visitors often remark how Bali is cleaner and nicer than the rest of Indonesia, saved from ruin when compared with the nearby atolls known as the Gili Islands (Lombok), which are home to bars, backpackers, and disintegrating coral atolls. As one study notes, the largest of these islands, Gili Trawangan, deals with the degradation of its coral reefs, beach erosion, and littering and trash issues.[149] Amid these problems are beautiful sunsets and health spas featuring Balinese massages and products.

Mystical tourism often features "traditional" peoples and occupations. In Bali, this might include a tour of a coffee or rice farm. At the Chinese destination Shangri-La, "Costumes, arts and crafts, architecture, festivals, religious rituals, and typical livelihoods act as markers of the 'backwardness' of the minorities."[150] In mystical tourism, the focus might be on the culture of the locals, who are presented as holding ancient wisdom, healing powers, and other mystical qualities. At Shangri-La, tourists can purportedly buy cures for their ailments from those who hold the secrets that have been lost to the West (and to the rest of China). In one example, "Their tour guides then introduce them to a row of booths in which white-robed Tibetan doctors consult with them individually and prescribe various herbal and mineral medicines that are conveniently available for purchase."[151]

Bodies from the Orient are a common fixture in advertisements connected to mystical tourism. Often a beautiful woman, perhaps Thai, Balinese, or Moroccan, is cast as the therapeutic or spiritual key to wellness and enlightenment. The sexual power of the Oriental woman (and to a lesser degree, man) is a colonial standby, situated in eighteenth- and nineteenth-century descriptions of foreign lands that rely on the idea of the noble savage. Today, the native model is a prominent fixture in mystical tourism. As one study of Thai tourism notes: "On the 'Unseen Paradise' website, the central picture is a Thai woman, her back, smeared with mud or sand, to the camera, looking halfway over her shoulder at a temple-style painting of a traditional Thai dancer. Both the dancer and the woman are topless. The caption reads: 'Heaven is now possible and right here within your grasp.'"[152] This woman is the symbol of what the tourist can hope to gain—sexual conquest and mystical enlightenment.

In Bali, meditation is presented as a multi- or trans-religious activity in much of the tourist literature as both Hindu and Buddhist, or simply spiritual. As we will learn, Bali has a confused imagery that often conflates religious symbols to provide a general aesthetic of exoticism. In contrast, Thailand's meditation business is identified with Buddhism. As Brooke Schedneck points out: "Advertisements utilizing social imaginaries of Thailand and meditation signal to the international community the Romantic nature of this practice, where one can escape into an exotic, timeless activity, removed from modern ills and malaise."[153] Thailand's romantic allure is tied to the appeal of Buddhism in the West, a topic further explored in Chapter Four.

Bali's tourist industry peddles a diversity of symbols—the muddled Orientalism discussed at length in Chapter Three. These are often translated into a relativistic language with keywords like spiritual and mystical, and packaged to make money. A shift away from organized, institutionalized religion to the foreign and exotic is an important part of these modern mystical landscapes. As one scholar notes: "A posttraditional world of increased pluralism, relativism, and tolerance virtually assures a shift in perspective on truth and ontological certainty."[154] The remainder of this book takes us on a journey through these landscapes, from the jungles of Bali to the desert sands of Tatooine.

4

Hindu Hippies and Boulder Buddhists

During the Chicago riots in 1968 where [Allen Ginsberg] had chanted "Om" for seven hours to calm everyone down, an Indian gentleman has passed him a note telling him his pronunciation was all wrong.

Deborah Baker[1]

At 2004's Burning Man, the group Gamelan X participated in the sunset Opening Fire Ceremony wearing black-and-white checkered sarongs with the silver and gold sashes popular in Bali.[2] Once they gathered in a circle, a woman named Rose led an initiation ceremony that focused on the Burning Fire/Man that was within each person.[3] This spectacle mixed elements of Hinduism, the costume of the Brahman class in Bali, and Gamelan music with American culture and a female priestess (in Hinduism, only men can be Brahmans). It is typical of what takes place at Burning Man, reflecting what we find in many of the translations of Buddhism and Hinduism found in modern mysticism. This chapter looks at Hinduism, the guru, American styles of yoga, Buddhism, the mindfulness industry, the mystical marketplace, and some of the intersections between these topics. Hinduism and Buddhism are placed in conversation with each other in this chapter, in part because they often appear in the same religious spaces, but more so because they exist within the muddled Orientalism that characterizes much of modern mysticism.

The role of visual piety, which is found in religions around the world, contributes to the ways in which Hinduism and Buddhism are imagined by mystical seekers. David Morgan has described visual piety as "the set of practices, attitudes, and ideas invested in images that structure the experience of the sacred."[4] The accumulation of objects tied to Hinduism and Buddhism is one way the consumer can perform a spiritual identity without committing to hours of intense language study, meditation, or committing themselves to other rituals. Modern mysticism allows people to pick and choose what they want from religious traditions. In some cases, the outward symbols characterize a mystical lifestyle, through a Buddha T-shirt, Free Tibet bumper sticker, or Prana yoga mat.

The erasure of gender issues in Hinduism and Buddhism is one aspect of the recasting and whitewashing of these religions, which are often presented through white bodies in advertising. At times, art performances invert these translations. At 2003's Burning Man, artist Ken Hamazaki's performance of a Japanese tea ceremony featured the artist dressed in costume as a Buddhist monk serving tea.[5] His "whiteface" may be read as a reversal of the whitewashing of religious traditions associated with Orientalism and the mystical marketplace.

Hinduism and Buddhism are identified with mysticism in ways that often ignore the more problematic aspects of religious life. Individuals who claim an allegiance to Hindu teachings often have a romantic view of its teachings. Spoken references to dharma, karma, and *moksha* in common speech often rely on oversimplified (or incorrect) understandings of these concepts. In the case of karma, only the first part of the concept—actions and their outcomes—is referred to. As Vinay Kumar Srivastava points out, the second part of karma "prepares one to suffer" and to "withstand, and also to transcend" life's suffering.[6] This part is seldom invoked when people talk about karma. People often employ incorrectly, in phrases such as "He has good karma." In Hinduism, karma is cumulative. It is not something that is wholly good or bad, but more like an accounting of all one's actions in this life and other lives. This is one of numerous misappropriations of religion that mark the immediatism and muddled Orientalism that lie at the center of much of modern mysticism.

UNDERSTANDING HINDUISM

Hinduism is one of the most complex religions in the world, with rich texts, rituals, and traditions and deep historical roots that go back thousands of years. It is a religion with a sophisticated intellectual history that few non-practitioners and non-scholars understand. Within Hinduism, yoga's definitions include "one of the two ways of the cessation of the mind's working," "a method of making the mind silent," "a state of complete separation of the *purusa* (self) and *prakti* (primordial nature)," and "the union of the *jīvātman* and the *paramātman*."[7] As anyone who has taught a course in world religions can attest, Hinduism is a challenging topic whose framing in the study of religion is complicated by its colonial history. Like other religious traditions, Hinduism has been subject to regimes of power that have constructed knowledge in ways that are less objective than one would hope for. As Dibyesh Anand points out: "Starting with Said, the enterprise of postcolonial theory has unpacked the notion of neutral academic expertise and highlighted how Western knowledge and representations of the non-Western world are neither innocent nor based on some pre-existing 'reality,' but implicated in the West's will to power, and its imperial adventures."[8]

Orientalism has played a major role in Hinduism's status as a primordial form of spirituality, which is complicated by modern anxieties about religion that include an aversion to its regimes of power. As one scholar suggests: "When thinking of this in the Hindu context, we might look to the ways in which a variety of modern *guru* movements have purported to represent their own versions of ancient and 'authentic' Vedic tradition as a solution to the crises of modernity."[9] Hinduism's appeal, in other words, is in part predicated on its exoticness.

Hinduism, while imagined as part of the exotic East, is also subjected to whitewashing. The de-ethnicizing of Hinduism is seen in white yogis as well as in the dislocation of Hinduism from gurus such as Osho and Amma.[10] American mystics like Eckhart Tolle also distance themselves from Hindu influences, instead choosing to state "a strong connection" to Hindu teachers, or in the case of Deepak Chopra, branding himself as the spokesman for the universalist form of mysticism that is so popular today.[11]

In modern mysticism, Hinduism is often obfuscated by, or confused with, Buddhism. As mentioned above, concepts central to Hinduism such as karma and dharma may be familiar to those who profess an admiration of the Buddha and his teachings, but these individuals often have an unsophisticated understanding of their meanings. How to talk about the relationship between these two religions is a central concern of scholars, who have asked provocative questions such as "Is Buddhism a Hindu schism?" While I leave these scholarly debates to others, it is important to be aware of the ways in which these two religions are intertwined. Traditions like yoga are also difficult to define, existing as "meditative ascetic practices frequently associated with the god Shiva in Hindu teachings" as well as with Buddhist and Jain traditions.[12]

As discussed earlier, scholars of religion have played a major role in this framing of Hinduism as a kind of ancient and eternal mysticism. Scholars invented "Hinduism" as a term to cover many of the religions in India, a move that was later adopted by the British and eventually by Indian nationalists. Historically, Hinduism's mystical framing has been part of a larger missionary project. "Thus, for some, describing religions of the East as 'mystical' is a way of differentiating the essential historical truth of Christianity from its inferior rivals—and implicitly to attack those within Western Christianity who might want to focus upon the 'mystical' dimensions of their own tradition."[13] Today, a homogeneous, ahistorical Hinduism is equated with the wisdom, spirituality, and mysticism of India and its number one export—yoga. As John Hutnyk argues: "India becomes the biological/genetic/conceptual repository and archive for values, concepts, styles, and 'life essence' considered absent in the individualistic 'developed' West."[14]

Mircea Eliade saw Hinduism as a universalistic form of mysticism. Eliade and Sivananda crossed paths in Rishikesh, India, in large part because of Eliade's interest in yoga.[15] As Sarah Strauss writes, the importance of Rishikesh in the imagination of Eliade and others—including later, the Beatles—is huge. "Its fame as a 'place of saints and sages' led Mircea Eliade—as well as that most famous of 'export gurus,' Swami Vivekananda—to visit Swami Sivannanda and others settled there."[16] Without digressing into a long history of Eliade and his time in India, it is worth noting that he had a love affair with the daughter of Dasgupta (a famous philosopher), which likely influenced his romantic views of India and Hinduism.[17] Like other important early scholars of religion, Eliade influenced generations of scholars who saw the East as a site of romantic academic engagement.

HINDUISM IN AMERICA

The largest waves of immigrants from Asia to America came in the mid- and late-twentieth century, encouraged in part by the Hart-Celler Act of 1965 that expanded openings for Asians seeking a new life in the United States.[18] These immigrants included many from India. Hinduism is not typically considered what we would call a missionary or evangelistic religion. Generally, one has to be born a Hindu, and although today, yoga and Ayurveda are popular in the West, there is considerably less allegiance to Hinduism than to Buddhism. This may be a relief for those who want to protect their traditions from converts. The Vishwa Hindu Parishad (Universal Indian Council) is one example of the desire to protect Hindu identity; with ties to the BJP (Bharatiya Janata Party), the conservative Hindu political party, which sees India and Hinduism as being one and the same.[19] Of course, this does not represent all Hindus in North America.

Hinduism has a rich visual culture that has produced an incredibly rich array of material culture and art forms including dance, sculpture, painting, and graphic narratives. The material culture identified with Hinduism is in part due to the use of idols, which are believed to be living gods that the individual sees—and that see the individual human. *Darśan*, which occurs when one sees the gods and they look upon the Hindu, helps us understand how the production and worship of idols are key parts of the Hindu tradition. However, likenesses of Hindu gods are not always used religiously by Hindus. Like non-Hindus, they are used decoratively. As Semontee Mitra reminds us, the Indian-American market carries a huge variety of these goods, from food to idols. "What is most striking here is that the statues of gods are not always made for worship, some are made for decorative purpose. Gods have been deprived of their godly statuses and reduced to merely decorative items placed beside jewelries, utensils, and teddy bears and bunnies. This reflects not just the attitudes of the producers but also of the consumers who buy and use them."[20]

Hindu imagery is commonly featured in the marketplace, especially in ethnic fashion and fitness gear. This imagery is popular with the white, affluent yogini or New Ager living in Boulder, Santa Fe, or Sedona. As Vineeta Sinha points out: "Interestingly,

Hindu symbolism and imagery are now also embossed and imprinted on a variety of everyday secular objects such as wallets, lockets, pendants, key chains, T-shirts, notebooks, bags, pens, hand-phone covers, lunch-boxes, car decals, stickers, etc, which are not necessarily rendered 'sacred' because of these divine associations."[21] Sinha sees these as aesthetic objects or decorative items, suggesting the appeal of "the East" includes its religious imagery as accouterment, fashion item, or house décor. Is a yoga mat with OM on it sacred? What about a T-shirt with Vishnu on it? Or are these simply aesthetic objects?

In addition to the production of idols and other religious objects, Hinduism is part of the American economic system in other ways. *Pujaris* are imported from India to train men in the priesthood, conduct rituals in the homes, and often are housed in larger temples—along with their families.[22] Organizations like ISSO (International Swaminarayan Satsang Organization) and BAPS (Bochanwasi Shri Akshar Puroshottam Swaminarayan Sanstha) market themselves to religious consumers and arrange for visits by sadhus from India, to "keep the bond strong."[23] As we shall see, the guru is not only important to Hindus, but to those individuals who have adopted or borrowed from Hinduism for profit.

YOGA

Indian gurus play an important role in the history of representations of Asian religion, especially those related to mysticism. As Iwamura's work shows, the character of the "Oriental Monk" is an especially powerful cultural figure found in literature, news media, television, and film. In her book on this character, Iwamura explains how Hinduism was introduced to American popular culture in the 1960s through him. This era witnessed the rise and fall of the most popular Indian guru in American history, Mahesh. In many ways, his popularity and status as an object of criticism reflect the contradiction inherent in Orientalism—the allure of the East and the threat it poses to Western culture. Like other Oriental monks, Mahesh embodied both "a long-gone India" and "present-day Asia," in the undeniable lure of Eastern mysticism and the challenges it posed when housed in a brown body.[24] These all contributed to the explosion of the yoga industry that we see today.

Deepak Chopra gives us an inventive version of the Hindu sage. He is tied to the Maharishi through his involvement with his line of Ayur-Veda herbal curatives.[25] Over recent years, his relationship to both the Maharishi and Ayurveda has been largely severed.[26] Even though Chopra presents a different kind of spiritual guide—clean-cut, New Age, with watered-down Hindu teachings—he also utilizes many of the same "representational dynamics" as Mahesh.[27] Chopra walks a careful line that sells his authenticity as a yogi-type of teacher while downplaying the fact that many of his therapies are Hindu. For example, he makes no references to Maharishi Ayurveda, but advocates the use of Ayurvedic therapies that are reframed as "spiritual" or "wellness" practices.[28] Chopra and others like him have remade Hinduism into a wellness lifestyle that is *just* far enough removed from its Indian origins for consumers to be comfortable in adopting it.

Yoga is an incredibly popular practice in America. Its success is in large part due to its whitewashing, which has erased its Hindu origins while capitalizing on its Eastern imagery. Reconstituting Hinduism as a kind of white, affluent style, yoga walks a precarious line between exoticism and white respectability. "The contemporary marketing of yoga of whatever type, however, often appeals to the exoticism and 'counter-cultural cachet' of yoga as a key selling point—except in those cases where to appear too 'mystical,' 'religious', or 'ethnic' and might put off customers looking for some light relief from the stresses of their busy urban lives."[29]

The aversion to the ethnic side of yoga is related to long-held anxieties surrounding yogis in the early twentieth century. Documented in numerous cases of individuals sent to mental asylums due to their commitment to yoga, Baha'i, or another newfound religious practice in the West, yogi-phobia was also expressed in numerous films featuring a sinister Hindu man. Mirroring the vilification of other non-white men, Hindus were subject to accusations of sexual perversion, religious fraud, and more. Hollywood capitalized on the hysteria with films such as *The Love Girl* (1916), *Sinister Hands* (1932), *Sucker Money* (1933), and *Religious Racketeers* (1938).[30]

Yoga is the most popular Hindu tradition in North America, with Ayurveda a close second. As scholars have shown, yoga came back into fashion as a modern practice in India due to its popularity in North America and Europe. As Askegaard and Eckhardt state: "This 'grandmothers' practice' was deemed not suitably modern by the growing urban and youthful middle classes constituting the class of an emerging consumer culture. However, yoga has become increasingly in vogue as an important part of a modern South Asian consumer lifestyle. Based on the West's stamp of approval, yoga has become a trendy activity for the nouveau rich in Asia to take part in."[31]

Yoga is one of many popular fitness programs focused on spirituality and promises of an improved individual, body, and soul.[32] Crossfit is another popular health regimen, promising personal transformation, health benefits, and help with psychological issues like depression and anxiety. Both Crossfit and yoga are examples of "therapeutic cultures" that mimic religion, often borrowing from their symbolic systems (Crossfit famously got into trouble with many followers after it posted a parody video of Jesus) and offering direct access to a "greater power" (perfect health), and encouraging transformation.[33] The idea of *spirit* is at the center of many of these cultures, reminiscent of Paul Tillich's definition of the spirit as a life-giving force that characterizes the human experience.[34] In both yoga and Crossfit fitness programs, an improved *spirit* is linked to fitness.

The origins of yoga, unlike Crossfit, are in the East. Literally meaning "to yoke," *yoga* is both a philosophy (one of the six *darśanas*, or traditions, in South Asian thought) and a religious discipline (Hindu, Buddhist, or Jain).[35] The true meaning of yoga is no simple matter, given its long history of speculative philosophy and ancient writings. Its reference to "yoke" and "union" is situated in numerous Hindu texts. In the Rig-Veda, yoga refers to the connection between the words of a verse and in the Atharva-veda, it is used to refer to the work of bullocks and a plow.[36] In the Bhagavad Gita, yoga is defined as *samatva* (when one is free from bringing about any result), as a method for improving behavior, and as the greatest state of spiritual attainment.[37] There are many varieties of yoga in Hinduism, including *bhakti yoga*, *karma yoga*, *raja yoga*, *hatha yoga*, *laya yoga*, and *mantra yoga*—all of which involve serious meditation, at times with breathing, at other times with other practices.[38]

The history of yoga in North America has been the subject of numerous studies that point to its relationship with universalistic and perennial religious movements like Unitarianism and theosophy. Swami Vivekananda (1863–1902) presented Vedanta as a model religion, promoted Hindu nationalism, and criticized yogis who he viewed as suspicious, in favor of "samadhi (higher consciousness) and moksha (spiritual liberation)."[39] He promoted raja yoga as the antithesis to hatha yoga, which he viewed as too body-centered.[40] Vivekananda was followed by others, including Krishnamacharya, who rehabilitated hatha, and whose hatha troupe "functioned both as cultural ambassadors and circus-like entertainers."[41] Eventually the more body-centered yoga practices won out, seen today in yoga's popularity at health clubs, community centers, and wellness resorts.

The story of how yoga was transformed from a complex philosophical system into goat and wine yoga is long and interesting, involving Indians such as Vivekanda and Krishnamacharya as well as numerous other individuals, among them Europeans and Americans. One of the most important women in the history of yoga was Indra Devi (1899–2002), a Latvian who traveled to India, starred in Bollywood films, convinced Krishnamacharya to take her to America, and eventually opened a yoga studio in Hollywood, introducing it to Greta Garbo, Jennifer Jones, and Gloria Swanson, among others.[42] Transcendental Meditation® (TM) remains popular among Hollywood's elite, credited for reducing anxiety, depression, creating balance, and more. Transcendental Meditation® (TM) has followers like director David Lynch and actress Jennifer Aniston. As William Bainbridge points out, it is one of many mystical traditions that evades religious classification:

> With respect to cults, this may mean that many of them avoid the label of religion, and the line between religion and science fades. Among familiar examples, Transcendental Meditation presented itself as a science rather than a variant of Hindu religion, and Scientology presented itself as religion rather than a variant of psychotherapy. This is not to say any of them was wrong, if *religion* is a socially constructed category.[43]

TM illustrates how quickly Hinduism stopped being a religion and started being something else.

The fitness yoga of today is connected to several figures, including the Maharishi Mahesh, whose popularity was eventually matched by his dramatic fall from grace. Mahesh's later life was precipitated by scandal, although he had faced critics for years. It was the Beatles–Mia Farrow episode that did the most damage, however.

> Transcendental Meditation®, the brain child of the Maharishi Mahesh Yogi, emerged on the public radar only

> when Donovan and the Beatles made a much-publicized pilgrimage to his mosquito-infested ashram in India, a New Age haj that ended disastrously when the grizzled guru made sexual overtures to another dabbler in TM®, Mia Farrow, and then asked the Fab Four to tithe a substantial portion of their income into his secret Swiss bank account.[44]

In fact, it was not just the Beatles who tithed. Everyone who received a mantra had to give a week's salary to the Mahesh as payment.[45] Despite this history, Transcendental Meditation® remains a popular practice in North America, among Hollywood's elite as well as the general public.

SYDA (Siddha Yoga Dham Associates), which remains extremely popular in Hollywood today, and has centers around the world, has also been plagued by scandal. When its founder Muktananda passed away, it emerged that he'd had sexual relationships with numerous female students including teenagers.[46] However, this did not close the doors of SYDA completely—indeed, they still have a presence in thirty countries today—suggesting that the power of mysticism continues to be a seductive force.[47]

HINDU HEALTH AND WELLNESS

The history of North American yoga includes many famous people, including poets, movie stars, musicians, and artists, whose experience with Hinduism was not plagued by scandal. Ralph Waldo Emerson and other writers had encounters with the religion through their interest in transcendentalism, theosophy, and European and North American mystical movements. Today, most Americans practice hatha yoga, one of six major traditions (Raja, Jnana, Karma, Bhakti, Mantra, and Hatha) that has been, at times, associated with "weird, fanatical, licentious, ungovernable, dangerous" behaviors, such as self-mortification and levitation.[48] Hatha yoga is none of these things today. Today, it is typically a streamlined, slickly commodified practice focused on burning calories and alleviating anxiety. As Jared Farmer writes: "In its mainstream form, Hatha has been cleaned up and partially de-enchanted. The typical American yoga instructor says 'namaste' and chants a perfunctory OM with her students, but does not teach tantric physiology. She is much more likely to give a testimonial about yoga's beneficial effects on the medical body."[49]

Yogamillionaires market their practices by removing just enough of the Hindu (as well as Buddhist and Jain) origins of the practice to make it palatable to North Americans and Europeans, but not so much that it loses its exotic appeal. The key to this translation project is to make it culturally accessible by removing just enough of its foreign origins so that it does not offend white sensibilities. As Suhag Shukla points out, commercial enterprises like *Yoga Journal* and the yoga industry in general avoid using the H-word and instead rely on the vocabulary of modern mysticism and New Age spirituality—"Eastern" and "Sanskritic."[50] Deepak Chopra is a great marketer of contemporary corporate yoga, which is described as "spiritual" instead of "Hindu" or "religious."[51]

CHAKRAS AND TANTRA

The chakra is another Hindu concept used in mystical and spiritual products, New Age religion, and alternative healing practices. Understood by Hindus as a "wheel" that exists as a system, there are seven chakras that correspond to different parts of the body.[52] The commodification of chakras is far-reaching and includes beauty products, exercise programs, and New Age festivals. Chakras are often cited by medical intuitives, healers who claim they can telepathically diagnose someone by observing or examining them. Alison Anton, a Boulder healer, is one of many entrepreneurs who advertises "medical intuition" as a diagnostic tool. Chakras are also part of popular feminist thought and are included in Oprah's spiritual teachings. As one scholar puts it: "Once again, Oprah distills complex charts of chakra points, horoscopes, and archetypes to their most basic premise."[53]

Non-embodied chakras are believed to be located at certain places, which are then visited by consumers seeking mystical experience. Glastonbury, England, is described as a "heart chakra" of the earth.[54] At chakra centers, great effort is made to connect the East with local histories and mythologies. At Glastonbury, Hinduism is even connected to Britain. "Since the 18th century, some writers and practitioners have drawn connections between Hinduism and Druidry by identifying Druids and Brahmins with one another."[55] Glastonbury also offers *darśan* (the Hindu ritual of seeing the gods and goddesses in icons) with His Holiness Gyalwa Jampa, along with shops containing products like images of Hindu deities and statues of various Boddhisatvas.[56] At Glastonbury, Hinduism is part of New Age spirituality, appealing to spiritual shoppers, modern mystics, and yoginis.

Chakras have also found their way into Oriental dance. In belly dance, they exist alongside Islamic patterns and calligraphy, in the choreography of Maria Sangiorgi. "The exploration of the chakra system with a focus on areas of connecting nerves throughout the spinal column provides an avenue for increased awareness of tensions and potential release of those tensions within the spinal vertebral system."[57]

Ayurveda is another Hindu practice that is commodified by non-Hindus, who often reap great financial benefit. In its original form, it is "the systematization of the Vedic medical knowledge and healing practices that were present during the Vedic era. The word *ayurveda* consists of two Sanskrit terms: 'veda' means 'knowledge' or 'science,' while 'ayu,' means 'life' or 'duration of life.'"[58] Today, Ayurveda is marketed in teas that promise healing and wellness, foods that advertise the restoration of the humors, and other therapies. Ayurveda is part of the romanticized and generalized Orient that offers a cure for the ills of modernity.[59] Ayurveda is often found at health spas, including at the Dragontree franchise, which has locations in Portland, Oregon and Boulder, Colorado. The Boulder location is decorated with saffron and red hues borrowed from an Indian palette, features natural treatments (no pedicures or chemicals), and offers a large number of products based on Ayurvedic principles as well as planners, Dreambooks, and Dreambook stickers with such phrases as "Feel your Focus."

In Germany, Ayurvedic medicine is dispensed by *heilpraktiker*, a homeopathic healing therapist whose diagnosis may include a "reading" of the patient's bodily systems through the use of headphones, wires, a computer, and a laser, resulting in a color-coded printout of the therapy needed.[60] One study describes the therapy as including "homeopathic sugar pills," thus combining the European therapy of homeopathy with Ayurvedic medicine.[61] As noted in several medical studies, homeopathy has been shown to be of no medical benefit. In one investigation, the "essential matter" in homeopathic drops was found to be nothing but sugar water.[62] Narainda's account of the *heilpraktiker* tells us that therapies from the East may lend credibility to otherwise dubious medical or therapeutic practices. In some cases, Ayurvedic psychotherapy is administered, or some form of Global Ayurveda is used on patients—therapies that are not found in the classical texts, and not practiced in India.[63]

Tantra is another misunderstood aspect of Hinduism. In the West it is often associated with sexual practices (the Kama Sutra, and Sting's famous interview in which he extolled the virtues of yogic sex are two examples). In reality, a *tantric* is something quite different. "In both classical and contemporary descriptions, a tantric is commonly portrayed as someone who is constantly searching for power and is rejecting norms, whether by human sacrifice and cannibalism, or through sex. In both scenarios, transgression lies at the core. And in both depictions, a Tantric lives compassion and love."[64] More recently, vaginal treatments like steaming and the use of *yoni* (Sanskrit for 'womb') stones point to the linking of Hinduism to sexual pleasure and spiritual transformation. Vaginal steaming is often cited as a practice situated in "Eastern mysticism" whose validity is due to its exotic and (supposed) ancient use in the Orient.[65]

EAT, PRAY, PAY: AYURVEDA AND MYSTICAL TOURISM

Ayurveda is a common feature of mystical tourism. Vedic Village, located outside Kolkata (Calcutta), is a luxury spa that offers villas and rooms surrounded by water, Ayurvedic therapies, massages, wellness therapies and of course yoga.[66] As Nazrul Islam points out, the mystical marketplace influences the practice of Ayurveda: "Under these new values, the orientalist discourse of Ayurveda has been 'deconstructed' and is no longer in dispute with conventional Western medicine."[67] Visitors might start their day by praying to a Hindu god, doing oral hygiene, taking a walk, followed by a yoga session and a hot-oil massage, which are thrown together in such a way that they represent a "contaminated" form of Ayurveda.[68] Vedic Village's website illustrates some of the ways in which Ayurveda is marketed as a wellness (and beauty) therapy, much like the Dragontree spas in Portland and Boulder. Here is content from their website:

> A tranquil sanctuary with a unique ambience of tradition, art and nature on one hand and on the other with ample international style leisure, sports activities, wellness facilities.
>
> Water bodies. Green pastures. Adventure. Spa. Bonfires. Sunsets. Boating. ATV Riding. Bowling Alley. Zorbing. Segway's. Kayaking ... the list goes on!
>
> A collection of exclusive hand-picked accommodation, with extraordinary villas and private homes, plus premium hotel rooms for those who expect excellent value, personal service and supremely comfortable accommodation.
>
> Brilliant gourmet experiences await you at the award-winning regional cuisine restaurant or through farm to fork organic meals at the all-hour restaurant, or even through the simplicity of the rituals at the tea lounge. And for after-hours there's always the romantic poolside bar or the pulsating nightspot.
>
> And finally, serenity awaits you at the private Sanjeeva Ayurvedic Spa. Only a short amble along the gardened pathways leads you to the temple of the holistic wellness retreat ... that starts the moment you check in![69]

Vedic Village is one of many mystical touristic resorts in India, Bali, and elsewhere that feature Ayurveda alongside luxurious villas and a "pulsating nightspot." In Bali, wellness resorts are marketed as luxury retreats with names such as Puri Dajuma Eco-Resort Spa, Bagus Jati Health and Wellbeing Retreat, Mava Ubud Resort and Spa, Rama Candidasa Resort and Spa, and Sukavati Ayurvedic Retreat and Spa. Sukavati offers programs with yoga sessions, facials, a fruit basket, and a stay in a luxurious villa starting at $1,900 for three nights.[70] The ashram, which is intended to be a place of serious religious study for Hindus, is now marketed as a retreat or resort. Nowadays, people can visit posh ashrams that are more luxury resort than Hindu religious retreat;

these are called *spashrams*: "Ashrams are now glorified spas called 'spashrams,' luxury resorts that boast swimming pools, golf courses, and 'zennis' courts."[71] The book and film *Eat, Pray, Love* helped to popularize both Indian mysticism and Balinese spirituality among contemporary spiritual seekers. As Ruth Williams points out, an entire industry of "EPL tourism" emerged after the release of the Julia Roberts film adaptation of the book. These included "visiting the Ganges ghats in Varanasi, India in order to 'feel the beating heart of the Hindu universe,'" and "experiencing dinner at a restaurant in Bali that features 'dreamy tables overlooking a rice field.'"[72]

One Earth, One Sky, Anand Krishna's ashram and retreat in Sunter, Indonesia, is popular with Indonesian Muslims who are Sufi-oriented but who do not want to join a more traditional Sufi order (*tarekat*, in Indonesian).[73] Krishna's religious biography is diverse—trained by both Hindu and Islamic teachers, a sojourn in India, and an encounter with a Tibetan lama—helping him to market himself to a community of followers who are encouraged to benefit from his wellness therapies.[74] One Earth, One Sky is an example of mystical tourism and it has broad appeal, both to North Americans and to others, including Muslims from Indonesia.

BUDDHISM IN THE WEST

> *I would say Asia is where I would go to discover me. I just think there's a lot of beliefs, languages and practices to embrace living. Especially when it looks like this … [*points to the beach*].*[75]
>
> Norman, 32 (Belfast, Ireland)

The story of Buddhism in the United States involves immigrants, yoga enthusiasts, and converts to Zen, Tibetan, and other schools of Buddhism. Today, it has a powerful presence in popular culture. Commodified forms of Buddhism are often joined with more serious practices through educational institutions like Boulder's Naropa University and the Shambhala Center, as well as in the lives of Buddhist converts. In some cases, the interest in Buddhism is joined with efforts to "save" Buddhist practices and people; this is especially true with Tibetan traditions. Following the work of Lopez who argues that Tibet functions as a site of special knowledge, Craig Janes writes: "Extending Lopez's argument to Tibetan medicine, it may be argued that among some groups in the West Tibet-as-Shangri-La is imagined as a threatened source of exceptional, disappearing knowledge for maintaining physical and spiritual health."[76]

The magazine *Tricycle* began in 1991, in a decade that saw the flourishing of Buddhism in popular culture, including among celebrities. As one study notes, even Oprah got in on the revival of Buddhism in America; one episode of her TV program featured a Seattle boy who claimed to be the reincarnation of a Tibetan Buddhist mystic.[77] One of the downsides of Buddha-mania is what religious scholar David Chidester calls "authentic fakes," the title of his 2005 book on popular culture and religion. In the case of Asian religions, these abound. "In American popular culture, Asian spirituality, the lure of the mystic East, has been capitalized on, Western style, by a fraud such as Eugen Herrigel, misrepresenting the Zen master Kenzo Awa; an imposter such as Cyril Hoskin, posing as Lobsang Rampa; and an invented, fictitious Internet guru such as Sri Vendra Yallah."[78]

In some instances, Buddhist communities have willingly joined the economic market, gaining followers and making money. In Scotland, the Tibetan organization Rokpa Scotland (RS) combines religious instruction with commodified forms of the religion. "One way in which Tibetan Buddhism adapts to consumer culture is by providing a range of culturally relevant services and commodities for a given fee. For example, RS sells a broad range of dharmas, retreats, therapies, books, vegetarian cookery courses and Tibetan Buddhist objects."[79]

The marketing of Zen is not limited to North America. In Denmark, the commodification of Zen includes books on therapy, psychology, management, gardening, and more.[80] None of this is new, of course; Buddhism is a missionary religion that was spread through conquest, traveling monks, and later, through cinema. As Peter Hansen writes, this was one benefit of the proliferation of documentary and dramatic films about Tibet over the last century: "The dancing lamas of Everest in the 1920s may have gone to London out of similar 'missionary' motives. These media enabled such monks to spread their message to other parts of the world as Buddhist monks had been doing for hundreds of years within Asia."[81]

Like Hinduism, Buddhism is widely misunderstood by many North Americans. It is a complex and diverse religion with numerous schools of thought, practices, and traditions that involve the worship of Hindu gods, tantric/mystical texts, visions, and philosophical movements. In Thailand, Buddha is the highest god in a large pantheon that includes Brahma, Vishnu, and Indra, who figures prominently in spirit altars and is the "most powerful Lord in the Thai spiritual world."[82] Tibetan Buddhism is strongly focused on tantras, "practices derived from esoteric texts stressing cognitive transformation through visualizations, symbols, and rituals" that are believed to help one reach higher spiritual states—even enlightenment.[83] Such differences are lost on spiritual consumers, who often obtain their knowledge about Buddhism from books in the travel literature section of bookstores. As one scholar puts it: "In bookshops, Buddhism-related books are to be found under the category 'Body and Mind' alongside books about popular psychology, new age, spirituality, and healthy living."[84]

BUDDHISM IN THE WESTERN IMAGINATION

Buddhism is often thought of in simplistic terms in North America, shaped by visions like Shambhala (the Buddhist "heaven"), the Buddha of cinema (à la Keanu Reeves), and the myth of Shangri-La popularized by the famous film. These three cultural moments are all identified with Tibet, which looms large in the Western imagination of the East as a land full of magical monks and mystical knowledge. Scholars in the nineteenth century described it as a sanctuary, and from the mid-twentieth century onwards it has often been depicted as "still uncontaminated by the ills besetting the modern world."[85] Many contemporary mystical consumers still hold these views, which were dismissed by scholars long ago. As Per Kvaerne notes: "Few serious scholars today would regard Tibet as a country somehow outside the rest of the world or as a mere repository of Buddhist culture long since lost in its land of origin. Inward-looking, exclusively text-oriented Tibetology is no longer viable (although some anthropologists occasionally seem to feel a need to flog dead horses)."[86]

Shangri-La is arguably one of the most powerful ideas in the Western imaginaire of Buddhism, influenced by the 1933 book by James Hilton titled *Lost Horizon*, the Frank Capra film that memorialized it (1937), and numerous other Hollywood productions that followed—including *Himalaya*, *Little Buddha*, *Kundun*, and *Seven Years in Tibet*.[87] Tibet's popularity is predicated, in part, on its presentation as the antithesis to Western modernity. As Donald Lopez writes: "Tibet operates as a constituent of romanticism in which the Orient is not debased but exalted as a surrogate self endowed with all that the West wants. Tibet is seen as the cure for an ever-dissolving Western civilization, restoring its spirit."[88]

Portrayals of Buddhism are also shaped by its history in the academy. Buddhism has often been framed as the antithesis to religions viewed as "violent" or "fanatical," such as Islam. The

Buddhist Oriental monk is a character that is modeled on serenity and peace. As Iwamura has shown, this fixture of popular culture in North America influences the ways in which Buddhism is understood by the lay public, even today. In early film, the Buddhist monk was often presented as a romantic character, such as in D. W. Griffith's *Broken Blossoms or the Yellow Man and the Girl* (1919). "The fact that Griffith associates peace, gentleness, sensitivity, and altruism to the Buddha and his followers constitutes a significant moment in popular consciousness."[89] The ideas surrounding Buddhism are powerful and often are far removed from reality. As Eske Møllgaard writes: "If we try to separate, say, real Tibet from virtual Tibet, then we may only be left with some scientifically sanitized ideal that has no relation to the Real of our existential, human and necessary human condition."[90] Gender is one place in which romantic notions are most evident. By obfuscating the patriarchy in Buddhism—seen in the long list of Oriental monks in America who are all men—and reconfiguring the religion as a philosophy, way of life, or self-help program, the gendered realities of Buddhism are hidden behind a veil of Tibetan prayer flags, meditation pillows, and yoga retreats.

The status of Buddhism as a "philosophy" allows it to be interwoven with other forms of mysticism like Sufism, which erases Buddhism's great diversity of clerics, rituals, and pilgrimages throughout the world. The modernization of Buddhism has involved a fair degree of historical revisionism, which includes silencing its gender biases, history of empire, and episodes of violence (seen today in Myanmar). As David MacMahan argues: "Modernists may openly refute certain elements of tradition or claim to be going back to the true, original tradition."[91] Buddhism has wrestled with these issues, at times reconstructing the religion as something quite different than what is represented in its texts, rituals, and traditions. This includes the wholesale transformation of Buddhism to a commodified product for the spiritual or mystical consumer.

It is not just that Buddhism exists as an imaginary field in the minds of many North Americans and Europeans. Its spiritual capital is a powerful example of the ways in which other people's religions become objects of consumption, corrupting its ethical foundations and contemplative practices. We see this in the products associated with mindfulness, which, as has been noted earlier, illustrate the misuse of Buddhist teachings.

However, the opportunistic elements warned against by Kabat-Zinn are surely underestimated here, and there is insufficient attention given to the ways in which such forces have managed to produce a grossly mutated version of mindfulness until it has now become a commodified consumerist product used to sell everything from colouring books and musical relaxation compact discs (CDs) to apps for mindful gardening, cooking, and driving.[92]

AMERICAN BUDDHISM

Buddhism, like many religions, is complex and diverse, determined by the communities, texts, and rituals that shape it. Different schools of Buddhism have commonalities such as the four noble truths, the eight-fold path, and the three jewels. In all schools the path to enlightenment through meditation is difficult, but individuals can find refuge in the three jewels—the Buddha, the teachings, and the community.[93] How these are defined varies, accounting for the diversity in Buddhist communities around the world. The practices found among Buddhist nuns in Tibet are highly ritualized, their texts are tantric, and their religion is heavily dependent on indescribable, ineffable experience—what some religious scholars would describe as "contemplative" or "mystical." Zen is different, with distinct rituals, texts, and different teachings; there are no mystical lamas or tantric texts.

The history of Buddhism in America is largely influenced by two factors: immigration and missionary activity. Buddhist immigration is often discussed in reference to the mainland, excluding the role of Hawaii, which is a major part of the story of Buddhism in the United States. In the United States, missionaries made an impact on non-ethnic Asians who become Buddhist. The period 1930–70 saw the beginnings of this, with small numbers of white followers of Jodo Shinshu in Hawaii in the 1920s as well as on the mainland at Gyomay Kubode's Buddhist temple in Chicago in the 1940s.[94]

In the first half of the twentieth century, Zen Buddhism was the most popular of the American Buddhist movements, garnering converts through meditation centers in New York, San Francisco, and elsewhere.[95] The popularity of meditation, new religious movements, and transcendental philosophy encouraged more converts to Buddhism, first to Zen, and later in the Tibetan school of Buddhism associated with Rinpoche, which is discussed in detail in the following sections. The majority of converts to Buddhism are white. The group known as Nichiren Shosu, with Tina Turner as its most famous follower, claims to have the largest number of followers of any school of Buddhism in North America.[96]

In North American media, Buddhism is presented as a predominantly white practice, with fewer Asians than one might expect, and minuscule numbers of Latino/as and African Americans. In the 2013 film *The Mindfulness Movie*, of the thirty-five people interviewed all were white except for Tich Nhat Hanh.[97] This imbalance is typical of North American presentations of Buddhism. In a survey of 100 mindfulness books, most feature natural imagery or some other non-human entity (like a statue or hands in pose).[98] While the majority of this book (and this chapter) focuses on North American mysticism and spirituality, it should be noted that Zen is broadly popular in Europe and other parts of the world. As Rocha points out, in Brazil it is used to market products with a wide field of meanings: "happiness, peace, tranquility, well-being, simplicity, harmony, and meditation on the one hand and modern, fashionable, and trendy on the other."[99]

TIBET, COLORADO

The individual most responsible for the development of Boulder, Colorado as a major center of Buddhism is Trungpa Rinpoche. A lineage holder of two of the major schools of Tibetan Buddhism—Nyingma and Kagyü—he founded the Naropa Institute, now a university, in 1974.[100] Trungpa's influence on American Buddhism is undeniable. He founded Vajradhatu in 1973, which later became Shambhala International and today operates over 100 meditation centers, a respected publishing house, and, of course, Naropa University.[101] Boulder is arguably the most popular site of Tibetan Buddhism in North America, even though Shambhala's headquarters moved to Halifax and its Gampo Abbey there has offered programs for corporations geared towards New Age goals like the creation of an "enlightened society."[102] A glance at Naropa University's offerings reflect the ways in which mysticism and spirituality are part of the translation project in Shambhala. Contemplative spirituality is reflected in the university's offerings, which include courses such as Spirituality and Creative Expression, Socially Engaged Spirituality, and Contemplative Intercultural Studies.

Trungpa was a very unconventional teacher, which was part of his appeal. As Fabrice Midal puts it: "For a master of crazy wisdom, the more intense the confusion, the greater the chances of entering into a relationship with this open space, without any major preconception. In such a situation, the ego's insanity is thoroughly exposed."[103] Identified with "crazy wisdom," a teaching model aligned with some Tibetan schools, Trungpa was known to be a philanderer, drunk, and grandstander. As Sandra Bell writes: "The large house that Chogyam Trungpa occupied in a high-class area of Boulder was known as The Kalapa Court. Disciples were admitted by invitation only. The residence was sumptuously appointed and organized to reflect a courtly hierarchy with followers eager to serve as cleaners, attendants, guards, cooks, flower arrangers, and so on."[104]

As previously discussed, Trungpa is known for his unconventional teaching style, excessive and exorbitant lifestyle, and sexual promiscuity. After his death, one of his students, Osel Tendzin (who led the community after Trungpa's death), transmitted HIV to numerous people in Boulder, including at least one young man who eventually succumbed to AIDS.[105] The crime of doing harm within a community that believes strongly in *ahimsa* (the principle of no harm) caused serious damage to the followers of Trungpa. The value of "crazy wisdom" came to be questioned, in part because Trungpa had promised magical protection to Osel when he revealed he was HIV-positive.[106]

Boulder Buddhists are a community of generally affluent, white Americans, largely insulated from Asian immigrant groups.[107] Lynn Eldershaw and other scholars point out that Shambhala faces challenges in surviving due to its mostly white followers, which comprises around seventy-eight percent of the overall community.[108] After the events surrounding the AIDS scandal and a reorganization, a new vision of Tibetan Buddhism was promoted that revitalized the membership which had dwindled after the AIDS scandal. At that point, Trungpa's community was re-envisioned as a New Age religion focused on meditation practices called the Shambhala Training, which had no requirement to be Buddhist.[109] As Sandra Bell explains: "The name is drawn from a Tibetan myth that features a kingdom of enlightened beings ruled by sagacious monarchs. The intention of the training is to create people capable of establishing a society in this world that mirrors the Shambhala kingdom. Participants can adhere to their own religious preferences and do not have to think of themselves as Buddhists."[110]

The question arises whether Shambhala is more of a religion or business model. The expression "Boulder Buddhists" is used by locals to describe the white, affluent, self-proclaimed Buddhists living in and around the city. Tumblr's *Stay Out of My Namaste Space* is one of the many ways in which the community is ridiculed. At the foundation of these jokes is a more serious concern about a community that is nearly eighty percent white, privileged, and embedded in New Age and contemporary cultures of mysticism and spirituality. As Lynn Eldershaw reminds us, this community is part of a larger project that exploits Tibetan culture and religion for profit:

> In an attempt to generate a "market edge," the movement has further expanded programming into areas of education, livelihood, and leisure, designed to appeal to contemporary Western tastes. A brief listing of some of these programs gives an indication of the breadth and variety currently offered throughout the movement: "Shamatha Yoga," "Zen Golf," "Shambhala Art," contemplative gardening, wilderness retreats, shaman retreats, leadership training, death and dying seminars, and programs for gay men and lesbians.[111]

The focus of Buddhism in Boulder is on Tibet; in particular, on the teachings associated with Trungpa. As we have seen, the West's fascination with Tibet far predates Trungpa. It is embedded in Orientalism and its reduction of indigenous people "to an essential idea," which in this case, sees "Tibetans as religious."[112] In films about Tibet, the people are also depicted as spiritual, often contrasted with European visitors.[113] These films, whether documentary or fictive and dramatic, often function as colonial experiences for the European and North American viewer. Like other parts of the Orient, Tibet is mystical. Unlike the West, which is rational, in Tibet we find the "arrested, fixated form of representation" that is an integral part of Orientalist discourse about so-called Eastern religion.[114]

One of the strategies used in creating a mystic Tibet was to combine myths, legends, facts, and rumors into "facts," creating a vision of place that was characterized by "strange ways and rare magical powers."[115] Today, the appeal of Tibetan Buddhism is situated in this history. It is also buttressed by the importance of tantric texts in Tibet, which are mystical, a fact that may explain the appeal of practices like Tibetan medicine, which have "New Age affinities."[116] Like many other religions, Tibetan Buddhism offers its mystical knowledge for a price. In Rokpa, Scotland, where a lama chooses who has access to the secrets of the tradition:

> In addition to limiting the adaptation of Tibetan Buddhism to consumer culture within the organization, RS manages the effect exogenous commodification has on the tradition by limiting access by external agencies to the depths of the tradition. For example, at the public lectures, Tibetan Buddhism is presented more as a philosophy of compassion than as a mystical religion, while access to the more esoteric and higher levels of teaching is controlled by the lamas through empowerment ceremonies. These empowerment ceremonies, of which there are many, are not open to the general public and are shrouded in secrecy. Only those taking the empowerment [ceremony] may attend and the content must remain secret.[117]

Tibetan Buddhism has been co-opted by many businesses that trade in New Age, alternative, and mystical products. The nature of the tradition, with its oracles, ascetics, and meditative practices, has great appeal for the individual who is looking for something different.[118] Tibetan Buddhism, its teachings, and its related products are an important part of the Buddhist character of Boulder, but Buddhism also exists as a New Age practice in the city, much as it does in other college towns that are imbued with a spiritualist edge.

BUDDHISM, INC.

Zen, Tibetan, and other schools of Buddhism are, as we have seen, linked to New Age, mysticism, and spirituality in numerous ways. While North American articulations of these connections are the focus of this chapter, they exist elsewhere. In India, the self-proclaimed "spiritual scientist" Subhash Patri cites Deepak Chopra and Carlos Castaneda as influences, runs meditation "camps," and builds pyramids that house items like Himalayan crystals (614 crystals in one alone) and large, contemporary artwork of the Buddha.[119]

Mindfulness is not the only way that Buddhism is commodified. Products featuring the Buddha include T-shirts, candles, bath products, the "pocket Buddha," wall friezes and canvas posters, beach towels (one product on the Café Press site features a Buddha in place of "beauty" and reads "Have a [Buddha]-ful Day"), shower curtains, incense burners, aprons on Zazzle.com, key chains, bags and purses, fountains, and watches. Some items are problematic due to the ritual rules surrounding the Buddha's image. In some parts of Southeast Asia, one is not supposed to point their feet toward an image of the Buddha, for example. Objects like the "Buddha Baby Bib" (Omfinite.com), the "Stars and Praying Skateboard" (Zazzle.com), and "'Breathe' Buddha Leggings" (Zazzle.com) mean someone is spitting up, riding on, or wearing an image of the Buddha.

Buddhism's popularity has been parlayed into a number of healing practices that appear to be ancient and authentic, but these are in fact new or refashioned practices that can be offered by anyone, including Western "healers." These include health programs, meditation practices, and transpersonal psychology. As one scholar notes, these can be intermixed in problematic ways:

> The common aspect of the different forms of mindfulness-based therapies is their use of some methods of Buddhist meditative practices. The success of mindfulness is however not due to a faithful transposition of Buddhism to modern psychology. As a matter of fact, eastern religious teachings are applied to mindfulness therapy without adopting Buddhist traditions and religious vocabulary, and most often, the translation of practices is conducted in highly unorthodox ways.[120]

Reiki is a popular healing method that is advertised as a way to transfer energy between the healer and patient. One would assume it to be an ancient Buddhist practice, originating in Japan or perhaps China. In fact, reiki is an invention of the Japanese Christian minister Mikao Usui that uses an old Buddhist practice to create a new healing method focused on a "universal life-force energy," or "white light."[121] This white light comes from another source—the universe or God. Obviously, there is no God in Buddhism. Reiki capitalizes on the American fascination with the Buddha and the New Age emphasis on energy. Reiki has also been translated into other types of energy healing, most notably "therapeutic touch," which explains *prana* as the material that makes us well—really healthy people have extra *prana* that can be used to help others be healed.[122] For energy healers, *prana* is repackaged and sold as a cure for emotional, psychological, and physical ailments. It is also the name of a high-end fashion brand founded by a supermodel.

Meditation is an extraordinarily popular practice in North America, illustrating both the appeal of "the East" and the co-opting of other people's religions for profit. As we have seen, Oprah Winfrey's brand of spiritual capitalism borrows from a number of traditions including Hinduism, Buddhism, and Islam. Meditation is often invoked in Winfrey's media empire as a central practice on her television network, social media, and in the monthly lifestyle magazine that bears her name. Oprah, as previously discussed, is an example of the broad interest in spirituality, mysticism, and the East. In her 2001 Live Your Best Life Tour, Oprah remarked, "I believe in meditating in the tub with some very nice bath products."[123] Not only is this a very different understanding of "meditation" than is found in Hindu and Buddhist practice, it is linked to material products that support "your best life."

Taoism is another tradition that is part of the mystical marketplace. Carrette and King list ten different genres of Taoist books ranging from New Age to business.[124] Reiki, touch therapy, meditation, Taoist business management, and other practices identified with Asia use the East as a source of wisdom, enlightenment, and healing, but often in a very sloppy fashion. In this vision of the Orient, Japan blurs into China, China blurs into India, Nepal blurs into Bali. As Said noted, essentialism is a hallmark of Orientalism. Today it is seen in the business of Eastern mysticism, in people such as Stephen Russell, the "Barefoot Doctor," whose success is built upon the "general 'pick and mix' approach that characterizes New Age orientalist approaches to Asian traditions."[125] Everything is thrown into the pot including acupuncture (China), yoga (India), meditation (Nepal), and herbalism (Europe and North America). One of the problems with the "pick and mix" approach is that core religious teachings are often misunderstood or ignored. In New Age Buddhism, the emphasis on cultivating the self is mistaken; for the point of Buddhist teachings is that the autonomous self (*atman*) is the problem to be solved—not the object to be cultivated.[126] Some scholars, like Carrette and King, have called this "a religion of the self," and even stronger approbations of these sorts of self-focused practices have been voiced by others.[127]

Japanese products are often identified with Buddhist traditions, whether or not this connection is genuine. One example of this is the *shakuhachi*—a flute traditionally made from bamboo that is commonly identified with Zen. There is little evidence to substantiate the claim that this instrument is associated with Zen. "While the 'spiritual' *shakuhachi* finds appeal among westerners, its Zen associations have little explicit relevance to its musical experts in Japan."[128] A wide range of items with Zen terminology are used to sell the instrument, and there are even tours like the "Bamboo Roots Pilgrimage" that take North American musicians across Japan on a spiritual tour—another example of mystical tourism.[129]

Zen has multiple meanings and uses due to its hypersignification. It is used to market breakfast cereal, music products, beauty creams, and furniture. Like other examples from the East, products associated with Zen promise things like a moment of Zen, relaxation, stress relief, and inner peace. Zen is also associated with nontraditional, eclectic, and creative moments. It is both "linguistically ubiquitous and semiotically ambiguous."[130] As Joshua Irizarry points out: "The most common usages paint *zen* as being synonymous with words such as *calm, peaceful, harmonious, natural, simple, relaxing, focused,* and *traditional.* But there is another side to zen which carries connotations of *deep, creative, energetic, inspirational, outside-the-box, unconventional, eclectic, contradictory, perplexing,* and *non-traditional.*"[131]

The polysemous nature of Zen makes it marketable to numerous consumer audiences, from those seeking inner calm in products from meditation music to yoga mats, to those who identify it with creativity, seen in the identification of Zen with Apple products. Zen is polysemous, open to a wide field of interpretations that allow for its consumption in numerous forms. Even the Celtic "spirituality" movement has entered the Zen landscape with the introduction of "Zen Druids."[132] It is sometimes associated with wealth, an antithetical reading of Zen that belies the idea of simplicity and anti-materialism at the core of Buddhism. This is seen in luxury Zen items ranging from jewelry and miniature rock gardens to the Fisher-Price Zen collection that advertises the use of "upscale materials" and "sophistication"—for an infant.[133]

Zen's association with the East and its exoticism is evidence of the branding power of mysticism. It is not identified with institutionalized Buddhism but, instead, with the individual's search for meaning. As one scholar points out: "And lastly, while *zen* may be associated with *spirituality*, *New Age*, or *mysticism*, it is virtually never associated with institutionalized religion."[134] The San Francisco Zen Center, which was originally identified with Suzuki Rōshi (Shunryu Suzuki, not to be confused with D. T. Suzuki), is another interesting case of Zen's transformation in the West. When Richard Baker became abbot (and before he was pushed out due to accusations that he'd had sexual liaisons with numerous women), the center had a vegetable farm and bakery, and was known for its vegetarian "hippie" cookbooks.[135] Today, the center has a satellite group in Sedona, Arizona. As discussed before, Sedona is a popular New Age site, believed to exist in a vortex that connects it to Glastonbury. New Age thinkers like Nicholas R. Mann claim that invisible "landscape temples" exist at these places, making it possible for individuals to transcend the real world through a mystic-spiritual experience. Sedona features a number of energy fields called "vortexes" including the Buddhist Amitabha stupa.[136]

Sedona resembles Glastonbury in its mystical appeal. Both sites are on supposed leylines, connected spaces that include Mecca, Ayers Rock (Uluru), the Great Pyramids, and Stonehenge, which are associated with "earth energy, power and sacredness."[137] At Glastonbury, Buddhism makes many appearances: individuals who claim they are the Maitreya (the new Buddha), the status of the town as a "heart chakra," and the linking of Jesus to the Buddha. As Marion Bowman points out: "Similarly, the myth of Jesus in Glastonbury is intricately woven into the worldview of the American believed by his followers to be an incarnation of both Jesus and Buddha, formerly known as His Holiness Tulku Buddha Maitreya Rinpoche, now His Holiness Gyalwa Jampa (Sanat Maitreya Kumara), Director of the Church of Shambhala Vajradhara Maitreya Sangha."[138] The Maitreya is a popular figure in other places. His appearance in the visions of Catholics in North America is well documented, as it is in visions of Catholics in Kenya. In Paolo Apolito's book on visions of Mary, he notes that the vision of Jesus speaking in Swahili "perfectly matches the appearance of the Maitreya when he was 'miraculously' photographed, in Kenya as well as many other places around the world."[139] Buddhism merges with New Age in other spaces. In the genre of ads geared towards "spiritually inclined consumers," an appeal is often made to spiritual seekers and Nones. As one study notes:

> Honda Accord ads portray a Zen-like moment of peaceful "simplicity," while MasterCard presents the card as a connection to priceless things that money can't buy. Ameriprise Financial commercials demonstrate how every dream can turn into a reality if you set your mind to it. The Ameriprise Financial ads appeal to spiritual audiences or the "seekers", those who are spiritual but not religious, perhaps are former hippies, and those who practice new age philosophies.[140]

The translation of Buddhism into a form of spirituality practiced by non-Buddhists reflects the popularity of modern mysticism. The number of North Americans and Europeans who practice Buddhism is relatively small in comparison to those who identify with mystical and spiritual practices. As Jørn Borup points out in the Danish case: "Buddhism in Denmark is very seldom described as a religion, and when this happens it is mainly related to individual converts or visits by the Dalai Lama. General portrayals are, however, mainly positive, especially when compared to other religions such as Islam and when indirectly referred to in articles about 'spirituality,' mindfulness or travel."[141] In other words, Buddhism proper is reserved for the foreigner while Buddhism for the European consists of Zen and mindfulness.

TRIPPING ON BUDDHA

In Buddhism, visual piety is important, whether it involves gazing at an icon or visiting a Buddhist temple. The construction of space using images of the Buddha involves a global retinue of images; as such, visual piety is often exploited in mystical tourism. In Bali, Buddhist imagery aids in the construction of the island as a place of power, spiritual energy, and exotic mystery. Bali is an excellent example of Foucault's Fourth Principle of the heterotopia, which is temporal, a temporary escape from the "real" world. He gives the example of the Polynesian resort, which both "abolishes time" and is also about the "rediscovery of time, it is as if the entire history of humanity reaching back to its origin were accessible in a sort of immediate knowledge."[142]

Bali is a site of muddled Orientalism whose participation in commodification is not limited to portable objects, but is also found in mystical tourism. Despite its majority Hindu population, Bali is often envisioned as a Buddhist space replete with tropical gardens, Buddha statues, meditation retreats, and mindfulness seminars. The idea of mysticism is at the center of the marketing of mystical tourism in Bali. As one "wellness writer" notes, Bali's "spirituality—specifically Hinduism—is woven into everything" alongside local Bintang beer, views of the jungle, Thai martial arts (like *pencak silat*), and luxurious accommodations.[143]

Buddhism is often featured at places identified with mystical tourism. In some cases, it stands alone as a mystical, contemplative form of spirituality that is the focus of a retreat, resort, or hotel. Buddhism may also exist alongside other religions at mystical centers such as Glastonbury, where the Archangel Michael's Soul Therapy Centre is now the Maitreya Monastery and which features products like assorted Bodhisattvas and therapies like Zen shiatsu and reiki.[144] At these places, Buddhism is often presented as part of a larger cornucopia of lifestyles, healing methods, and styles. Ethnic chic products like kurtas and caftans are inspired by the East and are found in shops alongside other products borrowed from an endless array of cultures. The dream catcher is ubiquitous, found everywhere from Glastonbury to Yogyakarta, Indonesia, existing as both "ethnic chic and spiritual tool."[145]

Bali is believed to be both a site of Hindu spirituality and a center of Buddhist mystical power. As we have seen, the conflation of different religions is apparent in the mystical tourism industry, which often combines therapies and rituals in the creation of new wellness practices. The imagery of the garden is an idea long connected to notions of tranquility, beauty, and of course, Paradise, powerful in the mystical tourism industry. As Foucault argues, the garden is the space that best exemplifies the Third Principle of the heterotopia—of superimposed places in one space. It is our happy place, whether located in our backyard or in a far-off island: "The garden has been a sort of happy, universalizing heterotopia since the beginnings of antiquity (our modern zoological gardens spring from that source).[146] Bali's image as a garden island, lush, tranquil, and spiritually authentic, is an illusion that falls apart as soon as one lands in the airport in Denpasar or spends time in busy areas like Kuta, site of a Hard Rock Café, nightclubs, bars, prostitutes, and other forms of reality.

The conflation of Buddhism with Hinduism, which erases the history of Indonesia's Hindu kingdoms and replaces it with a pan-Asian mysticism, is apparent in the wellness resorts that dot Bali's coastlines and are found in the interior of the island in places like Ubud. Buddhism is advertised in these resorts through names like Shambhala Oceanside Retreat, Blooming Lotus Yoga Spa, and inland, Ashoka Tree Resort Ubud. The foreign owners of the Shambhala Oceanside Retreat describe on their website how they settled in Bali: "Maybe you have already experienced the magical talent of the Balinese who know things in advance, who feel your thoughts, look straight into your heart, and who know the right timing. During a magical moment in October of 1999 on my second journey through Bali, I, Ilona Selke, met a very old seer in Ubud, maybe 115 years old, who gave me a reading."[147] This reading, it turned out, included the premonition that they would be neighbors, and because the "seer" gave an "immediately verifiable" reading to Selke's friend, she knew he was a true mystic.[148] Bali and its people are often identified as special and mystically powerful.

In Bali, mystical tourism presents indigenous people as bodies of power. "Framing this religiosity as residing (or not residing) in bodies" romanticizes the essentialized nature of the Balinese and maps racial differences.[149] Erik Cohen calls these travelers "nomads from affluence."[150] Artists like Walter Spies represent Balinese bodies as sensuous, much like the environment that surrounds them, which is often cast in luxuriant language: "The sensuous, sinuous bodies of the Balinese, as depicted, are continuous with the sensuous curves of the contoured rice terraces and of a tropical vegetation which itself has always been a Western metaphor for the languorous and sensual East."[151]

The landscape of Bali is considered mystically powerful because of its Hindu and Buddhist sites as well as its visual aesthetic. Bali looks and feels different from the streets of New York, Los Angeles, London, or smaller cities of North America and Europe. Foucault's Fifth Principle in his vision of heterotopias is "that they have a function in relation to all the space that remains."[152] He means that they create difference, an alternative reality for those who visit it, such as the tourists to spa and health retreats, meditation centers, and other places that offer a space which is "as perfect, as meticulous, as well arranged as ours is messy, ill constructed, and jumbled."[153] Nature becomes the perfection that normal life lacks, offering an escape from modernity that, in Asad's language, conscripts us.

Tourism in Bali includes "dangerous and effortful styles of tourism" that serve as a "self-imposed rite of passage."[154] Bali's mystical tourism industry capitalizes on the desire to go native by "slumming it." Slum tourism is the latest in a long history of travel trends that revolve around *difference*. More extreme examples include visits to urban poverty centers found in Central America, South America, and Africa. Tourists also slum it by adopting the temporary lifestyle of the local or native. Entrepreneurs have exploited this in clever ways, marketing difference as an attractive commodity. As one scholar explains: "Tourism lives on what is different. Its economic implications alone urge it to constantly create new products and open up new segments on the market. Tourism always looks for new places, inventing *sights* and *sites* which are then marked and marketed as tourist attractions."[155]

Scholars writing on health tourism have delineated two types—medical tourism (surgeries and other treatments are often cheaper in a foreign country) and wellness tourism (of which mystical tourism is one type).[156] Wellness tourism reflects the strong interest that North Americans and Europeans have in Asia as seen in shiatsu, t'ai chi, *onzen* (hot springs), and Chinese herbal treatments.[157] These practices are often identified with Asia's mystical traditions. Mystical tourism sells cultures, religions, and rituals to the consumer. As one scholar notes: "The product sold by the tourist industry, in its most general form, is a commodified relation to the Other."[158] More extreme mystical travelers may model the "pioneer endurance" that involves a "spirit quest."[159] Renting mopeds and living beachside is a popular example of the pioneer style in Bali. These are simulacra of Balinese life without the native people's poverty, lack of education, and struggles with problems like prostitution and political strife.

The presentation of Bali as a garden island, along with the mythologies that it is "disease-free" and cleaner than Java, evokes a tempting portrait of paradise and a history that denies its violent colonial past as well as more recent conflicts, including bloody terrorist attacks that have killed hundreds. "For the tourists in Bali, 'reality' can seem like something always withheld. Whole areas of the island's recent history are hidden from us. Equally, the reality of contemporary Balinese social life is veiled in layers of mythology developed to seduce us into believing we are present in a kind of paradise."[160]

Like other places that host mystical tourism, entrepreneurial New Age teachers often disconnect religious authority from the Balinese. If they did not, these teachers would have limited spiritual authority and fewer money-making opportunities.[161] These programs are often implemented through "a language about relationships and healing."[162] The emerging popularity of Authentic Relating (AR) is one new therapeutic model that relies on spiritualist code words and features an overwhelming number of white participants, as one can see on the various Facebook pages, websites, and other social media spaces that advertise its services. This movement promises a new way of relating and offers workshops in Bali, often advertised in terms of the island's mystical power, its propensity for healing, and its romantic allure.

In Bali, relationship work is parlayed into numerous other businesses that link bodily and spiritual work, including the sexual, tantric yoga offered at events like the Ultimate Goddess Retreat taught by Ronya Sebastian. Mentioned in the last chapter, Ms. Sebastian is also part of the Authentic Relating Team whose staff travel among locations that have "mystic" power like Boulder, Bali, and Santa Fe.[163] There is often an element of New Age in these practices, seen in another AR leader, Ryel Kestano, whose curated list of "The Most Influential and Life-Changing Books of All Time" is almost completely dominated by white authors.[164]

The sexual workshops offered by Sebastian represent one of many ways that sensuality is linked to Eastern mysticism. It is also likely that this identification of Buddhism with sexual gratification is situated in part on the confused lines drawn between Hinduism (where tantric sex is located) and Buddhism (focused more on celibacy, at least in more traditional readings of the practice). This hasn't stopped people from marketing Buddhism as a sexual practice. One example is "Orgasmic Meditation," or what is called "Om-ing".[165] In this case, the man pleasures the woman's clitoris with his finger while she listens to him "mindfully describing" the changes in color he observes and as one might expect, this requires products—OneStroke Lube, One Scrub All-Natural Salt, and OM Warmers long socks.[166] One can get a bundled deal with the OM Signature Kit, "which includes a 100% organic cotton blanket, zafu, two linen-covered pillows, lube, and three hand towels ($184.97)."[167]

Thailand also hosts a number of international meditation centers tied to sensuality and the idea of a romanticized Asia. Thomas Tweed has shown that the Romantic interest in Asia dates to the nineteenth century and involves "individuals interested in the exotic culture and aesthetics of Buddhist Asia, including its customs, architecture, and music, among others."[168] Romantic notions of Thailand are present today in tourist advertisements for meditation retreats, which often use ornate temple structures and other images. "From the glistening heads of dozens of golden Buddha statues to damp, lush forests, these images capture for the international meditator the idea of a Romantic and tranquil experience. Many images show sweeping landscapes of nature while others focus closely on bells, the hands of a Buddha statue, or a single flower."[169]

The design of southern Thailand's resorts intentionally demarcates space, creating a "very clear separation between itself and the outside world."[170] As Alex Tickell notes, this is a "heterotopian separation of the space of tourism" that creates a constructed utopia set apart from the outside world.[171] As we have seen, Burning Man, closer to home, is another space where these types of separations take place. In 2003, David Bests's *The Temple of Honor* (incredibly made from paper) was constructed as a place for forgiveness.[172] Appearing like a Buddhist temple in the Thai style, it offered an Orientalist space for pilgrims to Burning Man where they could achieve mystical transformation. The heterotopia of the tourist site, whether in Bali, Thailand, or Burning Man, provides a safe space for self-actualization exercises, yoga, Authentic Relating seminars, and sex therapies offered by the white teacher—the colonizer of territory, the holder of tradition, and the mystical expert.

5

Rumimaniacs

8:30 A.M. I have a series of spiritual exercises that I do every day. After reading Gathered Truths, I check out "Bowl of Saki" on my phone; it's delivered to my in-box every morning. It contains the teachings of the Sufis, a Middle Eastern sect that believes all paths lead to God and all religions are one, pointing to the same north star.

Oprah Winfrey[1]

Sufism is an Islamic tradition. According to Franklin Lewis, "Sufism entails a pious orientation toward religion, privileging the spiritual over the material, self-renunciation exercises and other forms of discipline (in addition, of course, to the ritual prayers and obligatory fasting required of all Muslims) as a means to approach God."[2] Sufism is not a Middle Eastern sect, and the North Star is not a commonly evoked image in Sufism. However, here, as in other places, Islam has been erased. Like other followers of multiple religious traditions, Oprah seems to see Sufism as a universalistic form of mysticism that provides spiritual benefits. She is not the first to do this; as we shall see, there is a long history of people arguing Sufism has no relationship to Islam.

Rumi, who wrote beautiful poetry, has a number of so-called quotes that are extraordinarily popular on social media platforms like Facebook and Twitter. They are often completely fabricated. Omid Safi calls this #FakeRumi and provides the following example: "Your task is not to seek for love, but merely to seek and find all the barriers within yourself that you have built against it." He points out that this quote is not from Rumi, but from a 1976 self-help book by Helen Schuman, who claimed the book was "dictated to her by … Jesus of Nazareth."[3]

ISLAM VS. SUFISM

These trans-religious presentations are often described as "universal Sufism."[4] Universal Sufism allows people to distance themselves from Muslims while adopting Sufism as a mystical identity. As discussed in the chapter on mysticism and the East, this erasure of Islam is not new; it is seen in the work of Alger and other later Orientalists. Early scholars of religion would try to explain Sufism as an Aryan, Hindu, or other tradition, disconnected from its Islamic origins. As Carl Ernst points out, one 1928 study makes the following claim: "No doubt can any longer remain that the teaching of Hallaj (d. 922) and his circle [in Baghdad] is identical with that of Samkara around 820."[5] Indomania, which included a romanticized fascination with Hinduism and Buddhism, at one time dominated the scholarship on Sufism, which thankfully was corrected by other scholars in more recent memory.

It is no wonder Oprah was confused, for Sufism is a misunderstood term involving contestations surrounding identity, practice, and religiosity. It is often identified as a form of mysticism that is set apart from Islam, even though it developed in the early centuries of the religion. In fact, the Sufi is an extra-devout Muslim. As Muhammad Hisham Kabbani notes, the tenth-century Sufi al-Junayd al-Baghdadi said: "The Sufi is the one who wears wool on top of purity."[6] Scholars including Carl Ernst, Ahmet Karamustafa, William Chittick, Sadiyya Shaikh, and Laury Silvers have all written about this early history.

In a 1994 issue of *Gnosis* focused on Sufism, Jay Kinney described the "Sufi Conundrum" that included the diversity of practices he observed between Bay Area hippies, the writings of Idries Shah, the Dances of Universal Peace, and Sufis from Muslim-majority countries.[7] The romanticizing of Sufism is well documented, seen in its casting as a universalistic, peaceful, "sect" as well as through older histories of the arts—painting, literature, and poetry. The stereotypes about Muslims are also found in these poems. As Walt Whitman famously wrote: "I hear dervishes monotonously chanting/interspers'd with frantic shouts/as they spin around turning always to Mecca."[8] Of course, Whitman also used Rumi's imagery of the rose garden and other Sufi themes in his poetry.

Scholars of Islam have taken issue with the ways in which Islam has been co-opted as a universalistic tradition.[9] Seyyed Hossein Nasr argues that those who remove Sufism from Islam are practicing "pseudo-Sufism."[10] Carl Ernst, one of the foremost scholars of Sufism, has written extensively about the Orientalizing of Islam in the academy and the classroom. He cautions against using "Sufism" as a broad descriptor since Islamic practices are specific to each order (*tariqa*).

> Sufism can refer to a wide range of phenomena, including scriptural interpretation, meditative practices, master-disciple relationships, corporate institutions, aesthetic and ritual gestures, doctrines, and literary texts. As a generic descriptive term, however, Sufism is deceptive. There is no Sufism in general. All that we describe as Sufism is firmly rooted in particular local contexts, often anchored to the very tangible tombs of deceased saints, and it is deployed in relation to lineages and personalities with a distinctively local sacrality. Individual Sufi groups or traditions in one place may be completely oblivious of what Sufis do or say in other groups.[11]

As we have seen, Sufism is often defined, adopted, corrupted, and presented as a contemporary religious and spiritual practice set apart from Islam. These presentations include a wide array of spiritual products such as meditation CDs, bumper stickers, T-shirts, and inspirational memes and posters, many of which misquote Rumi, Hafiz, and other Sufi poets. One company produces temporary tattoos with Rumi's words on them, billed as "Temporary on the skin" but "indelible on the soul."[12] Sufi tourism has its own "special niche" in which Islam is erased and replaced with the themes of "ancient and mystical knowledge."[13]

Thus, Sufism has been described as a sect of Islam, the core or essence of Islam, a tradition outside Islam (à la Oprah), and a pan-religious form of spirituality. In some cases, this involves efforts by Sufi teachers to make the tradition accessible to a broader audience. Lex Hixon, who took the name Shaykh Nur al-Jerrahi, was praised by the Beat poet Allen Ginsberg as a pioneer in the spiritual reawakening of America.[14] This reawakening involved the loosening of religious requirements found in Sufism, such as following shariah through the performance of rituals like *salat*, or daily prayer, and identifying as a Muslim. One Muslim who attended a Nur Jerrahi *dhikr* (ritual of remembrance) noted that participants arrived late, interrupted *dhikr* with casual conversation, and one person even laid down during the religious ritual and proceeded to take a nap.

The etymology of the word "Sufi" provides a platform for focusing this discussion on Sufism and Islam. Four possible origins of the term are *safa* (purity), *saff* (the first rank of humans before Allah), *Ashab al-Suffa* (the companions of the Prophet Muhammad who prayed on his veranda), and *suf* (the wool early Sufis wore).[15] Despite these etymologies, framing Sufism as an *alternative Islam* is very common. It allows people to claim they are "Sufi" and different from "other Muslims." The divisions between Islam and Sufism are at times similar to those found in modern Christianity, where mystics are defined as alternative/other Christians. As

April DeConick explains: "The newer story tells us that the Gnostic is an alternative Christian. The Gnostics' alternative Christianity died out because certain sociological and political factors favored nascent Catholicism and created an environment in which these alternative Christians could be suppressed and eradicated."[16]

WHITEWASHING SUFISM

In North America, non-Sufi Muslims often follow white Muslim teachers, typically rejecting immigrants and African Americans as spiritual guides, suggesting that when North American spiritual seekers say they are spiritual Sufis, racial politics is in play. The focus on Anglicized figures like Rumi and Hafiz allows one to engage Islam through racial and temporal distance, placing the wisdom of Sufism in the past. This is an example of what Johannes Fabian calls the denial of coeval Time.

Numerous examples of these New Age iterations of Sufism exist in North America, Europe, and elsewhere. They often focus on Rumi, who is presented as a universal teacher of a wisdom tradition rather than the Islamic scholar and poet he was. In fact, Rumi wrote these lines warning people against disassociating Sufism from its Islamic origins:

I am the slave of the Koran
While I still have life.
I am the dust on the path of Muhammad,
The chosen one,
If anyone interprets my words
In any other way,
I deplore that person,
And I deplore his words.[17]

One of the characteristics of Sufism, the belief in saints, involves an understanding of Islamic practice that includes prayer, pilgrimage, and the sanctity of holy bodies as well as the imagery related to them. In Islam, paintings of saints function as active bodies that have the ability to grant the follower *baraka* (blessing). Saints, known as *awliya*, are the "friends of Allah" who become loved through a process of acclamation, as opposed to a formal canonization procedure.[18]

The Islamic belief in sainthood is so strong that the spirits of the individual saints are believed to be incredibly powerful. One scholar tells a story of meeting the late Shaykh Nazim, head of the Naqshbandiyya-Khalidiyya order, and being touched by his followers afterwards. "By touching me or anything else that made contact with Nazim, including my backpack, they believed that they could benefit from the Baraka that God conferred to humanity through Nazim."[19] These powers are believed to survive death and may exist in the form of imagery. In Senegal, for example, even mass-produced images of the saint Amadou Bamba in the form of "posters, silkscreened banners, plaster plaques, photocopies, sand paintings" maintain his aura.[20] These communities are radically different from those often found in Western Sufism, which may not even require one to be a Muslim.

As we have seen, Sufism is popular in North America, but is often so removed from its Muslim roots that its followers reject (or are unaware of) any association with Islam. Some do not even know, or will deny, that Rumi, Hafiz, Rabi'ah, and Omar Khayyam were Muslims. Contemporary followers of New Sufism (sometimes called Neo-Sufism or Western Sufism) produce and purchase many objects and engage in many practices—music, inspirational calendars, glossy cards with quotes, and T-shirts. The search for spirituality through Rumi and other Muslim poets typically locates Sufism in the past, casting it as a solution to the ills of modernity. In reality, Sufism—Islamic Sufism included—has adapted to modernity quite well. In one encounter with Shaykh

Nazim, a scholar noted: "As he spoke, I noticed that one of Nazim's aides had begun to videotape his conversation with me—possibly to be posted on his Web site and included in one of the many videocassettes and CDs sold to his followers."[21] In another case, Nazim met a prospective student who was a German record producer and asked him which production methods for CDs were most profitable.[22] Nazim's self-marketing and use of technology illustrates how Islamic Sufism has adjusted to modernity.

As previously discussed, contemporary mysticism colonizes and whitewashes Sufism, separating it from Islam, marketing it as a form of spirituality, and profiting from its exotic allure. Like New Agers, Hindu yoginis, and Buddhist mystics, New Sufis have a large number of products to choose from. Sufi followers in North America often identify Rumi or Hafiz as spiritual guides while excluding other Muslims. African American Muslims, who have a huge impact on American culture through hip hop and other avenues, are never identified as part of these spiritual traditions. As one journalist pointed out in the early 1990s, many hip hop artists "have introduced some version of Afrocentrism, Black nationalism or Islam to Pop Culture" and they often dedicate their albums to "Minister Louis Farrakhan, the Honorable Elijah Muhammad, Malcolm X, Marcus Garvey, Clarence 13 X, Khalid Muhammad, the Five Percent Nation, The Nubian Islamic Hebrews, and the Moorish Holy Temple of Science."[23]

Non-Islamic Sufism functions as a de-racialized identity, negating its connections to a global population of largely Asian and African Muslims. The images of Rumi that portray him with Aryan features are only part of this story. Islam, as a religious identity, is framed as the antithesis of secularist modernity. Those who identify as "spiritual, not religious" Sufis are able to claim mysticism while tenuously holding onto a secular identity. This is the opposite of the ethic expressed in Islamic hip hop, whose artists envision themselves as part of a community "predicated upon faith rather than contemporary nation-state distinctions, or rather, on how colonizing cartographers cut up the global landscape."[24]

The cultural productions marketed to non-Muslim Sufis also erase Islam. Global music, New Age Rumi CDs, and the like often involve a complete misreading of Islamic cultural texts. Contemporary Islam has a rich tradition of music, including contemplative music, that is not on the radar of neo-Sufis. As discussed above, American hip-hop is one example—a genre heavily imbued with Islamic themes, vocabulary, and personalities, whether through the naming of artists or dedications to American Muslim leaders like Malcolm and Clarence. Beyond this, a wider field of Islamic inspirational music includes *nashids* (odes to Prophet Muhammad), *qawwali* (a South Asian genre of Sufi music), and the Senegalese music associated with the Tijāniyya Sufi order. As Joseph Hill points out, Senegalese rappers "use hip-hop music to convey deep Islamic—and more particularly Sufi—truths."[25] These truths, despite their resonance with Muslims, are ignored by many who call themselves Sufis.

SUFISM IN THE WEST

The history of Sufism in North America and Europe has received considerable academic attention in recent years. The connections of Western Sufism to theosophy, perennialism, and universalism are strong. At times, individuals discovered Sufism as part of a larger spiritual search, and in other cases, they fabricated their initiation into an order (Gurdjieff) or claimed to be chosen to carry on a secret lineage (Shah). G. I. Gurdjieff is more famous for his eccentricities and wild teaching style than his connections to Sufism. As Kate Zebiri has shown, he was not only a self-proclaimed spiritualist, but a charismatic figure whose claims are partially fictitious. "The 'Sarmoung' Sufi Order of Central Asia from which he claimed to have received his initial esoteric training and to have learned the spiritual exercises which he taught was almost certainly fictional."[26]

The French thinker René Guénon, who initially saw Sufism as a perennial and transcendental form of spirituality, later converted to Islam and adopted a Muslim identity. Guénon was a seeker and in his early days he tried out a number of traditions, including various esoteric movements and Eastern religions.[27] It was through "esotericism," not "Islam," that he discovered Sufism, and then through it and his marriage to an Egyptian woman he discovered Islam.[28] After Guénon's death, his community became splintered between those who identified as Muslim and those for whom Islam was not even remotely important. Among these latter followers is the order of Nazim Qabrisi, who conduct *dhikr* (the Islamic ritual of remembrance of Allah) at an organization called the East-West Centre instead of a mosque, and Frithjof Schuon, who considered Christian sacraments as part of the initiatory test.[29]

Studies of Western Sufism often include lengthy discussions of the ways in which perennialist thought, Traditionalism, esotericism, and universalism capitalize on Islamic devotional traditions. Seyyed Hossein Nasr is one of many scholars who have critiqued Sufi universalism. While Nasr has been accused by some of being a perennialist, in his critique of Schuon, he makes important distinctions that differentiate himself from many other Sufis living in the West. Nasr is a Traditionalist, aligning himself not with universalism, but with the traditional Arab and Persian philosophy of the Imperial Iranian Academy of Philosophy.[30] Today, the term "traditional" gets thrown about in studies of Islam. In this case, it refers not to a literalist Islam, but a bridging between Western academia and Islamic philosophy, religion, and culture. As one author described it, Traditionalism represents the linking of scholarship with Islamic thought (which was interrupted by the Iranian revolution in 1979).[31]

This story of Iranian intellectuals, mystics, academics, and their role in the revolution is important in understanding modern Sufism and its fault lines. Schuon saw Islam as a distraction from the essential esoteric work at the heart of Sufi practice. "For Schuon, then, the dogmatic and moralistic tendencies of Islamic theology can distract aspirants from pursuing the realization of metaphysical knowledge."[32] Schuon reportedly had a vision of Mary in 1965, named his order the Maryamiyya after her, and also lauded the initiatory rituals of Native Americans.[33]

Schuon was also known for ritualizing primordialism and holding so-called "Indian Days" where he dressed up like an Indian chief.[34] His interest in Native American rituals occurred after reading *Black Elk Speaks* (1932), and he incorporated some Lakota practices into his rituals.[35] Schuon was rumored to conduct naked rituals, which were unfairly blamed on the influence of Native American traditions, and resulted in famous Maryamiyyas distancing themselves from Schuon.[36] In the years since his death, Schuon's community, headquartered in Bloomington, Indiana, has become something of a curiosity.

In addition to his impact on individuals like Schuon, Guénon is important for another reason. He and his followers maintain Sufism is the "true" Islam, and his *tariqah* is the "true" order, thus effectively co-opting a part of Islam that is complicated, diverse, and global.[37] In these organizations, Sufism often becomes a transcendent form of mysticism that is removed from Islam and its many rituals like *dhikr/zikr* and *sama/sema* (the remembrance of God and the auditioning for Allah), and instead is part of perennial Unitarianism. The erasure of Islam is situated in centuries-old efforts to universalize Sufism. As Carl Ernst wrote, early scholars of religion "saw Sufism as an attractive system precisely to the degree that it denies the law of Muhammad and approaches Christianity."[38]

In some cases, self-proclaimed Sufis dabble in Islam for a very short time—so brief that there is no way they could possibly learn its complex rituals, liturgy, and teachings. They then proclaim themselves as masters of Sufism. One such example is Reshad Field. As Kate Zebiri notes:

> Notwithstanding the possible didactic use of humor, the redeployment of such stories as entertainment in the context of a mass audience (even if reading is largely a solitary pursuit) could be viewed as part of a process of desacralization. Second, at the level of the actual roles of the disciples and teachers themselves (whether as subjects or objects of the narratives in question), Field's period of "discipleship" was relatively brief—being only of a few weeks' duration; despite his erstwhile involvement with the Sufi Order (and, after with acquaintance with Rauf, the Mevleviya), like Shah he is not formally associated with any recognized Sufi order (nor does his teacher claim to be a Sufi *shaykh*) and, after his involvement with Rauf came to an end, did not teach in that kind of setting.[39]

Field is not the only one who has written on the topic of a Sufi psychology, repackaging Islam as a form of New Age therapy. As discussed elsewhere in this book, the Shahs, in particular, Idries Shah, present a system of Sufi psychology that is divorced from its Islamic roots.

Attempts to use Sufism as a therapeutic tool are wide-ranging. The work of Idris Shah, discussed more fully later in this chapter, is open to criticism in part due to his mysterious and controversial "lineage." Other efforts at articulating a Sufi psychology that speak to modern therapeutic models are more serious. Gretty Mirdal makes a persuasive argument for a psychology that includes Rumi. As she argues:

> Shifting attention away from the Self to the Other is another important concept in Rumi's teachings. The process is

> similar to "disidentification" where one ceases to identify with one's own feelings and images. This process is similar to Piaget's "decentration," Safran's "decentering," Bohart's "detachment," Deikman's "observing self," Tart's "dehypnosis," Teasdale's "metacognitive awareness," Wilber's "differentiation and transcendence," and Kegan's "de-embodying."[40]

This shift toward others while letting go of one's ego (*nafs*), which eventually brings one into a more loving, less self-absorbed state, is a key Sufi theme. Theoretically, the therapist is likened to a Sufi master in this model—someone who leads the individual through stages that focus on this work. Mirdal takes a middle road when discussing Rumi, at times describing him—correctly—as Muslim, then making statements about his "philosophy and poetry" (instead of his "theology and poetry") or about the "spiritual" aspect of Sufism.[41]

Reza Arasteh is one of the most important and interesting proponents of Sufi psychology. In his work, he sees objects of desire as the source of neurosis and anxiety that originate in the separation of humankind from Paradise in the garden.[42] Even more interesting is Arasteh's view of Sufism as a vehicle for therapy. As he explains it, finding a guide or teacher and living in the Sufi lodge (*khanaqah*) allows the patient to separate him or herself from old patterns and participate in the "existential moratorium" that allows for spiritual growth and psychological recovery.[43] Arasteh gives the possibility of a cross-cultural, inter-religious therapeutic model that does not participate in colonial practices. Instead, it embraces the source—Sufism—as the path to wellness.

Some North Americans identifying as Sufis also define Islam in interesting ways. Yannis Toussulis is associated with the Malamati-Naqshbandi order and while insisting that there is no Sufism without Islam, he also proposes that Sufism is not necessarily tied to shariah, seeing Islam as "an inherently dynamic tradition that changes over time, and as such takes on a variety of forms, not all of which correspond to what is considered orthodox."[44] He cites Traditionalists as antithetical to modern Sufism, suggesting that a division exists between Muslims who follow Islamic teachings closely and those who do not. Such qualifications support the Good Muslim/Bad Muslim dichotomy.

The adoption of Sufi figures like Rumi, new forms of whirling like the Dances of Universal Peace, and the proliferation of new "orders" identified as Sufi are part of contemporary Sufism in the West. Sufism in North America and elsewhere includes a number of important Sufi teachers—the traditional Sunni (Shaykh Kabbani), the reformist Shi'i (Nimatullahi), the universalistic (Inayat Khan), and those who fall under the scope of pseudo-Sufism (Idries Shah). Muslim Sufi orders often urge their members to use Islamic practices such as cleanliness, prayer, and meditative chanting, called *dhikr*. According to the late Shaykh Nazim Adil al-Haqqani: "You can't do anything without wudu. If you want to pray to Allah, you must clean yourself. Abdest, ablution, that is first."[45] Others would not do this. Idries Shah viewed Islamic rituals as "automatic practices" that were emotional, useless, and simply "conditioning."[46] One of the questions this raises is—what remains Sufi when all of its rituals are excluded?

New forms of Sufism often have their origins in old, recognized orders. The Chishti Sufi Hazrat Inayat Khan (d. 1927), whose teachings in North America and Europe were dominant until the countercultural movement of the 1960s, brought new forms of spirituality to the forefront of popular culture. Inayat Khan saw Sufism as an expansive spiritual path. The Chishti Order, which he is linked to, is one of the most important *tariqat* (lineages or orders) in Asia. Like many other Sufi teachers, Inayat Khan's teachings focused on love and the spiritual awakening of each individual. Eventually, his teachings became directed toward the love of humanity through peace-building. As other scholars have noted, Khan's teachings include a reliance on Hindu concepts like *darśan* (seeing the divine) and *wasifas* (similar to mantras).[47] This is not unusual for South Asian schools of Sufism, which are strongly influenced by the cultural milieu in India and Pakistan.

The movement Hazrat Inayat Khan inspired—titled the Sufi Movement—has received criticism for its focus on universalism and lack of adherence to some Islamic traditions.[48] In contrast, Zia Inayat-Khan, who leads the Inayati Order, is deeply embedded in Islam; his order includes many Islamic rituals that would not be found in more universalistic, or New Age, orders. He assumed control of the order through his father, Vilayat Inayat Khan. As Mark Sedgwick has written, Vilayat used words like "spiritual," "cosmic," "love," and "energy," and had certain days dedicated to different religions.[49] His son Zia renamed the order and as one scholar remarked, has taken it in a new (more religious) direction.[50]

The story of this family is in some ways the story of Sufism in America. It includes the traditionally Islamic, the universalistic, New Age, and humanistic interpretations that mark much of modern Sufism. The influence of Hazrat Inayat Khan on the fabric of American Sufism is important and long-lasting. Like Shah and his relationship to the Naqshbandi order, the Khan family, which includes Zia, are linked to the Chishti Order. No scandal surrounds the Khan family and there are no questions surrounding Inayat Khan's religious credentials. Both Shah and Khan are linked to the East through their claims of Sufi lineage.

Sufism's history in North America is tied to the countercultural and hippie movements of the 1960s to a lesser extent than Hinduism and Buddhism. Samuel L. Lewis was a student of Hazrat Inayat Khan and became known as "Sufi Sam" in San Francisco.[51] Lewis claimed to have received a revelation appointing him as the spiritual teacher of the hippies, and is famous for his Sufi Choir, which performed with the Grateful Dead.[52] Lewis was also a Zen master, according to his followers, and used Sufi whirling as well as Western choreography in his spiritual dances.[53] The inclusion of Hindu mantras and Zen teachings is not limited to Lewis and his followers. Neo-Sufi movements often develop practices and rituals that appeal to a cross-section of prospective followers. In Santa Fe, hippies have been observed walking the streets proclaiming the *shahada* (the proclamation of faith in Islam) as a casual song, unaware that they are uttering words that identify them as new Muslims—accepting the Islamic faith. The meditations available on mobile apps include one, "La Ilaha Ill'llah" that includes reciting the *shahada*, which was met with much enthusiasm from its users, including comments like "I love this mantra" and the inclusion of heart and peace-sign emojis.[54]

Public Sufi chanting, Zen–Hindu–Sufi teachers, and the growing popularity of poets like Rumi and Hafiz are due in part to the 1960s countercultural movement, which embraced Eastern spirituality at large. As Lewis explains:

> The Maharishi Mehash Yogi had temporarily won John Lennon, Mia Farrow, Donovan Leitch and other celebrities to Transcendental Meditation. George Harrison had helped popularize both Ravi Shankar and the Krishna Consciousness movement, and the books of gurus from Ram Das to Satya Sai Baba and J. Krishnamurti filled up the shelves in the chain bookstores of America, while classes on various forms of Yoga proliferated.[55]

By the 1970s, Muslim Sufi orders and Western Sufism had become part of the religious landscape of America, for better or worse.

Gurus, like those detailed in earlier chapters on Hinduism and Buddhism, also populate the Sufi landscape. Much like Trungpa, these individuals generally rose to prominence and then fell out of fashion. Idries Shah is one such figure; his enormous popularity was later challenged by accusations that he was not aligned with any Sufi order, and reviews of his books describe his "incursions into the higher lunacy, magic, witchcraft, and numerology."[56] Shah identified himself with the Naqshbandi order, but avoided identifying Sufism with Islam, instead insisting that it was a tradition with many names. He also claimed that Sufism was beyond Islam, found earlier, in a kind of universalistic spirituality that had no name. Shah also claimed to represent a "secret" branch of the Naqṣhbandiyya, and even though he did not claim to establish an order, his followers refer to him as "the Grand Sheikh of the Sufis."[57] His followers today often refer to their rituals in vague, non-Islamic terms as "spiritual practices," and do not identify as Muslim, insisting that Sufism is "beyond religion."

Some Muslims view Shah as something of a charlatan, owing in part to his claims to belong to a "secret branch" of the Naqshabandiyya order that has never been located by scholars, including those doing work in Afghanistan, its putative location. In a rather blatant form of cultural colonialism, Shah not only claimed that Sufism was primordial and non-Islamic, but that it was also responsible for traditions clearly outside Islam such as Zen Buddhism.[58] Adding to these controversial statements, in an incident in 1966, he convinced Gurdjieff's longtime disciple J. G. Bennett to sign over Gurdjieff's home and teaching center, which Shah quickly sold, using the funds to establish his own center.[59]

Israel's diverse Jewish population includes many spiritual seekers; some of them interested in coexistence. In Israel, the activist Eliyahu McLean joined with Sufi (Arab Muslim) conversation partners in his search for an "alternative Islam."[60] Sufi orders in Israel like The Path of Abraham and others that follow the whirling dervishes of Turkey and center on the popularity of Rumi are largely Jewish, representing the "structural inequalities that exist between Jews and Arabs in Israeli society."[61] Like other examples of the borrowing of different people's religions, even in cases where well-meaning individuals seek positive social change, they still rely on "the 'cultural capital' of Arab Sufis."[62]

Community masjid in Abiquiu, New Mexico (courtesy of the author).

Sufis living in Europe and North America, as well as other places, also include many individuals who proudly identify as Muslim. As one example, the northern New Mexico village of Abiquiu hosts a small but vibrant community of Naqshbandi Muslims.

Islamic Sufism offers curative treatments for illness. Historically, Sufis offered remedies based on Islamic medicine and theories of health; this is very different from the offerings made by the online Sufism available to the spiritual consumer today, which often promises a healthier life through the consumption of products or through the utterance of Sufi poetry in English translation. Among these modern palliatives, the ones associated with Rumi are the most popular.

RUMI, INC.

Rumi is the most popular poet in the world today. Many of his admirers do not know he is Muslim, or if they do, dismiss it as a minor detail in his life. In fact, Rumi was a devout Muslim who dedicated much of his life to seeking an understanding of Allah. As one scholar points out, "when Rumi invited his listener or reader to leave the yeses and nos of conventional beliefs behind, he did so as a Muslim who unquestionably accepted Mohammed as the Prophet and the Koran as God's last word."[63] Rumi was the son of a famous theologian and jurist from Balkh (in present-day Afghanistan). The family lived in Konya, Turkey, and in his mid-twenties Rumi became an important teacher, with many followers. He married and had children. In his mid-thirties, he met his teacher, friend, and companion Shams (Shamsettin) of Tabriz.[64] As scholars have noted, at this point his life changed in profound ways. The relationship between Rumi and Shams was intense and somewhat controversial. One story of their meeting describes how Rumi fainted, then was unconscious for an hour, and after this, the two men did not part for forty days.[65]

The tradition of whirling is specific to Rumi's order. It has been adopted by numerous New Age practitioners and followers as well as Nones, Unitarians, Jews, and dancers. In its classical form, the ritual of whirling is known as *sema*, part of a larger set of practices involving music and dance.[66] As Annemarie Schimmel explains, *sema* is literally "hearing," in the singing of quatrains of poetry that "was recited with musical accompaniment" and which created an ecstatic state for its listeners.[67]

The Dances of Universal Peace are popular with Unitarian Universalists, New Agers, and people of other faiths who dabble in universalistic Sufism. An American woman named "Sheikha Khadija," who was initially brought to Israel by a social entrepreneur named Ronen Yizkhaki, leads dances in Israel on an annual basis, mostly for Jewish Israelis.[68] Like other spiritual teachers who offer Islam as a commodity, she may be a true believer who wants to bring the benefits of her religion to others. However, in a modern state where Islam is often vilified, the popularity of Sufism raises interesting questions. Among them—can an Israeli Jew be a Sufi? The fact that scholars describe non-Muslims as Sufis says something very powerful about the ways in which religious identities are elided, transcribed, and created. The activities of one Jewish Sufi as listed on his website includes the line, "Led Interfaith Rituals for Peace in Europe (Auschwitz), USA Kabbalat Shabbat & Sufi Zikr with Palestinian Sufi Sheik in Lakota Sundance."[69] The collapsing of all these traditions illustrates how Sufism, like other religions, has been co-opted by mystical capitalism.

Music is another place where Rumi's status as a mystical figure is apparent. The reed flute called the *ney* is strongly associated with the poet because of his use of the instrument in his work. The genre known as "Sufi music" reflects a number of styles, sources, and influences that may not actually be Sufi. As a scholar writes about one musician: "The Sufi 'elements' in his music do not share anything in common with the *tekke* music repertoire … nor with the basic structural elements of that musical tradition such as its *makam* (modal) system."[70]

Sufi music is often marketed as universalistic. The musical duo Pearls of Islam utilize a spiritualist language that appeals to a wide audience: Silk Road is "Sufi inspired acoustic folk-rock," and Sami Yusuf has described his style as "Spiritique."[71] The appeal to spirituality is not just stylistic, but is seen in the vocabulary used in the lyrics. In some cases, the erasure of Islam from Sufi music is achieved through marketing, where it is cast as yet another "spiritual" or "mystical" tradition, played in spas alongside other musical styles sold as "world music." As Philip Bohlman writes: "Stated somewhat differently, Sufi music represents spirituality, not religion, whereby it can enter a realm cohabited by other world musics, for example the New Age sound of Native

American flute that surrounds one in the growing number of shops that sell Native American art."[72]

"Rumimania" is the term coined by William Rory Dickson and Meena Sharify-Funk to describe products including the poems of Coleman Barks, choreography and modern dance (including the aforementioned Dances of Universal Peace), contemporary music, and restaurants that have profited from Rumi's popularity. Rumi, like the Buddha, is open to numerous commodification strategies. His poetry can be found on the cover of journals and notebooks (redbubble.com has the largest collection of these products), plaques, and pillows. More creative uses of Rumi include a tray and tea set shaped like a whirling dervish (available on Etsy) and a wall clock (redbubble.com). Many of these products feature fake Rumi quotes, not found anywhere in his poetry; in some cases, these are easily traced to other religious personalities.

Coleman Barks is the most famous propagator of #FakeRumi—the fictitious Rumi quotes that are found on social media and in numerous products ranging from bumper stickers to wall art. His "translations" are actually "interpretations" that often rely loosely on the Persian original. Of course, all translations offer some interpretation; but in academia, this work requires at least some effort to learn the primary language one is translating *from*. Franklin Lewis describes Barks as perhaps the most successful of the Rumi reciters, with books, sound recordings, and other products that may feature music like the flute and drums.[73] Barks also has published translations of Hafiz who, like Rumi, is popular on the internet as a New Age and spiritual teacher.

Deepak Chopra, who markets himself as a Hindu–Buddhist–Sufi teacher all wrapped into one, has several Rumi products, including a book that features Barks' "translations." In keeping with the universalistic themes Chopra advertises, his 1998 CD titled *A Gift of Love* includes a fold-out cover, a cardboard dust jacket, a pouch with a color booklet, and a bonus: "A recessed slot holds the hot-pink compact disc which, when removed, reveals a photograph, of a henna-dyed pattern, in keeping with the Eastern Indian theme."[74] Madonna is also identified with a project on Rumi, a 2008 CD produced by Deepak Chopra titled *The Complete Idiot's Guide to Rumi Meditation*, which features Madonna, Demi Moore, and others reciting English translations of Rumi's poetry to create a "sincere and potent" mystical experience.[75]

Rumi's appeal as a universalistic figure is also apparent outside music. Numerous restaurants bear the name of Rumi. The Montreal eatery Restaurant Rumi offers a study in muddled Orientalism, offering Persian, Indian, Turkish, Moroccan, and Afghani food in a space with Pakistani, Indian, Turkish, and Moroccan décor.[76] Contemporary and modern styles are on display at other Rumi restaurants. I have eaten at Rumi's Kitchen in Atlanta numerous times. While the food is classically Persian, the décor is contemporary, with a few Eastern touches like water fountains, complete with waiters' uniforms that consist of pants and a black T-shirt with Persian script (assumedly of Rumi's poetry) available for purchase. Rumi's Café, located in Sherman Oaks, California, features an image of Rumi dancing on the surface of a coffee cup.[77]

TRIPPING ON RUMI

Rumi, as well as Sufism in general, is also used to promote travel. An important distinction should be made between religious tourism geared toward self-identifying Muslims, who may go on *hajj* and *umrah*, *rihla*, or *ziyarat*, and individuals who are interested in "exploring" Sufi figures like Rumi and Hafiz, which we call mystical tourism. As one study argues, Muslims engage in religious tourism through a number of journeys that include religious pilgrimages as well as "festivals, seminars, and conferences" that are "organized to draw Muslims together to integrate their professional, spiritual, and intellectual capabilities."[78] Halal food festivals, cultural events centered around Muslim holidays such as the Prophet's birthday and Eid, and gatherings selling Islamic goods are often open to non-Muslims and can serve as examples of the marketing of "spiritual tourism products."[79]

Muslims also use religious tourism as a way to engage non-Muslims and introduce them to the faith of Islam. As Farooq Haq and Ho Yin Wong explain, this form of religious tourism is modeled on *tableegh*: "Tableegh has its origins in early twentieth century India, a tradition of Muslim men travelling and staying in various mosques around the world to meet all Muslims and remind them about the spirit and spiritual practices of Islam."[80] Today, *tableegh* exists in numerous forms, including Sufi conferences that are open to both Muslims and non-Muslims. One of the most interesting examples of contemporary *tableegh* is Sout Ilaahi in Singapore. Operated by Khalid Ajmain, this organization hosts numerous conferences, classes, and workshops on Islam. It hosts a social-service organization whose work includes campaigns against drug use and domestic violence. Khalid Ajmain's religious practices include prayer (*salat*), pilgrimage (*ziyarat*), and rituals like *dhikr*—the chanting meditative practice of Sufism. Seen as therapeutic, these are not simply religious duties.

Mystical tourism for non-Muslim Sufis tends to focus strongly on Sufism, but it is presented in universalistic terms. Sufi-centered mystical tourism is typically led by individuals who aren't necessarily Muslim but do identify as Sufi, mystical, or spiritual. Numerous examples of mystical tourism are found in Muslim-majority countries as well as those with colonized Muslim populations, like Israel.

Egypt looms large in the imagination of Europe and North America. Orientalism is said to have begun there with Napoleon's invasion. The imposition of Western fantasies on Egypt has a long history in tourism. As John Urry notes: "Egypt became scripted as a place of constructed visibility, with multiple, enframed theatrical scenes set up for the edification, entertainment and visual consumption of 'European' visitors," seen in expressions like "Paris-on-the-Nile."[81] Today, Egypt hosts many tours that focus on the mystical qualities tied to its location in the East.

Morocco has also long been romanticized by European and American travelers as a site of exoticism and danger. The writer Paul Bowles is one of many authors, artists, and fashion designers who have lived in Morocco part-time or as full-time expatriates. Morocco has been a popular site for mystical tourism in recent years. Like many other places that sell the promise of good health and spiritual enlightenment, inequity is at the core of the industry. As one scholar notes: "The logic of tourism is that of a relentless extension of commodity relations and the consequent inequalities of power between center and periphery, First and Third Worlds, developed and underdeveloped regions, metropolis and countryside."[82]

Within this inequity lies the allure of the exotic East—a site of mysticism and danger. In a 2017 issue of *Mantra* magazine, Maranda Pleasant describes the allure of Marrakesh. The city and its souvenirs are "intoxicating," it has a "soulful wildness that will drive you mad yet will still have you asking for more," but it is also dangerous—walking alone at night can be "stressful" and "it can be exhausting, uncomfortable, and at times, unsettling."[83] Pleasant also suggests one take a buddy as a safeguard against the dangers of Muslim lands, which are represented on the page with a collage of images associated with the riches of the Orient—baskets overflowing with spices, bowls of dyes in bright colors, rose petals in every imaginable color, textiles, and ceramics.

Mantra's one-page exposé on the good and bad of Marrakesh communicates a number of common tropes about the East—exotic and dangerous, a place where one can eventually "feel comfortable walking alone" and "listen to our spirit."[84] Mystical tourism often capitalizes on the inner spiritual voice through a number of health and mystical practices tailored for the foreign traveler seeking new experiences and, hopefully, a transformation of the self.

Individuals who emigrate to Marrakesh and other cities in Morocco from Europe and North America often adopt a neocolonial lifestyle complete with servants, hired help, or what is described as domestic help. One study describes an Englishwoman who moved to Morocco because of its slower rhythm of life, which is made possible by hiring local personnel.[85] However, this is not always the case; some individuals travel to Morocco as part of a spiritual or mystical journey. Scholars describe some of these immigrants as "quest migrants" whose search for "elsewhereness" includes a change in lifestyle that is not necessarily better, and may in fact be worse than the standard of living they experienced in Europe or North America.[86] This often entails "an attraction to some forms of spirituality evoking a kind of otherness."[87] Yoga and Sufism (and conversions to Islam) are among the forms of mystical quest available in Morocco.[88]

The success of the annual sacred festival in Fes has aided the development of "Sufi tourism." Tours of Sufism function as forms of pilgrimage, and are "highly orchestrated capitalist events" that exploit the existing tourist economy.[89] As Deborah Kapchan argues: "They [Sufi tours] have included postfestival tours to the Sahara Desert to participate in Sufi dhikr ceremonies and specialized tours for groups of new-age adherents from the United States and France."[90] Many tour companies offer "mystical tours" of Morocco. Spirit Quest Tours, for instance, teases clients with promises of "the gleam of sumptuous materials, the charm of exotic and mystical objects," "the rhythms of the spirit," and the Sufi experience: "Sufi culture, beliefs, and rituals show a different face of Islam: gentle, mystical, blissful."[91]

Mystical tourism in Indonesia is largely focused on the Hindu island of Bali. Many people do not even identify Bali as being part of Indonesia, an unconscious decoupling from its Muslim neighbor islands. Tourism is most developed on Bali, which is often described by its visitors as "cleaner" and "more developed" than Java and other islands in Indonesia. Bali is associated with Hindu and Buddhist spirituality and stands as an outlier within the most populous Muslim nation in the world. The Spirit Quest Tours website advertised an "Eat, Pray, Love Bali" tour that teased, "You read 'Eat, Pray, Love.' And you loved it. And you wanted to change your life, too. But who can take a year off to travel? How about a week to experience some of the marvelous changes author Elizabeth Gilbert enthralled us with in her memoir?"[92]

Muslim sites in Indonesia dominate Java and are visited in high numbers by citizens and tourists. Abdullah Gymnastiar's Daarut Tahid complex is perhaps the best example, a site popular with *wisata rohani*, "spiritual spiritualists," who seek blessings from Aa Gym and buy religious products like head scarves and blessed honey.[93] Aa Gym is a Sufi figure whose life story includes dreams in which he claims he was visited by the Prophet Muhammad, which allows him to exist outside more established religious authorities.[94]

Another example of mystical tourism in West Java is the Anand Ashram and One Earth One Sky retreat center near the mountain resort area of Puncak. The appeal of this retreat and wellness center lies in its founder's religious biography, which includes Hindu, Buddhist, and Muslim influences. Most of Anand Krishna's followers are Javanese Muslims who practice a localized form of Islam imbued with Hindu elements. The fluidity that is so inherent in Indonesian Islam allows for the practice of other traditions, and Krishna's ashram fits this model perfectly. As Howell points out, they can "cultivate, with guidance and support, a practical engagement with their own mystical tradition, Sufism."[95]

The contrast often drawn between the two Indonesian islands, Bali and Java, is important. It shows how mystical tourism can be marketed for one group of tourists—Westerners—in a way that powerfully maps sacred geographies. This illustrates why Bali is viewed as its own country separate from the rest of the nation, as "cleaner" and more developed than Java. The bifurcation of Bali from the rest of Indonesia is so strong that scholars often have to point out that it is indeed part of the same country. In Anca-Luminata Iancu's work, she makes a point of this where she uses "Indonesia/Bali." As she writes of *Eat, Pray, Love*: "On her journey of self-discovery, Liz is determined to discover the pleasures of life in Italy, to pray and develop spiritually in India, and to spend some time in Indonesia/Bali, learning more about herself and trying to find some emotional balance in her life."[96]

While Southeast Asia has Thailand and Bali as its prime mystical touristic locations, Eurasia has Turkey, which is perhaps more strongly identified with Sufism than anywhere else on earth. The image of the whirling dervish is everywhere—on posters, T-shirts, CD covers—functioning as the "emblem of Turkey" despite the state repression of Sufism.[97] Sufism is also located at mystical tourist centers like Sedona and Glastonbury, where it exists alongside Buddhist, Hindu, Native American, African, Celtic, and other traditions, which are all part of a huge mystical marketplace. Sometimes Muslims capitalize on the popularity of these places, such as when Sheikh Nazim al-Haqqani declared Glastonbury the "spiritual heart of Britain," which led to the Naqshbandiyya having a presence in the town through the opening of the Healing Hearts Charity Shop, run by a Sufi named "Zero."[98] More commonly, Sufism is present at these places not as a formal Sufi order but as one of many options for the mystically inclined customer.

The marketing of Islam is not limited to travel. Muslim fashion is a huge business, existing in the blogosphere and on the runway, in stores from London to Jakarta, and on the streets in *mipster* (Muslim hipster) fashion. Muslims, like other religious people, participate in consumer practices. *Dejabbing* (removing the veil), dewigging, and dehatting exist alongside fashion on platforms such as Facebook, Instagram, and YouTube.[99] Ethnic wear, including tunics and caftans, is often inspired by Muslim fashion, which is a serious affair. As Liz Bucar writes, *pious fashion*, which describes the way Muslim women dress, is a kind of "performance practice" that involves role-playing within particular cultural and social restraints.[100] Dressing in an ethnic or bohemian style, which borrows from Islamic fashion, is another performance practice, but one that role-plays the Orient within the bounds of white normativity.

I started this chapter with Oprah and I would like to end with her. Oprah is important for many reasons—as a cultural icon, genius marketer, and contemporary mystic. On this last point I would like to introduce the next chapter, which is concerned with mysticism in popular culture. The appeal of the mystic is powerful and real. We see it in the rituals, products, and services that are inspired by the East. The mystical is also a part of North American culture as seen in individuals like Oprah whose charisma, leadership, and personality have broad appeal. As Karlyn Crowley points out, "her audiences do want to touch her clothing or get close to her."[101] The promise of personal transformation is apparent in the mystic quality attached to Oprah's body, as well as other bodies discussed in this book, such as Trungpa's radiating light and the fascination with the Dalai Lama. These imaginary relationships—with individuals and with the forms of mystical entertainment examined in the next chapter, are evidence of the power of the mystical in the modern world.

6

Lost, *Star Wars*, and Mystical Hollywood

> *It centered around God, what is God, but more than that, what is reality? What is this? It's as if you reach a point and suddenly you say, "Wait a second, what is this world? What are we? Who am I?"*
>
> George Lucas, reflecting on his own mystical experience at age six[1]

Throughout this book, we have looked at the ways in which the search for meaning in contemporary North American society is linked to a fascination with mysticism. Yoga, mindfulness, Dances of Universal Peace, Tibetan medicine, Ayurvedic spas, and fake Rumi memes are evidence of the allure of the East. The seductive power of modern mysticism is also a symptom of the malaise that surrounds modern life. In this final chapter, I will look at visual narratives that allow a sense of escape through mythical and mystical narratives, symbols, and characters.

Entertainment is one of the richest spaces in which the images, themes, and narratives associated with the Orient are found. As Antonio Gramsci predicted, "subversive ideologies disseminated by small, marginalized groups are often reincorporated into the dominant culture's contextual framework over time, often repackaged for mass consumption."[2] This book concludes with a meditation (no pun intended) on the expression of Eastern mysticism in television and in film. The previous two chapters focused on distinct religious traditions—Hinduism, Buddhism, Islam. Here I focus on some of the mystical themes identified with these religions and the expression of their imagery in popular culture. The production of mystical themes in entertainment illustrates that the Orient remains a fixture of the popular Western imagination.

I am sympathetic to a longing of relief from the pressures of daily life and the constant assault of technology. I readily admit that I seek out the Dragontree Spa when visiting Boulder and I have visited Bali not just once, but numerous times. For many living in the age of modernity, the East and its exotic attributes are viewed as salvific. Western Buddhism allows us "fully to participate in the frantic pace of the capitalist game, while sustaining the perception that you are not really in it, that you are well aware how worthless the spectacle is—what really matters to you is the peace of the inner self to which you know you can always withdraw."[3] These withdrawals take place in meditation and yoga, belly dance, and Rumi reading groups as well as at destinations that are part of the mystical tourism industry.

Entertainment also provides a source of escape and mysticism, especially television and film. Here we see the religious and cultural fields collapse, with heroes, villains, saints, and the supernatural circulating through narratives that are both fantastic and beautiful. As Jørn Borup explains: "Consumers of media and popular culture are thus engaged with already circulating scripts, master narratives and collectively shared webs of meaning. Such containers of stories, ideas and metaphors are products of circular transformations between East and West, tradition and modernity."[4] These stories often focus on good triumphing over evil. Luke Skywalker, Jack Shepard, or another hero is often placed in an exotic setting—a faraway planet, a secret island, or futuristic world may be the setting for the hero's story. Often, Orientalism and mysticism play central roles in these narratives.

Spiritual products have great appeal in today's mystical marketplace. In fact, in recent years the market has realigned itself to account for this consumer group. In some cases, images from the East are utilized; in other cases, an appeal to universalistic spirituality is made. Advertising often identifies purchasing power with a better existence: "These commercials emphasize concepts such as nature, relationships, personal/individual lifestyle, and limitless dreams that come true."[5] Television and film producers, writers, and directors understand this market as well, creating entertainment that features numerous religious symbols and themes, frequently representing the creative force borne by Orientalism.

The spiritual quest is often tied to the importance of place. Egypt, Morocco, India, Bali, Thailand, and Tibet are all powerful symbols of the exotic that hold the promise of knowledge, healing, and wellness. To this day, India is described in Orientalist language, with a "profusion of romantic palaces, impressive forts and extraordinary temples" that are among the countless "wonders of India's fabled shores."[6] The literature of postcolonial India is replete with these images. Scholars have pointed to the "consumable" quality of India on the page, part of the larger "Indo-chic" fad that includes yoga, mystical retreats at luxurious ashrams, and the mass marketing of Ayurvedic medicine.[7] These places are often recreated in television and film, at times using visual imagery that is obviously Moorish, Persian, or Orientalist.

As discussed in earlier chapters, the entrance of yogic religion into American popular culture dates to the late nineteenth and early twentieth centuries. The yogi with superhuman powers is found in books, television, and film.[8] This character is connected to far-off lands. India, Nepal, and Tibet are popular motifs in entertainment, featured in biopics about Everest, Buddhism, and the Dalai Lama and playing a prominent role in adventure fantasy films such as *Indiana Jones and the Temple of Doom* (Steven Spielberg, 1984). In this film, Jones and his cohorts survive a fantastic plane crash in the Himalayas, find themselves in India, and encounter a sacrificial Hindu cult that enslaves children. The plane crash is reminiscent of earlier fictionalized treatments of Tibet and its long history of miraculous survival stories.[9]

The storyline of this film communicates numerous ideas about Hinduism—it is mysterious and powerful, there are "good" and "bad" Hinduisms, and India is a supernatural and dangerous place full of poisonous snakes, crocodiles, and cannibals. Other films are connected to opium and the spiritual enlightenment it promises. In *Batman Begins* (Christopher Nolan, 2005), Batman disappears into the Himalayas where he is trained by a Ninja cult leader named Ra's Al-Ghul (a Muslim name). The magical flower that appears throughout the film is the poppy, connected to mystical experiences in the East.[10] Other examples of Tibet's starring role in Hollywood films include *2012*, Roland Emmerich's 2009 film that features a series of small arks in Tibet on which people survive as the rest of the world is flooded with water and beset with earthquakes and erupting volcanoes.[11] And of course, *Lost Horizons*, discussed in a previous chapter, was one of the first such movies, creating the legendary Shangri-La for audiences seeking magic.

MYSTICAL MOVIES

Brent Plate coined the term "mythical mash-up" to describe what we see in some of the more fantastic and creative example of television and film.[12] As I discuss in the following pages, the East plays a prominent role in these mash-ups. I focus on two visual narratives—ABC's *Lost* and the *Star Wars* franchise, visual texts that include complex readings of myth and feature the requisite heroes and monsters. These are fairly complicated narratives. Both *Star Wars* and *Lost* reflect a "mystification of the enemy," seen in *Star Wars*'s Darth Vader, an ominous and homicidal father figure, and *Lost*'s mysterious monsters and its dangerous world of "shadowy, unpredictable enemies."[13] *Star Wars* films have always been full of Orientalist imagery, although in recent years with films like *Rogue One*, with its heroine wearing hijab through much of the film, they have taken an anti-colonial, subversive turn that reflects a sympathy with Muslims and other colonized people.

Lost features many themes found in literature, reflecting classic texts like *The Tempest*, *Frankenstein*, and *Lord of the Flies*, where an island is colonized and transformed from "the natural into the supernatural," offering a "self-contained possible world for the colonial imagination, a place where anything unexpected can happen."[14] Island literature is often focused on otherness, which *Lost* revels in—monsters, the supernatural, black smoke, giant polar bears, and alternative spatial realities. *Lost* also suggests a kind of extreme, mystical tourism, which is often envisioned as a liminal, mystical space where transformation is possible.[15] Above all, it is a narrative about spiritual journeys and mystical experiences. The series ends with a lesson on letting go (or working through) physical and spiritual pain, a central theme in Hindu, Buddhist, and Islamic religious teachings.

Star Wars is strongly mythical. It has been interpreted as Christian, as argued by Brent Plate's remarks on the Christological imagery in the first film, *A New Hope*. *Star Wars* also has Buddhist and Islamic themes. Ample literature exists on the former, while the latter case merits a book-length study (indeed, this is a book I plan to write). The adventures in *Star Wars* are inspired by Joseph Campbell's books, which reflect George Lucas's perennialist views on mythology and mysticism. The universalistic aesthetic that runs through Campbell may explain why *Star Wars* is difficult to decode, although there is certainly a strong dose of Orientalism in the desert planet of Tatooine and the frequency with which veiling is used by its many heroes. Yet, questions remain such as: Is Luke a Buddhist monk or a Sufi dervish? Is the myth of the Jedi about Hindu *samsara* or Buddhist samurai culture? Is Obi Wan Kenobi Jesus or the Mahdi (the Muslim messianic figure)?

Mystical films are often set in exotic spaces that do not look like an American city or a European state; these include outer space (*Star Wars*), an alternate reality (*Lost*), and a mythical past world (*The Hobbit*). In particular, science fiction and fantasy television shows and films are populated with mystical places, characters, and themes. Mystical films are not usually about one religion—they are about a mash-up of religions and myths, presenting a generally mystical world filled with Hindu, Buddhist, Christian, and Islamic imagery and themes. They often reflect the universalism so popular in the mystical marketplace.

At first glance, *The Matrix* appears strongly Christian. Released at Easter, it features the hero Neo, a messianic "promised deliverer" who is the product of a Virgin birth (in a machine that includes a womb-like vat and umbilical-like cables), tempted by evil forces (the Agents who want Neo to betray Morpheus), who sacrifices his life for Morpheus—like the sacrifice of Jesus as a "ransom for many" (Mark 10:45).[16] *The Matrix* also expresses Buddhist and Hindu themes such as emptiness and cyclical time—found in both Hindu and Buddhist visions of birth, death, and rebirth (*samsara*). Morpheus remarks that "attachment" leads to delusions of reality, signifying the Buddhist focus on the illusory world, and Neo is told that he is not "The One," but maybe in his next life he will be, suggesting reincarnation.[17] Is *The Matrix* a Christian or Buddhist story, or is it Sufi? Islam has a messianic figure as well, and teaches that the ego (the *nafs*) creates false illusions of the world. One of the goals of the Sufi path is *fana* (annihilation of the ego), which necessitates a radical love of the world, and ultimately a kind of mystical union with Allah (God). *The Matrix* is set in a futuristic world and the sets reflect a kind of super Zen-style. At the same time, its absence of Orientalist imagery makes it a particularly interesting case in the world of mystical cinema.

LOST

Television has witnessed an explosion of creativity since the introduction of cable and satellite, expanding the viewing options for an enormous, worldwide audience. In recent years, shows like *Lost* (ABC, 2004–10), *Big Love* (HBO, 2006–11), and *The Leftovers* (HBO, 2014–17) have explored religious themes, often centering on mystical themes like communicating with God or the Divine and encountering death and rebirth. Shows like *Lost* and *The Leftovers* use the mystification of time as a plot device, altering linear time and space and creating a cycle, or even successive spirals of time, more reminiscent of Hindu and Buddhist thought than of a secular worldview that subscribes to the myth of progress and a linear progression of history. *Lost* features a great deal of Christian imagery—in Jack's last name "Shepard," the use of the number 23, which likely refers to Psalm 23, "The Lord is my shepherd," and the Catholic visions connected to Charlie, that include a dream in which Andrea de Verrocchio's painting *The Baptism of Christ* is recreated featuring Claire (his love interest), and his mother.[18]

Lost's use of spirals of time, mystical experiences, apparitions, and Eastern imagery to create a frightening heterotopia is both fantastic and beautiful. It's a complicated show, not without its critics, with enough literary references, from *Watership Down* and *Lord of the Flies* to Huxley's *Island* and Dickens's *Our Mutual Friend*, to merit a book-length study.[19] Even the creators of the show admit it is a mythical mash-up, with philosophy, literature, theology, and mythology all woven into the scripts, often in the same episode. As co-creator Damon Lindelhof put it:

> One of the things that we completely own is that in many ways *Lost* is a mash-up/remix of our favorite stories, whether that's Bible stories from Sunday school or *Narnia* or *Star Wars* or the writings of John Steinbeck. Carlton and I both had to take Philosophy courses when we were in college, and we talk about philosophy, so when certain ideas started to present themselves on the show, we just want to let the audience know that these philosophers are in our lexicon as storytellers.[20]

To address *Lost*'s various plotlines, themes, characters, and mysteries as they relate to religion (in particular, to Eastern imagery) would be impossible in a single chapter, so here I reflect on some of the ways the Orient appears in the show, the journeys of a few key characters, and the religious themes their stories touch upon.

Lost has numerous mystical elements in its plotlines. To begin with, *Lost* features ample Oriental vocabulary and imagery. The clandestine program known as the Dharma Initiative is a central part of the storylines in *Lost*. It is not accidental that dharma is the word for Buddhist teachings: its study is one of the ways to reach nirvana. As scholars have surmised, the Dharma Initiative's name may point to one of the key mystical messages in the series: "Just as you leave your car behind when you reach your destination, you should abandon the need for absolute rules once you are ready to 'move on' in loving community to the afterlife."[21] The Temple, one of several Dharma Initiative stations on the island, is another reference to the Orient and its high priest (or leader), Dogen, is named after the famous thirteenth-century Buddhist thinker. As the leader of those stationed at The Temple, he may symbolize the search for ultimate understanding of reality—or Enlightenment. The appearance of megalithic stone statues on the beach is one of the clearest references to Egypt and as such, is another example of the connective tissue between the exotic space of the island and the muddled Orientalism we find in modern mystical visions.

Lost begins with an airplane crash (Oceanic Flight 815) with seventy-two survivors (seventy-one humans and one dog). Not everyone survives for long, and a core group of characters appear, disappear, and reappear throughout the show's six seasons. Their lives and deaths occur in mysterious time cycles that may refer to the endless cycle of births and deaths featured in Hindu and Buddhist concepts of time. Sayid Jarah is one of the most compelling characters in *Lost*, a former member of the Iraqi Republic Guard who was a torturer during the Persian Gulf War (1990–91). As Todd Green points out, at first glance, Sayid represents yet another "bad Muslim" in a long list of Islamophobic characters in Hollywood television and film. He seems naturally predisposed to violence: "Here again we have an example of simplified complex representation. But it is telling that the Muslim character is the only prominent character on the show to struggle with the question of whether he (or she) is inherently prone to violence."[22] This may in fact be a teaching about the *greater jihad*—the *jihad al-nafs*—the war against the worst part of ourselves.

Interestingly, the creators of the series envisioned Sayid as a positive character. They struggled with how to present a Muslim to an audience habituated to negative portrayals of Islam and its followers. Damon Lindelof remarked: "It was always our intent to make Sayid heroic, intelligent and romantic. The fact that he's also Iraqi was never meant to define him, it was simply a way of making audiences potentially question their own ethnic/religious stereotypes as they (hopefully) fall in love with Sayid as much as we did."[23] Throughout the show's six seasons, Sayid is shown to be capable of love, heroism, and great sacrifice. In the end, he is like the other survivors of Oceanic 815—on a spiritual journey that requires him to deal with his past. Sayid is ultimately a major hero, carrying a bomb away from his friends that detonates and kills him. In this final act, he fulfills the duty of an Islamic *shahid* (martyr) who sacrifices his life for a great, moral cause—in this case, the survival of his friends. Sayid's "unqualified willingness to die for the sake of his comrades and to spare Jack, the community's most treasured human asset" represents his heroism, but this is limited by the centrality of the white hero.[24]

Lost has many heroes in addition to Sayid. Of these, Jack perhaps has the most mystical themes. Throughout the series, his impulse to be heroic results in an inability to let go of pain, loss, and disappointment. The last scene of *Lost* finds Jack lying in a bamboo forest dying, with a plane flying overhead. This is interspersed with scenes of him at Locke's funeral, surrounded by his friends from the island, and accompanied by their loved ones (including characters who had died in earlier seasons). Here Jack's father, who is named Christian, reappears. The last scene fits in with a major theme of the show, which is a loving community. Lindelhof admits this is a major arc of the show. He says: "In order to redeem yourself, you can only do it through a community."[25] In season two, Jack says that they will either live together or die alone. In many moments in the six years of *Lost* we see characters die for each other, sacrificing for a community built on friendship and love. The penultimate scene is one of the most overtly religious episodes in the six-year run of the series. Jack has performed his final act of heroism. Having placed a boulder on a light, that if set free will release the island's malevolence on the earth, he dies for the world.

> This final surgery is a selfless act that sends Jack, on the brink of death, back to the bamboo field in which he woke after the crash of Oceanic flight 815. He stumbles, collapses, and finally closes his eyes exactly where he had first glimpsed the island. Jack's narrative, which began with him regaining consciousness just after the plane crash, comes full circle, with him dying just after seeing the plane carry the remaining castaways from the island.[26]

The intellectual content of *Lost*—its connections to European philosophy (it has characters with names such as Locke, Milton,

Bentham, and Rousseau), the extensive Buddhist content (the Dharma Initiative, the Zen teacher Dogen), and the mythical mash-up (heroes, death, birth, redemption)—is impressive. It is also strongly mystical. The first question surrounding *Lost* is—what *is* the island where the survivors of Oceanic Flight 815 are trapped? Ultimately this is a question about reality and our relationship with the world.

Limbo is one theory that has been very popular with fans (but was strongly and publicly dismissed by the show's creators), with the characters stuck in between heaven and hell. This would explain why they desire to go home and why they are constantly tested by nefarious humans (called "the Others"), monsters, and other supernatural forces. Christian and Islamic notions of heaven and hell are somewhat similar in their inclusion of a messiah; for Christians, it is Jesus and for Muslims, it is the Mahdi. Jack is the most messianic of the characters; indeed, he sacrifices himself for his friends and for the world at large, which sounds a lot like Jesus (or perhaps Husayn, the proto-martyr of Shi'i Muslims).

Several other possibilities for decoding *Lost*'s mysteries lie outside the Christian–Islamic eschatological system, which are found in Hindu and Buddhist thought. The island may be a microcosm of the endless cycle of *samsara*, which includes an inescapable cycle of death and rebirth. As a professor once told me in graduate school, what makes *samsara* terrifying is the endlessness of it all. The monsters on the island—the giant polar bears, the black smoke—may in fact be the illusions of death that the Buddha teaches we must all overcome.

Buddhism's focus on cycles of suffering is at the center of the series, expressed in each character's storyline, from Charlie's drug addiction to Kate's past abusive relationships. In fact, *Lost* is filled with Buddhist references, the most famous being the secret government organization called the Dharma Initiative (DA) mentioned earlier. The DA is a shadowy organization with ties to corporate greed (through the character Penny, who is Desmond's long-lost love) that serves the role of game master, controlling things like some enormous, all-powerful, omniscient divine force.[27] Hinduism's concept of dharma is focused on obligation to caste and society, whereas in Buddhism it is the pattern of behavior that leads to enlightenment.[28] This is not the only reference to Buddhism's mystical path. There is the number 108 (the hatch's computer requires someone to reset the computer every 108 minutes or doomsday will be unleashed by the island's nefarious forces)—the standard number used in Buddhist meditation.[29]

Death is at the center of *Lost.* Jack is haunted throughout the series by his father, who wanders the island as a ghost. In one scene, Jack's father appears and he quickly follows him into the jungle, only to find a cove with potable drinking water—symbolizing the thirst for forgiveness and the resolution that Jack is searching for.[30] Visions of the dead are, of course, common in mysticism—in dreams, apparitions, and during ecstatic moments that take place during episodes of deep contemplation. Jack is not the only person on the island to have these visions, suggesting that death surrounds these characters and foreshadowing the possibility that they are, in fact, *already* dead but not at rest until they have spiritually progressed and let go of their attachments to the world.

Lost is deeply embedded in Western philosophy, especially in the work of the philosopher Rousseau (who has a character named after him) and DeLeuze. The island is built upon these two philosophers' complementary visions of the island—as a place to pull away and separate, and a place to start over again.[31] This is circular time (like *samsara*) and a collapse of the past with the present (the mysterium, or mystical experience) cohabitating one space—the island of *Lost.* As McManus explains:

> Rousseau concentrates on time as experienced by the individual and describes it as a flattened expanse of circular time—an eternal present—where past moments are relived, while Deleuze, drawing on the mythological, sees

> time on the island as a spiral series, where the past—and an un-past—is gathered up into the present and moved forward into the future. If one overlays Deleuze's conception of time with that of Rousseau's, then the collective narratives of the desert island—past, present, and future—are contained and enclosed in a circle, mirroring the geography and mythology of the island itself.[32]

In this way, the island is a heterotopia, a *tabula rasa* for all the fears, anxieties, wishes, and fantasies that are part of the mystical quest. Foucault famously writes about the utopia and the heterotopia being in a relationship with each other, and in a sense, the island is a perfect microcosm of this tension. Like the resorts of mystical tourism, "the passage of time continually recurs in an enclosed system" for different visitors, whether they be a castaway like Desmond, the scientists in the Dharma Initiative, or the survivors of Oceanic 815.[33] They are all on a mystical quest, whether alive or already dead, seeking understanding, enlightenment, or salvation.

In Said's critique of Orientalist discourse, the "Other" is the Oriental—the Muslim, the Hindu, the Arab—who functions as the object through which the European or North American defines and identifies himself. As one scholar notes: "An Other is a psychological foil created as a repository for characteristics, ideas and urges that one wishes to disown, and hence Others serve as projections of what we do not want to be."[34] *Lost* inverts this convention, choosing instead to present the Other not as the racial subaltern, but as us—a conservative, malevolent America whose privilege and malice is situated in paranoia. The survivors, who include many international characters—Sayid, Jin, Sun, and Eko—are often exoticized, even vilified (both Sayid and Eko are violent expressions of the Orientalized man), but these characters reflect "the impressive stunt of recalibrating numerous modes and tropes of Othering."[35] This radical rereading of identity and politics is at the center of the drama in *Lost*.

This drama sets up an interesting binary between Occident and Orient through its American hero and other characters. The myth of the white hero is central to the arc of the story and the pathos and grief at his self-sacrificial passing at the end of the series is deeply painful. However, it is the "hybrid liminal space" of the island that makes a religious argument about mystic experience.[36] Mysticism is often connected to liminality, whether in the idea of communion with the dead (believed to occur at gravesites by Muslims), miraculous visions (such as the Buddha's numerous experiences), or in seeing God or gods (the sight of gods in idols and vice versa that takes place in the Hindu universe through *darśan*).

As mentioned above, the nature of the island is a central, running question in the series. Is it purgatory? An alternate reality? A site of anxieties and wishes? A strong possibility is that *Lost* is about none of these things, or all of these things—limbo, *samsara*, a parable about the quest for truth, a heterotopia. All of these possibilities are mystical in nature, involving the search for meaning, an understanding of life, and contemplation of the unknown. One of the ways the creators of *Lost* present these possibilities is through visions of the past and the future—through what are known as flashbacks and flash-forwards. This "operational aesthetic" is important, for it "demands dual attention to both the story and the narrative discourse that narrates the story," which presents a confusing vision of time that is thought to be in the past, but is in fact the future.[37] The destruction of linear time is a mystical notion, seen in the stories of mystics that live in numerous ages, are reborn, or see the future.

The paranormal and magical occurrences on the island also support the notion that the island is a mystical space. One magical element is the giant polar bear on the tropical island; another is the black smoke. Jack's father, or someone he thinks is his father, appears repeatedly, then disappears into the jungle. We find out at the end of the series that these visions are premonitions, for his father is an important part of the final scene. Jack's fear of death is represented in his dead father and, as such, is a way of signaling "The End." This is the end for us all. The possibility of healing, leading to the restoration of wellness, is another mystical quality of the island. John Locke is perhaps the best example of the healing power of the island, which in his case, restores his ability to walk. As scholars have pointed out, such storylines result in numerous analyses of *Lost*'s genre: "Is it a supernatural thriller, a scientific mystery, a soap opera in the wilderness, a religious fantasy, or all of the above?"[38] The idea of the magical island is an old one, and literary examples of magical islands and their monsters, angels, and miracles can be found throughout numerous cultures.

As I suggested earlier, the end of the series may provide some final clues about *Lost*'s mystical messaging. In the last scene, Jack dies on the island, which is interspersed with vignettes of a funeral. Everyone is dead. The significance of the church is important. It purposely displays the symbols of different religions—and this suggests that they are all in the same place, a universalistic form of heaven.[39] This mystical Neverland is nowhere and everywhere. The characters have reached another space—not the island, not the real world—but a place that offers an ending.

What does this ending mean? The death of the ego, or the self, is one of the central lessons in the religious traditions examined in this book. The Buddha teaches his followers to accept the world as it is and let go of illusions. "Dharma is a Sanskrit word meaning 'the essence of nature.' What is to be hoped for is the absolute repose of our being, nothingness."[40] In Islam, the Prophet Muhammad says, "Die before you die," which was then repeated by Rumi and made famous. In this way, *Lost* is a Muslim show—suggesting that humans let go of their *nafs*—the bad part of the ego—the thing that creates monsters on the island we are lost upon. It is only then that we can be free.

STAR WARS

Star Wars, like *Lost*, is a rich cultural text. Articles and books on *Star Wars* exist, but they pale in comparison to the wide-reaching impact the franchise has both in North America and around the world. What has been written on religion in the series has largely focused on its Buddhist themes, imagery, and teachings, while its Christian, Orientalist, and Islamic/Sufic elements have been largely ignored. The lack of attention to Orientalist style in the films is unfortunate, and this is where most of my analysis lies, for I believe it reveals much about the popularity of not just Buddhism, but also elements of Islam.

Not all films create a veritable religion. *Star Wars* doesn't just exist on the silver screen. Jediism is considered a religion by some of its followers and most of its rituals and community events exist online in spaces like the Institute for Jedi Realist Studies (a website) and the Jedi Church (a Facebook group).[41] In fact, the Jedi Doctrine sounds very much like universalist Sufism, with its one absolute principle about God: "This is a concept that most religions of the world concur with. Some refer to it as their deity, some refer to it as a life force, but one thing nearly all religions agree with, is that there exists a single unifying force."[42] The language of Jediism reflects a vague, spiritualist vision that is strongly universalist.

Star Wars is perhaps the greatest mythic mash-up in modern cinema. The "complexity of symbolic expression and references" in the films make it amenable to different, almost endless religious readings.[43] George Lucas has been quoted in numerous interviews as saying that his creation is in part, a response to what he sees as the lack of mythology (what we might call "religion") in the modern world. Lucas studied anthropology in college, and it had a profound impact on him: "Myths, stories from other cultures. It seemed to me that there was no longer a lot of mythology in our society—the kinds of stories we tell ourselves and to our children, which is the way our heritage is passed down. Westerns used to provide that, but there weren't Westerns anymore. I wanted to find a new form."[44] That new form was space.

Star Wars has it all—heroes, villains, monsters, angels, death, rebirth, magic, and love. Considerable debate about which religion the films reflect, who the characters represent, and the heavy layers of Orientalism all point to the lure of modern mysticism. The Force is a strongly mystical concept. As Lucas is fond of saying, "The Force dwells within."[45] It is something both ethereal and material, a kind of energy field that all living creatures create, and that the Jedi can tap into and use to his (or her) advantage.[46] Like God, one cannot see it, but some people can feel it surround them and envelop them in mercy.

Buddhism has a strong voice in the *Star Wars* films through costuming, characters, and the narrative about the Force. Christian Fiechtinger argues that these elements can be understood as part of the overall mythic—and mystic—aesthetic Lucas creates: "Contents and values of Buddhist origin are presented as exemplary, but it is left to the audience's capability of intertextual thinking to identify them as Buddhist. What I venture to sustain is, that despite Lucas's sympathy for Buddhism, it is used rather as a resource of elements to create a *mystic* atmosphere in the movie."[47] Many North Americans reduce Buddhism to "oneness," a problematic reduction that ignores the complexity of Buddhist thought and furthermore, that does not fit into *Mahayana*, *madhamika*, or *yogachara*.

The Jedi might be a kind of samurai. Lucas's early vision of Kenobi surrounded his efforts to cast Toshiro Mifune as the aged master, and he also considered developing a character who was a Japanese princess.[48] The similarity to Japanese films, including Kurosawa's, is evident in the image of the Jedi as warrior as well as the Jedi fraternity existing as a veritable paraphrase of *jidaigeki*.[49] The costume of the Jedi is monk-like, similar to the habit worn by

Buddhist monks in Southeast Asian locations like Vietnam. The life of celibacy that marks many Buddhist orders is seen in the Jedi as well—Luke is never shown with a romantic interest and in *The Last Jedi*, he is a cantankerous, solitary monk who spends his days on an isolated island away from any human entanglements—including romantic ones. Kenobi, in addition to his Japanese-sounding name, is another solitary monk, wandering the desert in the first film, much like a solitary Buddhist monk or a Christian saint who has taken the vow of celibacy.

The theme of the suffering of Anakin, Luke, Leia, Rey, and others may also be linked to Buddhism. As Bortolin points out: "Throughout Star Wars we see the Jedi practicing mindfulness and concentration, and as they do they come to better understand themselves, the galaxy, their own personal suffering, and the dark side within."[50] This theme is seen early on in the story of Anakin, whose suffering destroys his life, and later in Luke, whose role in *The Last Jedi* is profoundly Buddhist. In this film, Luke is the lone monk, a *siddhu* who has reached the highest levels of focus and reflection. The Force can also be seen in Buddhist terms (and in the Hindu notion of Brahman) as "everything is Buddha."[51] The Force is not an either/or, and while there is a dark side and a light side, the theme of universal existence challenges the dualities in Luke's mind. Obi-Wan states, "Luke, you're going to find out that many of the truths we cling to depend greatly on our point of view."[52] In a sense, this is the lesson learned when Yoda raises Luke's sunken ship from the muddy waters. This task is impossible for Luke because he sees the world in terms of can and cannot.

Yoda teaches him, in this moment, that his immediate concerns will defeat his Jedi training. Luke is fixated on the rescue of his friends at this moment and as the pivotal scene in the cave reminds us, Luke is battling his own ego. In his mystical vision in the cave he strikes Vader down, and then Vader is revealed to be himself. This moment reveals a mystical truth—the ego is the enemy because it obfuscates reality and creates fear. According to Suzuki: "When we do something with a quiet, simple clear mind, we have no notion of shadows, and our activity is strong and straightforward."[53]

The Buddhist themes are compelling, but the Force is also, like much of *Star Wars*, an amorphous idea that fits many of the world's religious mystical traditions. As Baxter argues, it is "a belief roomy enough for Christianity, Buddhism and Islam to nestle in its ample folds."[54] The Force may be understood as a kind of *prana*, or life force, that flows through the universe.[55] Due to the close relationship of Hinduism and Buddhism, this *prana* may be connected to *pranayama*—one of the eight steps of yoga.[56] The training that various Jedi individuals go through, including Luke and Rey, is similar to yogic training, and the dangers posed by yogic/Jedi powers are similar.

The spiritual path Luke and other Jedis embark on is not only a Buddhist theme. On an eschatological level, the myth of the Jedis is millenarian, familiar to those who have a millenarian Buddhist or Christian worldview or for that matter, an Islamic one. Muslims believe in a figure called the Mahdi, a messiah who returns before the end of time. Buddhism has a similar idea of Shambhala: "Tibetan Buddhism carries a millenarian message for all mankind in the Kālacakra prophecy of the coming of Sambala."[57] In the end, Rey may emerge as the savior, trained by her teacher Luke who, in *The Last Jedi* is an apparition that tricks the villain Kylo Ren.

The Jedis share similarities with Christian knights of the Middle Ages; their quest for the Kiber Crystal is a kind of retelling of the story of the Holy Grail. At least one observer has pointed out that "May the Force be with you," may be code for the Christian expression, "May the Lord be with you, and with your spirit."[58] However, it could also be a version of the Muslim expression, "May Peace be upon you"—which is a translation of *Salam alaikum*. The preponderance of veils certainly suggests that at the very least, Islam plays a decorative role in the films of the *Star Wars* universe.

Scholars have not been as attentive to Hindu themes in film as one would hope. Hindu practice may in fact be a central part of *Star Wars* for, like Jedi training, "Yoga follows an ancient educational tradition involving a special teacher–disciple relationship."[59] This reflects one of the main points of mysticism in the modern world—it is about everything, but also about nothing specific. Lucas, an admirer of Joseph Campbell, expresses this in his films, where the idea that all religions have a common truth—perennialism—is woven with New Age thought, creating a "modern patchwork spirituality."[60]

Early versions of Lucas's script provide clues about the ways in which Orientalist and Islamic themes have been present in the Star Wars franchise from the start. In the beginning, the Force had a good side called Ashla, the good Jedi were known as the Bendu, and the Kiber Crystal (which is what destroys the Death Star) was a kind of Holy Grail that held incredible power.[61] Ashla is reminiscent of the Persian name Asla; Bendu may be a twist on Bandu, a province in Persia; and the magical crystal is likely named after the Khyber Pass in Central Asia, a place long identified with magic and mysticism. The planet of Tatooine is filmed in Tunisia and its inhabitants include Sand People, who are menacing and wear full hijab. And of course, the costuming is reminiscent of North African dress, especially the *djellaba*.

The costuming in *Star Wars* has received little attention from religious scholars despite its strong Muslim tones. While visiting the *Star Wars and the Power of Costume* exhibit (2016–17) at the Denver Art Museum, I noticed two elements that stood out in the costumes. The first is the Japanese aesthetic, seen in the strong, modern lines of many of the costumes, which were clearly inspired by Japanese clothing. The curators had examples of these Japanese styles alongside the costumes, presenting a very clear picture of the Asian aesthetic that drives many of the characters in the series.

The second element I noticed was veiling, which despite its constant presence in *Star Wars* films, has been completely neglected by scholars of religion. Princess Leia famously veils in the first film, wearing a white costume that reflects her purity as a female (who is later revealed to be a Jedi through her birth line). She wears an attached hijab—worn at opportune times, such as when she is in the presence of a spiritual leader. One of these occasions is the hologram played for Kenobi. Here, her veiling is a sign of her religious devotion in the presence of a religious master, a shaykh. As is the case in Islamic contexts, Muslim women often veil when in special situations—at the mosque, the graveyard, the shrine—as well as within the presence of a spiritual master. Leia is not the only one to wear a hijab, however, and different styles of veiling dominate the films. In *The Force Awakens*, Rey's veiling dominates the film. In the ad for the film, the main character is shown veiled, and her costume (in both this film and *The Last Jedi*) often incorporates some sort of hijab, or cover.

Rogue One's Islamic themes extend far beyond costuming—the main character Jyn Erso veils throughout much of the film. Ultimately, she sacrifices her life for the cause of the Rebel Alliance. Her martyrdom can be read as the action of a *shahid* in Islam, who dies for the cause of justice. Saw Gerrera, played by Forest Whitaker, is a freedom fighter from the Clone Wars. His character is likely inspired by the Islamic freedom fighter—violence has taken over his soul, but he is redeemable and ultimately dies for a just cause, freedom. Islamic themes are also dominant in *The Last Jedi*, which finds Rey struggling with her *nafs*, the dangerous part of the ego that leads to destruction. As she says, "Something inside me has always been there. But now it's awake. And I need help." Luke is cast as the mystical shaykh who teaches Rey in the style of the dervish. In the end, his appearance in two places at once reflects stories of Sufis who were believed to transmigrate across space and time. His magical powers remind this scholar of Islam of the Sufi tales of disappearing doors and other miraculous events, so central in Muslim religious histories from Persia to Indonesia.

Mysticism is strong in these films. As Brent Plate and others have suggested, the films also have strong Christological elements, including prophetic heroes, a messiah (Luke? Rey?), and strict codes of conduct reminiscent of the medieval orders of knighthood.[62] The Jedis are indeed a religious order, but do they resemble the samurai or the Christian knight, or something else? They can also be read as a filmic expression of the master–disciple relationship seen in Sufi orders (*tariqa*). The focus of the Sufi path is the annihilation of the ego (*nafs*), which causes humans to commit evil deeds through words and deeds that reflect a lack of love for Allah and the world. In *Star Wars*, even the chief villain of the early films—Darth Vader—is redeemable. As one scholar puts it: "We learn that even the Emperor's cruelest servant, Darth, was redeemable via love and faith, not power."[63]

Various religious readings of *Star Wars* suggest that Lucas's exposure to mysticism is expressed in his films; in particular, through the character of the Jedi and the idea of the Force. As other scholars have suggested, the Force is a mystic concept that is fluid and vague enough to fit into any number of religious, mystical traditions. In the early films, "The vague energy out of which all beings are created can appear mystical and fluid when it is not encumbered by definitions or limitations."[64] As we learn, the Dark Side is imbalance—and this idea is explored as the franchise develops.[65] The balance can be restored, but it requires an infusion of Light. Sufism has a strong and loud voice here through the ideas of *nur* and *silsila*. *Nur*, which is the Divine Light attached to prophets from Adam to Muhammad, is one reading of the Force's potential for goodness. After all, just as in Sufism, the Jedi must engage in practices in order to attune his heart toward goodness. When Yoda trains Luke, he admonishes him on his inability to focus on the necessary rituals that will lead him to clarity. In Islam, this is the path that leads to a complete understanding of Allah and an acceptance of *tawhid*—the unicity of creation. The Jedi order also has a lineage, reflecting the *silsila*—or line of transmission—that characterizes Sufi orders. Luke cannot be trained by just anyone—only Jedis like Kenobi and Yoda can teach him the way. These are the masters who teach Luke how to train his ego and accept the reality of the world—one of the central lessons of Sufism.

Television and film are imaginary spaces that provide a perfect tableau for the Orientalist fantasies and engagement with mysticism desired by the public. The success of *Lost* and *Star Wars* is due in part to their expert production, consummate acting, and cinematic genius, even with some missteps. One wonders also how much of the seductive quality of mystical entertainment is tied to the need for escape. I can remember clearly sitting in my TV room in Albuquerque, closing the door, and escaping my life for an hour on a tropical island full of adventure, romance, and mystery—the stuff of Oriental dreamscapes. These dreamscapes are very much a response to disenchantment, a subject I will say a few words about in the postscript.

Postscript

The East remains a place of wonder and enchantment in a world that has lost much of the magic that once inhabited it. One of the tragedies of the Enlightenment may in fact be the twilight of this magic. When people do yoga, or travel to India, when they look for Rumi in a dance performance in Turkey, they are searching for something that is missing. Talal Asad's analysis of our modern predicament is apropos here. As we march ahead as conscripts of modernity, as cogs in the wheel of a world ruled by technology and the panopticon of hegemonic power, perhaps a little enchantment is necessary to survive. Who doesn't feel drawn to the mysterious island of *Lost*, or the sweeping sands of *Star Wars*'s Tatooine? Even hardened and cynical scholars like myself get hooked on these fantasies, or return to Bali again and again, pulled there by some inexplicable force.

I've tried to explore some of this tension in this book. As this journey through modern mysticism ends, it is worth reflecting on the creative power of Orientalism in the world today. We see it in spas, airport book shops, alternative medicine, international tourism, fashion, television, and film. The seductive qualities attached to the Orient are part of our historical legacy and the fact that they remain in force says something powerful about the afflicted nature of our disenchanted world.

Some will say that I have been too harsh on those who adopt and follow these different brandings of modern mysticism, but they are missing the main point; I have tried to show here how unconscious these adoptions are. Magic and wonder are great things, but in modern mysticism, their sacred qualities are often overruled by a commitment to capital. In writing this book, I've wondered if it is possible to overcome the hegemonic power of modernity. Its gaze is so complete and overwhelming that its erasure of the cultures it poaches is often unconscious. As a wise teacher named Yoda once said, "In a dark place we find ourselves. And a little more knowledge lights our way."

NOTES

INTRODUCTION

1 Naraindas, "Of Relics, Body Parts and Laser Beams," p. 67.
2 Caplan, "The Fate and Failings of Contemporary Spirituality," p. 52.
3 Lucia, "Innovative Gurus," p. 235.
4 Mitra, "Merchandizing the Sacred," p. 114.
5 Winslow, "The Imaged Other," p. 253.
6 Ibid.
7 Rakow, "Religious Branding and the Quest," p. 216.
8 Ibid., p. 229.
9 Watson, "A Popular Indonesian Preacher," p. 776.
10 Borup, "Branding Buddha," p. 41.
11 Eberhardt and Freeman, "'First Things First, I'm the Realist,'" p. 304.
12 Anand, "Western Colonial Representations," p. 36. Also see Candler, *Unveiling of Lhasa*.
13 Sijapati, "Sufi Remembrance Practices," n.p.
14 Ibid.
15 Bowman, "Ancient Avalon, New Jerusalem," p. 174.
16 Sellers-Young, *Belly Dance, Pilgrimage and Identity*, p. 85.
17 Ibid., p. 53.
18 Bowman, "Ancient Avalon, New Jerusalem," p. 181.
19 Shirazi, *Brand Islam*, p. 1.
20 Hyland, "McDonaldizing Spirituality," p. 335.
21 Urry, *The Tourist Gaze*, p. 11.

22 Wheeler, "The Ethics of Conducting Virtual Ethnography," p. 165.
23 Ibid., p. 169.
24 Iwamura, *Virtual Orientalism*, p. 7.
25 Baudrillard, *Seduction: Cultural Text*, p. 153.
26 John Frow, "Tourism and Semiotics of Nostalgia," p. 128.
27 Ibid., p. 131.
28 Dawes, "The Role of the Intellectual in Liquid Modernity," p. 142.
29 Ibid.
30 Faubion, "From the Ethical to the Thematical (and Back)," p. 93.
31 Iwamura, *Virtual Orientalism*, p. 7.
32 Fabian, *Time and the Other*, p. 25.
33 Winslow, "The Imagined Other," p. 261.
34 Foucault, *Technologies of the* Self, p. 18.
35 Roof, *Spiritual Marketplace*, p. 35.
36 Foucault, "Of Other Spaces," p. 24.
37 Caplan, "The Fate and Failings," p. 52.

CHAPTER 1: HISTORIES OF RELIGION AND MYSTICISM

1 Gelberg, "The Call of the Lotus-Eyed Lord," p. 157.
2 Said, *Orientalism*, pp. 120–121.
3 King, *Orientalism and Religion*, p. 211.
4 Ee and Kahl, "My Soul and Soul Suspended," p. 6.
5 Ibid., p. 7.
6 Arjana, *Veiled Superheroes: Islam, Feminism, and Popular Culture*, p. 1.
7 Iwamura, *Virtual Orientalism*, p. 6.
8 Ibid., p. 26.
9 Iancu, "Spaces of Their Own," p. 446.
10 Ibid., p. 447.
11 Gilbert, *Eat, Pray, Love*, p. 92.
12 Guathier, "Intimate Circles and Mass Meetings," p. 264.
13 Chidester, *Savage Systems*, p. 254.
14 Hornborg, "Designing Rites," p. 407.
15 Maghbouleh, *The Limits of Whiteness*, p. 6.
16 Smith, *Imagining Religion*, p. xi.
17 Smith, *Drudgery Divine*, pp. 17, 21, 22.
18 Asad, *Genealogies of Religion*, p. 29.
19 Payne, "In Defense of Ritual," p. 81.
20 DeConick, *The Gnostic New Age*, p. 6.

21 Lipton, "Secular Sufism," p. 427.
22 King, *Orientalism and Religion*, pp. 25–26.
23 Lipton, "Secular Sufism," p. 430.
24 Ibid.
25 Vial, *Modern Religion, Modern Race*, p. 1.
26 Lipton, "Secular Sufism," p. 427.
27 Anand, "Western Colonial Representations," p. 34.
28 Kaschewsky, "The Image of Tibet in the West," p. 3.
29 Ibid., p. 7.
30 Tweed, *The American Encounter with Buddhism*, pp. 4–5.
31 Mannur and Sahni, "'What Can Brown Do for You?'" p. 182.
32 Carrette and King, *Selling Spirituality*, p. 283.
33 Mannur and Sahni, "'What Can Brown Do for You?'" p. 182.
34 Versluis, *American Gurus*, p. 4.
35 Iwamura, *Virtual Orientalism*, p. 9.
36 Vial, *Modern Religion, Modern Race*, p. 12.
37 King, "Orientalism and the Modern Myth of 'Hinduism,'" p. 164.
38 Schopen, "Archaeology and Protestant Presuppositions," p. 15.
39 Horsley, "Religion and Other Products of Empire," p. 16.
40 Ibid.
41 Ibid., p. 18.
42 Mann, Numrich, and Williams, *Buddhists, Hindus, and Sikhs in America*, p. 5.
43 Ibid.
44 Arjana, *Muslims in the Western Imagination*, p. 3.
45 Akman, "Sufism, Spirituality and Sustainability," p. 6.
46 Ibid.
47 Alger, *The Poetry of the East*, p. 64, quoted in Ford, "The Rose Gardens of the World," p. 16.
48 Fabian, p. 47.
49 Morris, "'Look Into the Book of Life,'" 396.
50 Amira El-Zein, "Spiritual Consumption in the United States: The Rumi Phenomenon," p. 75.
51 Kapchan, "The Promise of Sonic Translation," p. 468.
52 Ernst, "Ideological and Technological Transformations," p. 245.
53 Smith, *Map Is Not Territory*, pp. 94–95.
54 Ibid.
55 Osto, *Altered States*, pp. 22–23.
56 Ibid., p. 23.
57 Ibid., p. 187.
58 Ibid., p. 190.
59 Religious Studies as a field of academic study emerged as a consequence of the work of Orientalists and other scholars.
60 King, *Orientalism and Religion*, p. 7.

61 Maxwell, "Considering Spirituality," p. 264.
62 Ibid.
63 Ibid., p. 266.
64 Dickson, *Living Sufism in North America*, p. 175.
65 Borup, "Branding Buddha," p. 47.
66 Sijapati, "Sufi Remembrance Practices," n.p.
67 Joshi, "On the Meaning of Yoga," p. 53.
68 Askegaard and Eckhardt, "Glocal Yoga," p. 47.
69 Jain, "Who Is to Say Modern Yoga Practitioners Have It All Wrong?" p. 431.
70 Zaidman et al., pp. 610–611.
71 Kitiarsa, "Beyond Syncretism," p. 486.
72 Ibid.
73 Marmor-Lavie, Stout, and Lee, "Spirituality in Advertising," p. 6.
74 Ibid., pp. 8–11.
75 Roof, *Spiritual Marketplace*, p. 96.
76 Thomas, "Spiritual but Not Religious," p. 411.
77 Albanese, "The Aura of Wellness," p. 39.
78 Ibid., pp. 39, 41.
79 Ibid., p. 43.
80 Hodder, "Spirituality and Well-Being," p. 197.
81 Versluis, *American Gurus*, p. 13.
82 Pechilis, "Understanding Modern Gurus," p. 104. Guénon did, according to some scholars, adhere to specific practices, which makes his inclusion in this quote problematic for some scholars.
83 Coats, "Sedona, Arizona: New Age," p. 386.
84 Roof, *Spiritual Marketplace*, p. 97.
85 Ruthven, *The Divine Supermarket*.
86 Hodder, "Spirituality and Well-Being," pp. 198–199.
87 Ibid., p. 199.
88 Albanese, *The Aura of Wellness*, p. 33.
89 Brennan, *Light Emerging*, pp. 131–32, quoted in Albanese, p. 34.
90 Bram, "Spirituality Under the Shadow," p. 126.
91 Ibid.
92 Albanese, "The Aura of Wellness," p. 49.
93 Ibid.
94 Warikoo, "Shrines and Pilgrimages of Kashmir," p. 58.
95 Ibid.
96 Morris, "'Look Into the Book of Life,'" pp. 395–396.
97 Pike, "Selling Infinite Selves," p. 195.
98 Foucault, "Of Other Spaces," p. 24.
99 Baer, "The Work of Andrew Weil and Deepak Chopra," p. 235.
100 Islam, "New Age Orientalism," p. 224.
101 Escher and Petermann, "Marrakesh Medina," p. 29.

102 Bowman, "Going with the Flow," p. 168.
103 Bowman and Keynes, "Arthur and Bridget in Avalon," p. 22.
104 Béres, "A Thin Place," p. 397.
105 Ibid., p. 400.
106 Srinivas, "Highways for Healing," p. 482.
107 Miller, *Rumi Comes to America*, p. 17.
108 Howell, "Muslims, the New Age and Marginal Religions," p. 476.
109 Ibid., p. 480.
110 Strauss, "The Master's Narrative," p. 219.
111 Brown, *Regulating Aversion*, p. 43.
112 Apolito, *The Internet and the Madonna*, p. 179.
113 Ibid.
114 Fox, "Why Media Matter," p. 355.
115 Bell, "'Crazy Wisdom,'" p. 60.
116 Urry, *The Tourist Gaze*, p. 20.
117 Ibid.
118 Ibid., p. 181.
119 Ee and Kahl, "My Mind and Soul Suspended," p. 8.
120 Fox, "Why Media Matter," p. 369.
121 Mannur and Sahni, "'What Can Brown Do for You?'" p. 182.
122 Taylor, *A Secular Age*, p. 587.
123 Mannur and Sahni, "'What Can Brown Do for You?'" p. 182.
124 Bell, "'Crazy Wisdom'", p. 65.
125 Lynn P. Eldershaw, "Collective Identity," p. 78.
126 Bell, "'Crazy Wisdom'", p. 60.
127 Ibid., p. 66.
128 Root, *Cannibal Culture*, p. 40.
129 Johnson, "Authenticity, Tourism, and Self Discovery," p. 174.
130 Yoshihara, *Embracing the East*, p. 24.
131 Ibid., p. 18.
132 Fara, "Portrait of a Nation," p. 38.
133 Yoshihara, *Embracing the East*, pp. 35, 97.
134 Ertimur and Coskuner-Balli, "Navigating the Institutional Logic," pp. 51–52.
135 Carrette and King, *Selling Spirituality*, p. 599.
136 Zaidman, Goldstein-Gidoni, and Nehemya, "From Temples to Organizations," p. 606.
137 Mirdal, "Mevlana," p. 1210.
138 Sijapati, "Sufi Remembrance Practices," n.p.
139 See Arjana, *Muslims in the Western Imagination*. On hijab porn, see Moors, "NiqaBitch and Princess Hijab."
140 Bock and Borland, "Exotic Identities," p. 12–13.
141 Ibid., p. 12.
142 Huggan, *The Postcolonial Exotic*, p. 18.

143 Watson, "A Popular Indonesian Preacher," p. 777.
144 Gauthier, "Intimate Circles," p. 265.
145 Ibid.
146 See the following chapter for a more extensive discussion of Full Circle.
147 Jain, *Selling Yoga*, p. 74.
148 St John, "Civilised Tribalism," p. 5.
149 https://hanumanfestival.com/our-tribe/ (accessed September 17, 2018).
150 Ibid.
151 https://hanumanfestival.com/teachers-lineup/ (accessed September 18, 2018).
152 http://hanumanadventures.com/india/ (accessed September 18, 2018).
153 https://hanumanfestival.com/get-involved/vendor/ (accessed September 18, 2018).
154 http://hanumanfestival.com/teachers-lineup/gina-murdock/ (accessed September 18, 2018).
155 See Chapter Five for more #FakeRumi quotes.
156 Gauthier, "Intimate Circles," p. 265.
157 Sherry and Kozinets, "Comedy of the Commons," p. 136.
158 Ibid., pp. 136–137.
159 Ibid., p. 125.
160 Pike, "Selling Infinite Selves," p. 205.
161 Foucault, "Of Other Spaces," p. 26.
162 St. John, "Civilised Tribalism," p. 10.
163 Gauthier, "Intimate Circles," p. 266.
164 Pike, "Selling Infinite Selves," p. 191.
165 Ibid., p. 205.
166 Ibid., p. 201.
167 Badiner, "Dharma on the Playa," https://tricycle.org/magazine/dharma-playa/ (accessed September 17, 2018).
168 www.sunguardians.net/events/ (accessed September 18, 2018).
169 Ibid.
170 https://buddhacamp.wordpress.com/about/ (accessed September 18, 2018).
171 https://buddhacamp.wordpress.com/activities/ (accessed September 18, 2018).
172 Lofton, *Oprah*, p. 49.
173 Ibid.
174 Guy, *Art of Burning Man*, pp. 40–41.
175 www.shrinetheworld.com/about/ (accessed October 4, 2018).
176 Guy, *Art of Burning Man*, p. 47.
177 Ibid., p. 57.

178 Ibid., p. 117.
179 Ibid., pp. 124–125.
180 LadyBee, "The Outsider Art of Burning Man," p. 345.
181 Sherry and Kozinets, p. 127.
182 Lewis, Paul, "Welcome to Powder Mountain – a utopian club for the millennial elite," *Guardian* (March 16, 2018), www.theguardian.com/technology/2018/mar/16/powder-mountain-ski-resort-summit-elite-club-rich-millenials?CMP=Share_iOSApp_Other (accessed March 19, 2018).
183 Ibid.
184 Ibid.
185 Shippee, "Trungpa's Barbarians and Merton's Titan," p. 120.

CHAPTER 2: CULTURAL COLONIALISM, MUDDLED ORIENTALISM, AND THE MYSTIC POOR

1 Einstein, *Brands of Faith*, p. 161.
2 Kabbalah.com.
3 Einstein, *Brands of Faith*, p. 161.
4 Ibid., p. 158.
5 Ibid.
6 Harris, "Celebrity Spirituality," p. 102.
7 Shippee, "Trungpa's Barbarians," pp. 110–111.
8 Ibid., p. 111.
9 Trungpa, *Cutting Through Spiritual Materialism*, p. 7, quoted in Shippee, "Trungpa's Barbarians," p. 112.
10 Bell, "'Crazy Wisdom,'" p. 58.
11 Gelberg, "The Call of the Lotus-Eyed Lord," p. 150.
12 See Bucar, *Stealing Your Religion* (forthcoming).
13 Zarcone, "Rereadings and Transformations of Sufism in the West," p. 117.
14 Zebiri, "'Holy Foolishness' and 'Crazy Wisdom,'" p. 102.
15 Ibid., p. 105.
16 Sedgwick, *Western Sufism*, p. 211.
17 Sinha, *Religion and Commodification*, p. 199.
18 Ibid.
19 Akman, "Sufism, Spirituality and Sustainability," p. 7. Also see Rawlinson, "A History of Western Sufism."
20 Hyland, "McDonaldizing Spirituality," p. 347.

21 Hedstrom, "The Commodification of William James," pp. 129–130.
22 *The Oprah Magazine*, "The O List," March 2018, p. 43.
23 Jain, "Who Is to Say," p. 77.
24 Geczy, *Fashion and Orientalism*, p. 93.
25 Ibid., p. 154.
26 Tello, "Creating Your Nurturing Personal Sanctuary," p. 41.
27 Escher and Petermann, "Marrakesh Medina," pp. 37–39, 35.
28 Winslow, "The Imagined Other," p. 264.
29 Knudson, "The Purchase of Enlightenment," p. 67.
30 Gilbert, *Eat, Pray, Love*, p. 193.
31 Larasati, "Eat, Pray, Love Mimic," p. 92.
32 McKay, "'Truth,' Perception, and Politics," p. 82.
33 Zaehner, *Mysticism Sacred and Profane*, p. 160. Quoted in Ernst, "Situating Sufism and Yoga," p. 20.
34 Dickson, *Living Sufism In North America*, p. 188.
35 Chidester, *Authentic Fakes*, p. 203.
36 Dickson, *Living Sufism in North America*, p. 173.
37 Larasati, "Eat, Pray, Love Mimic," p. 91.
38 Pedersen, "Tibet, Theosophy, and the Psychologization of Buddhism," pp. 153–154.
39 Fields, *How the Swan Came to the Lake*, p. 87.
40 Ibid., p. 89.
41 Sedgwick, *Western Sufism*, p. 211.
42 Pedersen, "Tibet, Theosophy, and the Pyschologization of Buddhism," p. 159.
43 www.fullcirclevenice.org (accessed September 9, 2018).
44 www.avatarism.net (accessed September 9, 2018).
45 www.avatarism.net/artist-bio/ (accessed September 9, 2018).
46 Ibid.
47 Ibid. Andrew Keegan, the founder of Full Circle, also claims to have had a mystical experience at Burning Man.
48 www.fullcirclevenice.org/full-circle-reflections-future/ (accessed September 9, 2018).
49 www.fullcirclevenice.org (accessed September 9, 2018).
50 www.fullcirclevenice.org/community/ (accessed September 9, 2018).
51 Foxen, *Biography of a Yogi*, pp. 116–117.
52 Carrette and King, *Selling Spirituality*, p. 3.
53 Ibid., p. 87.
54 Coats, "Sedona, Arizona," p. 386.
55 Korom, "The Role of Tibet in the New Age Movement," p. 169.
56 Lopez, "The Image of Tibet of the Great Mystifiers," p. 198.
57 Ibid.
58 Møllgaard, "Slavoj Zizek's Critique of Western Buddhism," p. 175.
59 Bock and Borland, "Exotic Identities," p. 25.

60 Timalsina, "Encountering the Other," p. 285.
61 Bock and Borland, "Exotic Identities," p. 26.
62 Root, *Cannibal Culture*, p. 88.
63 Antony, "On the Spot," p. 350.
64 https://members.ronjasebastian.com/p/Hidden-Paradise-Ultimate-Goddess-Retreat (accessed November 2, 2018).
65 Rinpoche, "Buddhism in the West and the Image of Tibet," p. 387.
66 McDaniel, "Liberation Materiality," p. 402.
67 Miller, *Rumi Comes to America*, p. 3.
68 Ibid., p. 4.
69 Bohlman, "World Musics and World Religions," p. 67.
70 Irizarry, "Putting a Price on Zen," p. 62.
71 Ibid., pp. 52, 59, 60.
72 Rose Deighton, a religious scholar earning her doctorate at Emory University, saw this on the menu at a coffee shop near her home.
73 Knabb and Welsh, "Reconsidering A. Reza Arasteh," p. 45.
74 Hermansen, "Muslims in Performative Mode," p. 392.
75 Tourage, "Performing Belief and Reviving Islam," p. 211.
76 Crow, "Consuming Islam," p. 13.
77 Ibid., p. 10.
78 *Los Angeles Times*, June 18, 1988, Life & Style, Part E, p. 1. Quoted in El-Zein, "Spiritual Consumption," p. 73.
79 Sana Saeed, Twitter, 7/15/19, 9:50 p.m. *Sex and the City*, season 4, episode 11.
80 Bauman, *Liquid Modernity*, p. 57.
81 McKenzie, "Right Business, Right Consumption," p. 599.
82 Zaidman, Goldstein-Gidoni, and Nehemya, "From Temples to Organizations," p. 613.
83 Derrida, "Signature, Event, Context," pp. 307–330. Quoted in Tourage, "Performing Belief and Reviving Islam," p. 225.
84 Sellers-Young, *Belly Dance, Pilgrimage, and Identity*, p. 86.
85 Ibid.
86 Farmer, "Americanasana," p. 155.
87 Mirdal, "Mevlana," p. 1205.
88 Senay, "The Fall and Rise of the *Ney*," pp. 419–420.
89 Hermansen, "Muslims in the Performative Mode," p. 393.
90 El-Zein, "Spiritual Consumption," p. 75.
91 Khabeer, "Rep That Islam," p. 126.
92 Eberhardt and Freeman, "First Things First," p. 306.
93 El-Zein, "Spiritual Consumption," p. 75.
94 Knudson, "The Purchase of Enlightenment," p. 67.
95 Kopano, "Soul Thieves," p. 3.
96 Low, "White Skins/Black Masks," p. 215.
97 Ibid., p. 196.

98 Arjana, *Muslims in the Western Imagination*, p. 107.
99 Geczy, *Fashion and Orientalism*, p. 140.
100 Rasch, "Enlightenment as Religion," p. 117.
101 Ibid., p. 128.
102 Brown, *Regulating Aversion*, p. 153.
103 Mitra, "Merchandizing the Sacred," p. 116.
104 Sinha, *Religion and Commodification*, p. 38.
105 Timalsina, "Encountering the Other," p. 278.
106 Ibid., p. 279.
107 Pfadenhauer, "In-Between Spaces," p. 153.
108 Low, "White Skin, Black Masks," p. 93.
109 Kapchan, "The Promise of Sonic Translation," p. 470.
110 Ibid., p. 161.
111 Quote from a conversation with Blayne Harcey, the American scholar of Hinduism and Buddhism.
112 Low, "White Skins/Black Masks," p. 3.
113 Versluis, *American Gurus*, p. 177.
114 Ibid.
115 Ibid., p. 78.
116 Martin and Koda, *Orientalism: Visions of the East*, p. 51.
117 Said, *Orientalism*, p. 222.
118 Urry, *The Tourist Gaze*, p. 148.
119 Ibid.
120 Low, "White Skin, Black Masks," p. 89.
121 Martin and Koda, *Orientalism: Visions of the East*, p. 51.
122 Ibid.
123 Sellers-Young, *Belly Dance, Pilgrimage, and Identity*, p. 46.
124 *Harper's Bazaar*, "Oprah for President?" (interview), March 2018, p. 332.
125 Fields, *How the Swans Came to the Lake*, p. 90.
126 Farmer, "Americanasana," p. 155.
127 Larasati, "Eat, Pray, Love Mimic," pp. 92–93.
128 Mbembe, *On the Postcolony*, p. 2.
129 Geczy, Fashion and Orientalism, p. 59.
130 Korom, "The Role of Tibet," p. 172.
131 Yoshihara, *Embracing the East*, p. 25.
132 Ibid.
133 Silva, "Art and Fetish in the Anthropology Museum," p. 79.
134 Wharton, "Relics, Protestants, Things," p. 425.
135 Larasati, "Eat, Pray, Love Mimic," p. 94.
136 Foxen, *Biography of a Yogi*, p. 32.
137 Mitra, "Merchandizing the Sacred," p. 117.
138 Bowman, "Ancient Avalon, New Jerusalem," p. 166.
139 Mannur and Sahni, "'What Can Brown Do for You?'" p. 186.

140 Ibid.
141 Ibid.
142 MacCannell, *Empty Meeting Grounds*, p. 168. Quoted in Hill, "Inca of the Blood," p. 255.
143 Ibid.
144 Durham, "Displaced Persons," p. 203.
145 Ibid., p. 204.
146 Hutnyk, "Magical Mystery Tourism," p. 101.
147 Durham, "Displaced Persons," p. 203.
148 Logan, "The Lean Closet," p. 611.
149 Ibid., p. 613.
150 Ibid., p. 619.
151 Vandenburg and Braun, "'Basically, It's Sorcery for your Vagina,'" p. 472.
152 Shohat and Stam, *Unthinking Eurocentrism*, p. 192.
153 Llamas and Belk, "Shangri-La," p. 262.
154 Carrette and King, *Selling Spirituality*, p. 113.
155 Albanese, "The Aura of Wellness," p. 35.
156 Ibid.
157 Williams, "*Eat, Pray, Love*," p. 624.
158 Ibid., p. 613.
159 Ibid.
160 Larasati, "Eat, Pray, Love Mimic," p. 93.
161 Williams, "*Eat, Pray, Love*," p. 624.
162 Huang and Xu, "Therapeutic Landscapes and Longevity," p. 28.
163 Ibid.
164 Govers and Go, *Place Branding*, p. 223.
165 Llamas and Belk, "Shangri-La," p. 264.
166 Shop.goop.com (accessed June 20, 2019).
167 Ibid.

CHAPTER 3: MYSTICISM, INCORPORATED

1 Drury, *The New Age*, p. 128.
2 Lucia, p. 235.
3 Wilkins-LaFlamme, "How Unreligious are the Religious 'Nones'?" p. 478.
4 Baker and Smith, "None Too Simple," p. 721.
5 Ibid.
6 Yusuf, *Purification of the Heart*, p. 11.
7 Wilson, *Mindful America*, p. 137.

8 Ibid.
9 Ibid.
10 Ibid., p. 138.
11 Yoshihara, *Embracing the East*, p. 29.
12 Zarcone, "Rereadings and Transformations of Sufism in the West," p. 112.
13 Janes, "Buddhism, Science, and Market," p. 286.
14 Taylor, *A Secular Age*, p. 77.
15 Foxen, *Biography of a Yogi*, p. 15.
16 Hornborg, "Designing Rites to Re-enchant Secularized Society," pp. 403, 406.
17 Foxen, *Biography of a Yogi*, p. 15.
18 Llamas and Belk, "Shangri-La: Messing with a Myth," p. 260.
19 Wilkins-LaFlamme, "How Unreligious Are the Religious 'Nones?" p. 179.
20 Taylor, *A Secular Age*, p. 513.
21 Berger, *The Many Altars of Modernity*, p. 6.
22 Pfadenhauer, "In-Between Spaces," p. 150.
23 Berger, *The Many Altars of Modernity*, p. 28.
24 Bainbridge, *Dynamic Secularization*, p. 5.
25 Jafari and Süerdem, "An Analysis of Material Consumption Culture," p. 72.
26 Hyland, "McDonaldizing Spirituality," p. 344.
27 Jafari and Süerdem, "An Analysis of Material Consumption Culture," pp. 64–65.
28 Ibid., p. 65.
29 Bauman and Haugaard, "Liquid Modernity and Power," p. 115.
30 Bauman, *Liquid Modernity*, p. 134.
31 Crow, "Consuming Islam," p. 10.
32 Žižek, *The Puppet and the Dwarf*, p. 26.
33 Thomas, "Spiritual but not Religious," p. 405.
34 Albanese, "The Aura of Wellness," p. 30.
35 Ibid., p. 31.
36 Roberts and Roberts, "A Saint in the City," p. 55.
37 Geertz, *The Interpretation of Cultures: Selected Essays*, p. 90.
38 Chidester, *Authentic Fakes*, p. 13.
39 Ibid., p. 42.
40 Ibid.
41 Bowman and Keynes, "Arthur and Bridget in Avalon," p. 17.
42 Versluis, *American Gurus,"* p. 179.
43 Zarcone, "Rereadings and Transformations," p. 112.
44 Farmer, "Americanasana," p. 154.
45 Roof, *Spiritual Marketplace*, 34.
46 Mirdal, "Mevlana Jalāl ad-Dīn Rumi and Mindfulness," p. 1205.

47 Wharton, *Selling Jerusalem*, p. 45.
48 Geary, *Furta Sacra*, p. 45.
49 Wharton, "Relics, Protestants, Things," p. 414.
50 Ibid., pp. 421, 423.
51 Schmidt, *Consumer Rites*, p. 5.
52 Ibid., p. 45.
53 Huggan, *The Postcolonial Exotic*, p. 31.
54 Bock and Borland, "Exotic Identities," p. 8.
55 Lofton, *Oprah: The Gospel of an Icon*, p. 25.
56 Ibid., p. 29.
57 *Oprah Magazine* 19, no. 11, p. 66.
58 Ibid.
59 Ibid., p. 1210.
60 Morris, "'Look Into the Book of Life,'" p. 397.
61 Einstein, *Brands of Faith*, p. 197.
62 McClintock, *Imperial Leather*, p. 58.
63 Root, *Cannibal Culture*, p. 88.
64 Einstein, *Brands of Faith*, p. 200.
65 Ibid., p. 199.
66 Ibid.
67 DeConick, *The Gnostic New Age*, p. 17.
68 Shirazi, *Brand Islam*, p. 1.
69 Mannur and Sahni, "'What Can Brown Do for You?'" p. 179.
70 Wharton, "Relics, Protestants, Things," p. 425.
71 Ibid., p. 427.
72 Kapchan, "The Promise of Sonic Translation," p. 472.
73 Eberhardt and Freeman, "First Things First," p. 322.
74 Mitra, "Merchandizing the Sacred," p. 115.
75 Foxen, *Biography of a Yogi*, p. 47.
76 McClintock, *Imperial Leather*, p. 46.
77 Eck, "'*Tirthas*'", p. 336.
78 Heelas, *Spiritualities of Life*, p. 138.
79 Korom, "The Role of Tibet in the New Age Movement," p. 169.
80 Foxen, "Supermen, Mystical Women, and Oriental Others," p. 47.
81 Malhotra, *Instant Nirvana*, p. 36.,
82 Ourvan, *The Star Spangled Buddhist*, p. xviii.
83 Bowman, "Going with the Flow," p. 243. Emphasis is mine.
84 Roberts and Roberts, "A Saint in the City," p. 55.
85 Roof, *Spiritual Marketplace*, p. 91.
86 Logan, "The Lean Closet," pp. 600–602.
87 Martin and Koda, *Orientalism: Visions of the East*, p. 13.
88 McKenzie, "Right Business, Right Consumption," p. 606.
89 Zarcone, "Rereadings and Transformations," p. 114.
90 Ibid., p. 119.

91 Møllgaard, "Slavoj Zikek's Critique," p. 178.
92 Chidester, *Authentic Fakes*, p. 112.
93 Baker and Smith, "None Too Simple," p. 721.
94 Iwamura, *Virtual Orientalism*, p. 37.
95 Dickson and Sharify-Funk, *Unveiling Sufism*, p. 40.
96 Gelberg, "The Call of the Lotus-Eyed Lord," p. 155.
97 Dickson and Sharify-Funk, *Unveiling Sufism*, p. 40.
98 Maxwell, "Considering Spirituality," p. 267.
99 Tweed, *The American Encounter with Buddhism*, p. 49.
100 Graves, "Introduction" in Shah, *The Sufis*, p. 23.
101 Palmer, *Oriental Mysticism*, pp. x–xi.
102 Mirdal, "Mevlana Jalāl-ad-Dīn Rumi and Mindfulness," p. 1210.
103 Bauman, *Consuming Life*, p. 53.
104 Schedneck, *Thailand's International Meditation Centers*, p. 106.
105 Gauthier, "Intimate Circles and Mass Meetings," p. 266.
106 Foley, "The Naqshbandiyya-Khalidiyya, Islamic Sainthood, and Religion," p. 524.
107 Martin and Koda, *Orientalism: Visions of the East*, p. 46.
108 Low, "White Skin, Black Masks," p. 89.
109 Martin and Koda, *Orientalism: Visions of the East*, p. 13.
110 Ibid., p. 35.
111 Mannur and Sahni, "'What Can Brown Do For You?'" p. 182.
112 Ibid., p. 185.
113 Yoshihara, *Embracing the East*, p. 98.
114 Martin and Koda, *Orientalism: Visions of the East*, pp. 73–74.
115 Ibid., p. 55.
116 Baer, "The Work of Andrew Weil and Deepak Chopra," p. 240.
117 Gunderson, "Starting Over: Searching for the Good Life," p. 161.
118 Askegaard and Eckhardt, "Glocal Yoga," p. 53.
119 Featherstone, "The Body in Consumer Culture," p. 171.
120 https://dragontreeapothecary.com/collections/massage-oils/products/ayurvedic-massage-oil-8oz (accessed November 2, 2018).
121 Featherstone, "The Body in Consumer Culture," p. 187.
122 Gunderson, "Starting Over," p. 161.
123 https://dragontreeapothecary.com/products/peace-herbal-tea (accessed November 2, 2018).
124 Gunderson, "Starting Over," p. 162.
125 Wilson, *Mindful America*, p. 156.
126 Mickey, "'*Eat, Pray, Love*' Bullshit," p. 6.
127 Ibid., pp. 14, 18.
128 Ibid., p. 19.
129 Foderaro, "A Tonic for the Harried," p. 51.
130 Winslow, "The Imagined Other," p. 254.
131 Ibid.

132 Ibid.
133 www.joelosteen.com/Pages/Store-Messages.aspx (accessed July 2, 2019).
134 Hill, "Inca of the Blood," p. 256.
135 Frow, "Tourism and the Semiotics," p. 146.
136 Ibid.
137 Root, *Cannibal Culture*, p. 94.
138 Gunderson, "Starting Over," p. 169.
139 Ibid., p. 165.
140 Joshunda Sanders and Ana Mouyis, "Eat, Pray, Spend," n.p.
141 Ibid.
142 Bram, "Spirituality Under the Shadow of the Conflict," p. 125.
143 Hill, "Inca of the Blood, Inca of the Soul," p. 251.
144 Urry, *The Tourist* Gaze, p. 13.
145 Huang and Xu, "Therapeutic Landscapes and Longevity," p. 23.
146 Ibid., p. 24.
147 Ee and Kahl, "My Mind and Soul Suspended," p. 13.
148 Tickell, "Footprints on the Beach," p. 42.
149 Graci and Dodds, *Sustainable Tourism in Island Destinations*, p. 121.
150 Llamas and Belk, "Shangri-La," p. 264.
151 Ibid., p. 267.
152 Johnson, "Authenticity, Tourism, and Self-discovery," p. 163.
153 Schedneck, *Thailand's International Meditation* Centers, p. 103.
154 Roof, *Spiritual Marketplace*, p. 84.

CHAPTER 4: HINDU HIPPIES AND BOULDER BUDDHISTS

1 Baker, *A Blue Hand*, pp. 214–215.
2 Bowditch, *On the Edge of Utopia*, p. 211.
3 Ibid.
4 Morgan, *Visual Piety*, pp. 2–3.
5 www.youtube.com/watch?v=3XuEFj3zd1U (accessed October 19, 2018).
6 Srivastava, "Religion and Development," p. 346.
7 Joshi, "On the Meaning of Yoga," p. 58.
8 Anand, "Western Colonial Representations," p. 24.
9 McMahan, *The Making of Buddhist Modernism*, p. 223.
10 Ibid., p. 234.
11 Ibid., p. 240.

12 Ernst, "Situating Sufism and Yoga," p. 22.
13 King, *Orientalism and Religion*, p. 97.
14 Hutnyk, "Magical Mystery Tourism," p. 99.
15 Strauss, "The Master's Narrative," p. 220.
16 Ibid., p. 221.
17 Ibid., p. 227.
18 Mann, Numrich, and Williams, *Buddhists, Hindus, and Sikhs*, p. 32.
19 Ibid., p. 91.
20 Mitra, "Merchandizing the Sacred," p. 116.
21 Sinha, *Religion and Commodification*, p. 111.
22 Mann, Numrich, and Williams, *Buddhists, Hindus, and Sikhs*, p. 87.
23 Mitra, "Merchandizing the Sacred," p. 120.
24 Iwamura, *Virtual Orientalism*, p. 104.
25 Ibid., p. 109.
26 Baer, "The Work of Andrew Weil," p. 239.
27 Iwamura, *Virtual Orientalism*, p. 110.
28 Baer, "The Work of Andrew Weil," p. 239.
29 Carrette and King, *Selling Spirituality*, p. 119.
30 Foxen, "Supermen, Mystical Women, and Oriental Others," p. 54.
31 Askegaard and Eckhardt, "Glocal Yoga," p. 48.
32 Roof, *Spiritual Marketplace*, p. 107.
33 Ibid., p. 39.
34 Tillich, *Systematic Theology*, p. 24.
35 Farmer, "Americanasana," p. 145.
36 Joshi, "On the Meaning of Yoga," pp. 53–54.
37 Ibid., p. 57.
38 Ibid., pp. 61–63.
39 Farmer, "Americanasana," pp. 147–148;
40 Jain, "Who Is To Say," p. 442.
41 Farmer, "Americanasana," p. 149.
42 Ibid., p. 153.
43 Bainbridge, *Dynamic Secularization*, p. 4.
44 Harris, "Celebrity Spirituality," pp. 98–99.
45 Drury, *The New Age*, p. 137.
46 Jain, *Selling Yoga*, p. 87.
47 Ibid.
48 Farmer, "Americanasana," pp. 145–146.
49 Ibid., p. 147.
50 Jain, "Who Is To Say," p. 443.
51 Ibid., p. 444.
52 "The Seven Chakras," *Hinduism Today* 33, no. 1 (2011): 114.
53 Crowley, "New Age Soul," p. 44.
54 Bowman, "Ancient Avalon, New Jerusalem," p. 164.
55 Ibid., p. 170.

56 Ibid., pp. 167–168.
57 Sellers-Young, *Belly Dance*, p. 60.
58 Islam, "New Age Orientalism," p. 222.
59 Ibid., p. 224.
60 Naraindas, "Of Relics," p. 68.
61 Ibid.
62 https://nccih.nih.gov/health/homeopathy (accessed November 2, 2018).
63 Naraindas, "Of Relics," p. 81.
64 Timalsina, "Encountering the Other," p. 277.
65 Vandenburg and Braun, "'Basically, It's Sorcery for Your Vagina,'" p. 480.
66 Islam, "New Age Orientalism," pp. 221, 222.
67 Ibid., 228.
68 Ibid., pp. 228–229.
69 www.thevedicvillages.com (accessed May 23, 2018).
70 www.sukhavatibali.com/wellness/taste-of-wellness-3-day-program/ (accessed October 3, 2018).
71 Harris, "Celebrity Spirituality," p. 105.
72 Williams, "*Eat, Pray, Love*," p. 622.
73 Howell, "Muslims, the New Age," pp. 488–489.
74 Ibid.
75 Ee and Kahl, "My Mind and Soul Suspended," p. 10.
76 Janes, "Buddhism, Science, and Market," p. 284.
77 Mann, Numrich, and Williams, *Buddhists, Hindus, and Sikhs*, p. 30.
78 Chidester, *Authentic Fakes*, p. 218.
79 McKenzie, "Right Business," p. 604.
80 Borup, "Branding Buddha," p. 48.
81 Hansen, "Tibetan Horizon," p. 101.
82 Kitiarsa, "Beyond Syncretism," p. 477.
83 Powers, *Introduction to Tibetan Buddhism*, pp. 119–120. Quoted in McKenzie, "Right Business," p. 603.
84 Borup, "Branding Buddha," p. 48.
85 Kvaerne, "Tibet Images," p. 55.
86 Ibid., p. 59.
87 Llamas and Belk, "Shangri-La," pp. 257, 259.
88 Lopez, *Prisoners of Shangri-La*," pp. 202. Quoted in Llamas and Belk, "Shangri-La," p. 260.
89 Iwamura, *Virtual Orientalism*, p. 15.
90 Møllgaard, "Slavoj Zizek's Critique," p. 175.
91 McMahan, *The Making of Buddhist Modernism*, p. 28.
92 Hyland, "McDonaldizing Spirituality," p. 336.
93 Barker, "Men, Buddhism and the Discontents," p. 34.
94 Mann, Numrich, and Williams, *Buddhists, Hindus, and Sikhs*, p. 25.

95 Ibid.
96 Ibid., p. 28.
97 Wilson, *Mindful America*, p. 155.
98 Ibid., p. 154.
99 Rocha, *Zen in Brazil*, p. 131. Quoted in Borup, "Branding Buddha," p. 49.
100 Shippee, "Trungpa's Barbarians," p. 109.
101 Mann, Numrich, and Williams, *Buddhists, Hindus, and Sikhs*, p. 31.
102 Bell, "Scandals in Emerging Western Buddhism," p. 235.
103 Midal, *Chögyam Trungpa*, p. 163. Midal was a student of Trungpa's and his book does not include any of the controversies or scandals identified with his teacher and his community.
104 Bell, "'Crazy Wisdom,'" p. 62.
105 Ibid., p. 64.
106 Fields, *How the Swans Came to the Lake*, p. 365.
107 Eldershaw, "Collective Identity," p. 89.
108 Ibid., p. 91.
109 Bell, "'Crazy Wisdom,'" p. 72.
110 Bell, "Scandals in Emerging Western Buddhism," p. 234.
111 Eldershaw, "Collective Identity," pp. 89–90.
112 Anand, "Western Colonial Representations," p. 26.
113 Ibid.
114 Ibid.
115 Richardson, *Tibet and its History*, p. 61. Quoted in Anand, "Western Colonial Representations," p. 29.
116 Kraptchuk and Eisenberg, "Varieties of Healing," p. 200. Cited in Janes, "Buddhism, Science, and the Market," p. 282.
117 McKenzie, "Right Business," p. 607.
118 Richardson, *Tibet and Its History*, p. 12.
119 Srinivas, "Highways for Healing," pp. 490–491.
120 Mirdal, "Mevlana," p. 1212.
121 Albanese, "The Aura of Wellness," p. 36.
122 Ibid., p. 38.
123 Lofton, *Oprah*, p. 62.
124 Carrette and King, *Selling Spirituality*, p. 94.
125 Ibid., p. 89.
126 Ibid., p. 101.
127 Ibid.
128 Senay, "The Fall and Rise," p. 409.
129 Ibid.
130 Irizarry, "Putting a Price on Zen," p. 57.
131 Ibid.
132 Bowman and Keynes, "Arthur and Bridget," p. 17.
133 Irizarry, "Putting a Price on Zen," p. 60.
134 Ibid., p. 57.

135 Bell, "Scandals," p. 235.
136 Coats, "Sedona, Arizona," p. 386.
137 Bowman, "Ancient Avalon," p. 183.
138 Ibid., p. 171.
139 Apolito, *The Internet and the Madonna*, p. 180.
140 Marmor-Levie, Stour, and Lee, "Spirituality in Advertising," p. 2.
141 Borup, "Branding Buddha," p. 52.
142 Foucault, "Of Other Spaces," p. 26.
143 DeLaney, "Why This Wellness Writer Names Bali as Her Favorite Holistic Destination." Departures Newsletter. http://departures.com/travel/hotels/bali-wellness-retreats/ (accessed September 18, 2018).
144 Bowman, "Ancient Avalon," p. 168.
145 Ibid.
146 Foucault, "Of Other Spaces," p. 26.
147 www.baliseminars.com/vission-and-mission.html (accessed October 3, 2018).
148 Ibid.
149 Hill, "Inca of the Blood," p. 258.
150 Cohen, "Nomads from Affluence," p. 92.
151 Byrne, "Gateway and Garden," p. 35.
152 Foucault, "Of Other Spaces," p. 27.
153 Ibid.
154 Graeburn, *Ethnic and Tourist Arts*, p. 35. Quoted in Hill, "Inca of the Blood," p. 265
155 Steinbrink, "'We Did the Slum,'" p. 19.
156 Lee and Kim, "Success Stories of Health Tourism," p. 217.
157 Ibid., p. 222.
158 Frow, "Tourism and the Semiotics of Nostalgia," p. 150.
159 Graeburn, *Ethnic and Tourist Arts*, p. 36.
160 Byrne, "Gateway and Garden," p. 41.
161 Hill, "Inca of the Blood," p. 258.
162 Albanese, "The Aura of Wellness," p. 49.
163 www.authenticrelatingtraining.com/about-us/ (accessed October 19, 2018).
164 www.authenticrelatingtraining.com/blog/2018/3/25/the-most-influential-and-life-changing-books-of-all-time (accessed October 19, 2018).
165 Wilson, *Mindful America*, p. 139.
166 Ibid.
167 Ibid.
168 Schedneck, *Thailand's International Meditation Centers*, p. 103. Also see Tweed, *The American Encounter with Buddhism 1844–1912*, p. 70.
169 Schedneck, *Thailand's International Meditation Centers*, p. 120.

170 Tickell, "Footprints on the Beach," p. 43.
171 Ibid.
172 Bowditch, *On the Edge of Utopia*, p. 231.

CHAPTER 5: RUMIMANIACS

1 Silva-Jelly, "Oprah for President?" p. 332.
2 Lewis, *Rumi Past and Present, East and West*, p. 21.
3 Omid Safi's Facebook Page, August 17, 2018, used with permission of the author. See Safi's forthcoming book titled *Rumi's Masnavi: A Biography* (Princeton University Press, 2020) for more #FakeRumi quotes.
4 Dickson and Sharify-Funk, *Unveiling Sufism*, p. 25.
5 Ernst, "The Islamicization of Yoga," p. 200.
6 Kabbani, *Classical Islam and the Naqshbandi Sufi Tradition*, p. 647.
7 Dickson and Sharify-Funk, *Unveiling Sufism*, p. 23.
8 Ford, "The Rose-Gardens of the World," p. 15.
9 Dickson, *Living Sufism in North America*, p. 170.
10 Dickson and Sharify-Funk, *Unveiling Sufism*, p. 24.
11 Ernst, "Ideological and Technical Transformations," p. 22.
12 Dickson and Sharify-Funk, *Unveiling Sufism*, p. 35.
13 Kapchan, "The Promise of Sonic Translation," p. 476.
14 Dickson and Sharify-Funk, *Unveiling Sufism*, p. 11.
15 Akman, "Sufism, Spirituality and Sustainability," p. 3. Also see Mir Vali-ud-din, *The Quranic Sufism* (Lahore: Sh. Muhammad Ashraf Publishers).
16 DeConick, *The Gnostic New Age*, p. 6.
17 Friedlander, *The Whirling* Dervishes, p. 14. Quoted in El-Zein, p. 82.
18 Foley, "The Naqshbandiyya-Khalidiyya," p. 528.
19 Ibid., p. 523.
20 Roberts and Roberts, "A Saint in the City," p. 64.
21 Foley, "The Naqshbandiyya-Khalidiyya," p. 522.
22 Ibid., p. 542.
23 Alim, "Re-inventing Islam," p. 48.
24 Ibid., p. 46.
25 Hill, "'Baay Is the Spiritual Leader," p. 268.
26 Zebiri, "'Holy Foolishness,'" p. 100.
27 Zarcone, "Rereadings and Transformations," p. 112.
28 Ibid., p. 113.
29 Ibid., pp. 115, 116.
30 Sedgwick, *Western Sufism*, p. 204.
31 Ibid.

32 Dickson, *Living Sufism in North America*, p. 171.
33 Zarcone, "Rereadings and Transformations," p. 116.
34 Versluis, *American Gurus*, p. 170.
35 Dickson, *Living Sufism in North America*, p. 115.
36 Ibid.
37 Zarcone, "Rereadings and Transformations," p. 117.
38 Ernst, *The Shambhala Guide to Sufism*, p. 13.
39 Zebiri, "'Holy Foolishness," p. 113.
40 Mirdal, "Mevlana," p. 1209.
41 Ibid., pp. 1203, 1209.
42 Knabb and Welsh, "Reconsidering A. Reza Arasteh," p. 52.
43 Ibid., p. 54.
44 Dickson and Sharify-Funk, *Unveiling Sufism*, p. 27.
45 Al-Haqqani, *Heavenly* Counsel, p. 109.
46 Sedgwick, *Western Sufism*, p. 217.
47 Dickson and Sharify-Funk, *Unveiling Sufism*, p. 47.
48 Sedgwick, *Western Sufism*, p. 225.
49 Ibid., p. 232.
50 Ibid., p. 233.
51 Dickson and Sharify-Funk, *Unveiling Sufism*, p. 49.
52 Ibid.
53 Lewis, *Rumi Past and Present*, p. 518.
54 Sijapati, "Sufi Remembrance Practices," n.p.
55 Lewis, *Rumi Past and Present*, p. 519.
56 Sedgwick, *Western Sufism*, p. 219.
57 Shah, *The Sufis*, p. xx.
58 Dickson, *Living Sufism in North America*, p. 91.
59 Ibid.
60 Bram, "Spirituality Under the Shadow," p. 124.
61 Ibid., p. 131.
62 Ibid.
63 Mirdal, "Mevlana," p. 1205.
64 Ibid., p. 1204.
65 Ibid.
66 Ibid., p. 1203.
67 Schimmel, "Mystical Poetry in Islam," p. 70.
68 Bram, "Spirituality Under the Shadow," p. 132.
69 Ibid., p. 126.
70 Senay, "The Fall and Rise of the Ney," p. 418.
71 Morris, "'Look into the Book of Life,'" pp. 393, 397.
72 Bohlman, "World Musics," p. 67.
73 Lewis, *Rumi Past and Present*, p. 626.
74 Ibid., p. 627.
75 Dickson and Sharify-Funk, *Unveiling Sufism*, p. 35.

76 Ibid., p. 38.
77 www.larumicafe.com (accessed October 3, 2018).
78 Haq and Wong, "Is Spiritual Tourism a New Strategy?" p. 138.
79 Ibid., p. 144.
80 Ibid., p. 138.
81 Urry, *The Tourist Gaze*, p. 130.
82 Frow, "Tourism and the Semiotics," p. 151.
83 Maranda Pleasant, *Mantra Yoga + Health*, May/July 2017, p. 14.
84 Ibid.
85 Escher and Petermann, "Marrakesh Medina," p. 36.
86 Therrien, "French People in Morocco," p. 112.
87 Ibid., p. 115.
88 Ibid.
89 Kapchan, "The Promise of Sonic Translation," p. 472.
90 Ibid.
91 https://spiritquesttours.com/morocco/ (accessed October 3, 2018).
92 Williams, "'*Eat, Pray, Love*,'" p. 622.
93 Watson, "A Popular Indonesian Preacher," p. 777.
94 Ibid., p. 784.
95 Howell, "Muslims, the New Age," p. 489.
96 Iancu, "Spaces of Their Own," p. 445.
97 Kapchan, "The Promise of Sonic Translation," p. 476.
98 Bowman, "Ancient Avalon," p. 170.
99 Lewis, "Uncovering Modesty," p. 245.
100 Bucar, *Pious Fashion*, p. 18.
101 Crowley, "New Age Soul," p. 35.

CHAPTER 6: *LOST*, *STAR WARS*, AND MYSTICAL HOLLYWOOD

1 Pollock, *Skywalking*, p. 19.
2 Korom, "The Role of Tibet," p. 179.
3 Žižek, "The Prospects of Radical Politics," p. 254.
4 Borup, "Branding Buddha," p. 53.
5 Marmor-Lavie, Stout, and Lee, "Spirituality in Advertising," p. 2.
6 Huggan, *The Postcolonial Exotic*, p. 58.
7 Ibid., p. 59.
8 Foxen, "Supermen, Mystical Women, and Oriental Others," pp. 35–36.
9 Neuhaus, *Tibet in the Western Imagination*, p. 197.

10 Ibid.
11 Ibid.
12 Plate, "Star Wars," n.p.
13 Takacs, "Monsters, Monsters Everywhere," p. 15.
14 González, "Monsters on the Island," p. 15–16.
15 Tickell, "Footprints on the Beach," p. 42.
16 Bassham, "The Religion of The Matrix," pp. 111–112.
17 Ford, "Buddhism, Mythology, and The Matrix," p. 137.
18 Clark, "You Lost Me," pp. 327–328.
19 Jones, "Dickens on Lost," p. 71.
20 *New York Times* interview, quoted in Plate, "What the Lost Finale Is Really About," n.p.
21 Lee, "See You in Another Life, Brother," p. 141.
22 Green, *The Fear of Islam,* p. 253.
23 Twair, "ABC-TV's Hit Series, 'Lost,' Features Sayid," p. 52.
24 Newbury, "*Lost* in the Orient: Transnationalism Interrupted," p. 210.
25 Plate, "What the Lost Finale Is Really About," n.p.
26 McManus, "Protecting the Island," p. 4.
27 Jones, "Dickens on *Lost,*" p. 73.
28 Clark, "You Lost Me," p. 334.
29 Ibid.
30 Ames, "Where Have All the Good Men Gone?" p. 438.
31 McManus, "Protecting the Island," p. 13.
32 Ibid., p. 15.
33 Ibid., p. 12.
34 Gray, "We're Not in Portland Anymore," p. 223.
35 Ibid., p. 235.
36 Ibid., p. 237.
37 Mittell, "*Lost* in a Great Story," pp. 130, 131.
38 Ibid., p. 134.
39 Lee, "See You in Another Life, Brother," p. 141.
40 Fields, *How the Swans Came to the Lake,* p. 125.
41 Bainbridge, *Dynamic Secularization,* p. 138.
42 Jedichurch.org, quoted in Bainbridge, *Dynamic Secularization,* p. 138.
43 Feichtinger, "Space Buddhism," p. 29.
44 Seabrook, "Letter from Skywalker Ranch," p. 205.
45 Pollock, *Skywalking,* p. 139.
46 Ibid., p. 140.
47 Feichtinger, "Space Buddhism," p. 30.
48 Fielding, "Beyond Judeo-Christianity," p. 31.
49 Feichtinger, "Space Buddhism," p. 32.
50 Bortolin, *The Dharma of Star Wars,* p. 13.
51 Fielding, "Beyond Judeo-Christianity," p. 36.
52 Ibid.

53 Suzuki, *Zen Mind, Beginner's Mind*, p. 21.
54 Baxter, *Mythmaker: The Life and Work of George Lucas*, p. 244.
55 Malhotra, *An Introduction to Yoga Philosophy*, p. 93.
56 Ibid., p. 97.
57 Korom, "The Role of Tibet," p. 180.
58 Pollock, *Skywalking*, p. 148.
59 Malhotra, *An Introduction to Yoga Philosophy*, p. 94.
60 Feichtinger, "Space Buddhism," p. 40.
61 Pollock, *Skywalking*, p. 145.
62 Jamilla, "Defining the Jedi Order," p. 156.
63 Meyer, "Star Wars, *Star Wars*, and American Political Culture," p. 114.
64 Jamilla, "Defining the Jedi Order," p. 157.
65 Ibid.

BIBLIOGRAPHY

Akman, Kubilay. "Sufism, Spirituality and Sustainability: Islamic Mysticism through Contemporary Sociology." *Comparative Islamic Studies* 4, no. 1/2 (2010): 1–15.

Albanese, Catherine L. "The Aura of Wellness: Subtle-Energy Healing and New Age Religion." *Religion and American Culture: A Journal of Interpretation* 10, no. 1 (2000): 29–55.

Alger, William Rounseville. *The Poetry of the East.* Boston: Wittermore, Niles, and Hall, 1856.

Alim, H. Samy. "Re-inventing Islam with Unique Modern Tones: Muslim Hip Hop Artists as Verbal Mujahedin." *Souls* 8, no. 4 (2006): 45–58.

Ames, Melissa. "Where Have All the Good Men Gone? A Psychoanalytic Reading of the Absent Fathers and Damaged Dads on ABC's *Lost*." *The Journal of Popular Culture* 47, no. 3 (2014): 430–450.

Anand, Dibyesh. "Western Colonial Representations of the Other: The Case of Exotica Tibet." *New Political Science* 29, no. 1 (2007): 23–42.

Antony, Mary Grace. "On the Spot: Seeking Acceptance and Expressing Resistance through the *Bindi*." *Journal of International and Intercultural Communication* 3, no. 4 (2010): 346–368.

Apolito, Paulo. *The Internet and the Madonna: Religious Visionary Experience on the Web*. Chicago: University of Chicago Press, 2005.

Arjana, Sophia. *Muslims in the Western Imagination.* New York: Oxford University Press, 2015.

Arjana, Sophia. *Veiled Superheroes: Islam, Feminism, and Popular Culture.* Lanham: Lexington Books, 2018.

Asad, Talal. *Genealogies of Religion: Discipline and Reasons of Power in Christianity and Islam.* Baltimore: John Hopkins University Press, 1993.

Baer, Hans A. "The Work of Andrew Weil and Deepak Chopra: Two Holistic Health/New Age Gurus: A Critique of the Holistic Health/New Age Movements." *Medical Anthropology Quarterly* 17, no. 2 (2003): 233–250.

Bainbridge, William Sims. *Dynamic Secularization: Information Technology and the Tension Between Religion and Science.* New York: Springer, 2017.

Baker, Deborah. *A Blue Hand: The Beats in India.* New York: Penguin Press, 2008.

Baker, Joseph O'Brian and Buster Smith. "None Too Simple: Examining Issues of Religious Nonbelief and Nonbelonging in the United States." *Journal for the Scientific Study of Religion* 48, no. 4 (2009): 719–733.

Barker, Chris. "Men, Buddhism and the Discontents of Western Modernity." *Journal of Men, Masculinities and Spirituality* 2, no. 1 (2008): 28–46.

Bassham, Gregory. "The Religion of *The Matrix* and the Problems of Pluralism." In *The Matrix and Philosophy: Welcome to the Desert of the Real,* edited by William Irwin, 111–125. Chicago: Open Court, 2002.

Baudrillard, Jean. *Seduction: Cultural Text.* New York: Palgrave Macmillan, 1991.

Bauman, Zygmunt. *Liquid Modernity.* Cambridge: Polity, 2000.

Bauman, Zygmunt and Mark Haugaard. "Liquid Modernity and Power: A Dialogue with Zygmunt Bauman." *Journal of Power* 1, no. 2 (2008): 111–130.

Baxter, John. *Mythmaker: The Life and Work of George Lucas.* New York: Avon, 1999.

Bell, Sandra. "'Crazy Wisdom,' Charisma, and the Transmission of Buddhism in the United States." *Nova Religio* 2, no. 1 (1998): 55–75.

Bell, Sandra. "Scandals in Emerging Western Buddhism." In *Westward Dharma: Buddhism Beyond Asia,* edited by Charles S. Prebish and Martin Baumann, 230–242. Berkeley: University of California Press, 2002.

Béres, Laura. "A Thin Place: Narratives of Space and Place, Celtic Spirituality and Meaning." *Journal of Religion & Spirituality in Social Work: Social Thought* 31 (2012): 394–413.

Berger, Peter. *The Many Altars of Modernity: Toward a Paradigm for Religion in a Pluralist Age.* Boston: Walter de Gruyter/Mouton, 2016.

Bock, Sheila and Katherine Borland. "Exotic Identities: Dance, Difference, and Self-Fashioning." *Journal of Folklore Research* 48, no. 1 (2011): 1–36.

BIBLIOGRAPHY

Bohlman, Philip V. "World Musics and World Religions: *Whose World?*" In *Enchanting Powers: Music in the World's Religions*, edited by Lawrence Sullivan, 61–90. Cambridge: Harvard University Press, 1997.

Bortolin, Matthew. *The Dharma of Star Wars*. Boston: Wisdom, 2005.

Borup, Jørn. "Branding Buddha—Mediatized and Commodified Buddhism as Cultural Narrative." *Journal of Global Buddhism* 17 (2016): 41–55.

Bowditch, Rachel. *On the Edge of Utopia: Performance and Ritual at Burning Man*. New York: Seagull Books, 2010.

Bowman, Marion. "Ancient Avalon, New Jerusalem, Heart Chakra of Planet Earth: The Local and the Global in Glastonbury." *Numen* 52, no. 2 (2005): 157–190.

Bowman, Marion. "Going with the Flow: Contemporary Pilgrimage in Glastonbury." In *Shrines and Pilgrimage in the Modern World: New Itineraries into the Sacred*, edited by Peter Jan Margry, 241–280. Amsterdam: Amsterdam University Press, 2008.

Bowman, Marion, and Milton Keynes. "Arthur and Bridget in Avalon: Celtic Myth, Vernacular Religion and Contemporary Spirituality in Glastonbury." *Fabula* 48, nos. 1/2 (2007): 16–32.

Bran, Chen. "Spirituality Under the Shadow of the Conflict." *Israel Studies Review* 29, no. 2 (2014): 118–139.

Brennan, Barbara Ann. *Light Emerging: The Journey of Personal Healing*. New York: Bantam, 1993.

Brown, Wendy. *Regulating Aversion: Tolerance in the Age of Identity and Empire*. Princeton: Princeton University Press, 2006.

Bucar, Liz. *Pious Fashion: How Muslim Women Dress*. Cambridge: Harvard University Press, 2017.

Byrne, Denis. "Gateway and Garden: A Kind of Tourism in Bali." In *Heritage and Tourism: Place, Encounter, Engagement*, edited by Russell Staiff, Robyn Bushell, and Steve Watson, 26–44. New York: Routledge, 2013.

Candler, Edmund. *Unveiling of Lhasa*. London: Edward Arnold, 1905.

Caplan, Mariana. "The Fate and Failings of Contemporary Spirituality." *Revision Magazine* 5, no. 1 (2004): 26–33.

Carrette, Jeremy and Richard King. *Selling Spirituality: The Silent Takeover of Religion*. New York: Routledge, 1997.

Chidester, David. *Savage Systems: Colonialism and Comparative Religion in Southern Africa*. Charlottesville: University of Virginia Press, 1996.

Chidester, David. *Authentic Fakes: Religion and American Popular Culture*. Berkeley: University of California Press, 2005.

Clark, Lynn Schofield. "You Lost Me: Mystery, Fandom, and Religion in ABC's *Lost*." In *Small Screen, Big Picture: Television and Lived Religion*, edited by Diane Winston, 319–341. Waco: Baylor University Press, 2009.

Coats, Curtis. "Sedona, Arizona: New Age Pilgrim-Tourist Destination." *Crosscurrents* 59, no. 3 (2009): 383–389.

Cohen, Erik. "Nomads from Affluence: Notes on the Phenomenon of Drifter-Tourism." *International Journal of Comparative Sociology* 14, no. 1/2 (1973): 89–103.

Crow, Karim Douglas. "Consuming Islam: Branding 'Wholesome' as Lifestyle Fetish." *Islamic Sciences* 13, no. 1 (2015): 3–26.

Crowley, Karlyn. "New Age Soul: The Gendered Translation of New Age Spirituality on The Oprah Winfrey Show." In *Stories of Oprah: The Oprahfication of America Culture*, edited by Trystan T. Cotton and Kimberly Springer, 33–47. Jackson: University Press of Mississippi, 2010.

Dawes, Simon. "The Role of the Intellectual in Liquid Modernity: An Interview with Zygmunt Bauman." *Theory, Culture & Society* 28, no. 3 (2011): 130–148.

DeConick, April D. *The Gnostic New Age: How A Countercultural Spirituality Revolutionalized Religion from Antiquity to Today*. New York: Columbia University Press, 2016.

DeLaney, Brigid. "Why This Wellness Writer Names Bali as Her Favorite Holistic Destination." Departures Newsletter. http://departures.com/travel/hotels/bali-wellness-retreats/ (accessed 9/18/18)

Derrida, Jacques. "Signature, Event, Context." *Margins of Philosophy*, translated by A. Bass, 307–330. Chicago: University of Chicago Press, 1982.

Dickson, William Rory. *Living Sufism in North America: Between Tradition and Transformation*. Albany: State University of New York Press, 2015.

Dickson, William Rory and Meena Sharify-Funk. *Unveiling Sufism: From Manhattan to Mecca*. Bristol, CT: Equinox Publishing, 2017.

Drury, Nevill. *The New Age: Searching for the Spiritual Self*. London: Thames & Hudson, 2004.

Durham, Meenakshi Gigi. "Displaced Persons: Symbols of South Asian Femininity and the Returned Gaze in U.S. Media Culture." *Communication Theory* 11, no. 2 (2001): 201–217.

Eberhardt, Maeve and Kara Freeman. "'First Things First, I'm the Realist': Linguistic Appropriation, White Privilege, and the Hip-Hop Persona of Iggy Azalea." *Journal of Sociolinguistics* 19, no. 3 (2015): 303–327.

Eck, Diana L. "'*Tirthas*': 'Crossings' in Sacred Geography." *History of Religions* 20, no. 4 (1981): 323–344.

Einstein, Mara. *Brands of Faith: Marketing Religion in a Commercial Age*. New York: Routledge, 2008.

Eldershaw, Lynn P. "Collective Identity and the Postcharismatic Fate of Shambhala International." *Novo Religio: The Journal of Alternative and Emergent Religions* 10, no. 4 (2007): 72–102.

BIBLIOGRAPHY

El-Zein, Amira. "Spiritual Consumption in the United States: The Rumi Phenomenon." *Islam and Christian–Muslim Relations* 11, no. 1 (2000): 71–85.

Ernst, Carl W. "The Islamicization of Yoga in the 'Amrtakunda' Translations." *Journal of the Royal Asiatic Society* 13, no. 2 (2003): 199–226.

Ernst, Carl. "Situating Sufism and Yoga." *Journal of the Royal Asiatic Society* 15, no. 1(2005): 15–43.

Ernst, Carl. "Ideological and Technological Transformations of Contemporary Sufism." In *Muslim Networks: Medium, Metaphor, and Method*, edited by Miriam Cooke and Bruce Lawrence, 224–246. Chapel Hill: University of North Carolina Press, 2005.

Ernst, Carl. *The Shambhala Guide to Sufism*. Boston: Shambhala Publications, 1997.

Ertimur, Burçak and Gokcen Coskuner-Balli. "Navigating the Institutional Logics of Markets: Implications for Strategic Brand Management." *Journal of Marketing* 79 (2015): 40–61.

Escher, Anton and Sandra Petermann. "Marrakesh Medina: Neocolonial Paradise of Lifestyle Migrants?" In *Contested Spiritualities, Lifestyle Migration and Residential Tourism*, edited by Michael Janoschka and Heiko Hass, 29–46. New York: Routledge, 2014.

Fabian, Johannes. *Time and the Other: How Anthropology Makes Its Object*. New York: Columbia University Press, 2002.

Fara, Patricia. "Portrait of a Nation." *New Statesman*, October 6, 2003: 38–39.

Farmer, Jared. "Americanasana." *Reviews in American History* 40, no. 1 (2012): 145–158.

Faubion, James. "From the Ethical to the Thematical (and Back): Groundwork for an Anthropology of Ethics." In *Ordinary Ethics: Anthropology, Language, and Action*, edited by Michael Lambek, 84–101. New York: Fordham University Press, 2010.

Featherstone, Mike. "The Body in Consumer Culture." In *The Body: Social Process and Cultural Theory*, edited by Mike Featherstone, Mike Hepworth, and Bryan S. Turner, 170–196. London: Sage, 1991.

Feichtinger, Christian. "Space Buddhism: The Adoption of Buddhist Motifs in *Star Wars*." *Contemporary Buddhism* 15, no. 1 (2014): 28–43.

Fielding, Julian. "Beyond Judeo-Christianity: *Star Wars* and the Great Eastern Religions." In *Sex, Politics, and Religion in Star Wars: An Anthology*, edited by Douglas Brode and Leah Deyneka, 25–46. Lanham: Scarecrow Press, 2012.

Fields, Rick. *How the Swans Came to the Lake: A Narrative History of Buddhism in America*. Boston: Shambhala Publications, 1992.

Foley, Sean. "The Naqshbandiyya-Khalidiyya, Islamic Sainthood, and Religion in Modern Times." *Journal of World History* 19, no. 4 (2008): 521–545.

Ford, Arthur L. "The Rose-Gardens of the World: Near East Imagery in the Poetry of Walt Whitman." *Walt Whitman Quarterly Review* 5 (1987): 12–20.

Ford, James L. "Buddhism, Mythology, and *The Matrix*." In *Taking the Red Pill: Science, Philosophy, and Religion in The Matrix*, edited by Glenn Yeffeth, 125–144. Dallas: Benbella Books, 2003.

Foucault, Michel. (Translated by Jay Miskowiec). "Of Other Spaces." *Diacritics* 16, no. 1 (1986): 22–27.

Foucault, Michel. *Technologies of the Self: A Seminar with Michel Foucault*. Edited by Luther H. Martin, Huck Gutman, and Patrick H. Hutton. Amherst: University of Massachusetts Press, 1988.

Fox, Richard. "Why Media Matter: Critical Reflections on Religion and the Recent History of 'the Balinese.'" *History of Religions* 49, no. 4 (2010): 354–392.

Foxen, Anya P. "Supermen, Mystical Women, and Oriental Others: Dynamics of Race and Gender in Pop-Cultural Yogis and the Universal Superhuman." In *The Assimilation of Yogic Religions through Pop Culture*, edited by Paul G. Hackett, 35–58. Lanham: Lexington Books, 2017.

Foxen, Anya P. *Biography of a Yogi: Paramahansa Yogananda & the Origins of Modern Yoga*. New York: Oxford University Press, 2017.

Friedlander, Shems. *The Whirling Dervishes: Being an Account of the Sufi Order Known as the Mevlevis and Its Founder, the Poet and Mystic Jalau'uddin Rumi*. Albany: SUNY Press, 1992.

Frow, John. "Tourism and the Semiotics of Nostalgia." *October* 57 (1991): 123–151.

Gauthier, François. "Intimate Circles and Mass Meetings. The Social Forms of Event-Structured Religion in the Era of Globalized Markets and Hyper-Mediatization." *Social Compass* 61 no. 2 (2014): 261–271.

Geary, Patrick. *Furta Sacra: Thefts of Relics in the Central Middle Ages*. Princeton: Princeton University Press, 1990.

Geczy, Adam. *Fashion and Orientalism: Dress, Textiles and Culture from the 17th to the 21st Century*. New York: Bloomsbury, 2013.

Geertz, Clifford. *The Interpretation of Cultures: Selected Essays*. New York: Basic Books, 1973.

Gelberg, Steven J. "The Call of the Lotus-Eyed Lord: The Fate of Krishna-Consciousness in the West." In *When Prophets Die: The Postcharismatic Fate of New Religious Movements*, edited by Timothy Miller, 149–164. Albany, NY: SUNY Press, 1991.

Gilbert, Elizabeth. *Eat, Pray, Love*. New York: Penguin, 2006.

González, Antonio Ballesteros. "Monsters on the Island: Caliban's and Prospero's Hideous Progeny." *Atlantis* 21 no. 1 (1997): 15–20.

Govers, Robert and Frank Go. *Place Branding: Glocal, Virtual, and Physical Identities, Constructed, Imagined and Experienced*. New York: Palgrave Macmillan, 2009.

Graci, Sonya and Rachel Dodds. *Sustainable Tourism in Island Destinations*. Washington, D.C.: Earthscan, 2010.

Graeburn, Nelson, editor. *Ethnic and Tourist Arts: Cultural Expressions from the Fourth World*. Berkeley: University of California Press, 1977.

Gray, Jonathon. "We're Not in Portland Anymore: *Lost* and Its International Others." In *Reading Lost: Perspectives on a Hit Television Show*, edited by Roberta Pearson, 221–239. New York: I.B. Tauris, 2009.

Green, Todd H. *The Fear of Islam: An Introduction to Islamophobia in the West*. Minneapolis: Fortress Press, 2015.

Gunderson, Agnete. "Starting Over: Searching for the Good Life: An Ethnographic Study of Western Lifestyle Migration to Ubud, Bali." *New Zealand Sociology* 32, no. 2 (2017): 157–171.

Guy, N. K. *Art of Burning Man*. Cologne: Taschen, 2015.

Hansen, Peter H. "Tibetan Horizon: Tibet and the Cinema in the Early Twentieth Century." In *Imagining Tibet: Perceptions, Projections, and Fantasies*, edited by Thierry Dodin and Heinz Räther, 91–110. Somerville, MA: Wisdom Publications, 2001.

Harris, Daniel. "Celebrity Spirituality." *Salmagundi* 160 & 161 (2009): 98–108.

Haq, Farooq and Ho Yin Wong. "Is Spiritual Tourism a New Strategy for Marketing Islam?" *Journal of Islamic Marketing* 1, no. 2 (2010): 136–148.

Al-Haqqani, Shaykh Nazim Adil. *Heavenly Counsel: Journey from Darkness into Light*. Fenton: Institute for Spiritual & Cultural Advancement, 2013.

Hedstrom, Matthew S. "The Commodification of William James: The Book Business and the Rise of Liberal Spirituality in the Twentieth-Century United States." In *Religion and the Marketplace in the United States*, edited by Jan Stievermann, Philip Goff, and Detlef Junker, 125–144. New York: Oxford University Press, 2014.

Heelas, Paul. *Spiritualities of Life: New Age Romanticism and Consumptive Capitalism*. Malden, MA: Wiley-Blackwell, 2008.

Hermansen, Marcia. "Muslims in Performative Mode: A Reflection on Muslim-Christian Dialogue." *The Muslim World* 94, no. 3 (2004): 387–396.

Hill, Joseph. "'Baay Is the Spiritual Leader of the Rappers': Performing Islamic Reasoning in Senegalese Sufi Hip-Hop." *Contemporary Islam* 10 (2016): 267–287.

Hill, Michael. "Inca of the Blood, Inca of the Soul: Embodiment, Emotion, and Racialization in the Peruvian Mystical Tourist Industry." *Journal of the American Academy of Religion* 76, no. 2 (2008): 251–279.

Hodder, Jacqueline. "Spirituality and Well-Being: 'New Age' and 'Evangelical' Spiritual Expressions among Young People and Their Implications for Well-Being." *International Journal of Children's Spirituality* 14, no. 3 (2009): 197–212.

Hornborg, Anne-Christine. "Designing Rites to Re-enchant Secularized Society: New Varieties of Spiritualized Therapy in Contemporary Sweden." *Journal of Religion and Health* 1, no. 2 (2012): 402–418.

Horsley, Richard A. "Religion and Other Products of Empire." *Journal of the American Academy of Religion* 71, no. 1 (2003): 13–44.

Howell, Julia D. "Muslims, the New Age and Marginal Religions in Indonesia: Changing Meanings of Religious Pluralism." *Social Compass* 52, no. 4 (2005): 473–493.

Huang, Liyuan and Honggang Xu. "Therapeutic Landscapes and Longevity: Wellness Tourism in Bama." *Social Science & Medicine* 197 (2018): 24–32.

Huggan, Graham. *The Postcolonial Exotic: Marketing the Margin*. New York: Routledge, 2001.

Hutnyk, John. "Magical Mystery Tourism." In *Travel Worlds: Journeys in Contemporary Cultural Politics*, edited by Raminder Kaur and John Hutnyk, 94–119. London: Zed, 1999.

Hyland, Terry. "McDonaldizing Spirituality: Mindfulness, Education, and Consumerism." *Journal of Transformative Education* 15, no. 4 (2017): 334–356.

Iancu, Anca-Luminata. "Spaces of Their Own: Emotional and Spiritual Quests in *Under the Tuscan Sun* and *Eat, Pray, Love*." *Journal of Research in Gender Studies* 4, no. 1 (2014): 439–452.

Irizarry, Joshua A. "Putting a Price on Zen: The Business of Redefining Religion for Global Consumption." *Journal of Global Relations* 16, no. 16 (2015): 51–69.

Islam, Nazrul. "New Age Orientalism: Ayurvedic 'Wellness and Spa Culture.'" *Health Sociology Review* 21, no. 2 (2012): 220–231.

Iwamura, Jane Naomi. *Virtual Orientalism: Asian Religions and American Popular Culture*. New York: Oxford University Press, 2011.

Jafari, Aliakbar and Ahmet Süerdrm. "An Analysis of Material Consumption Culture in the Muslim World." *Marketing Theory* 12, no. 1 (2012): 61–79.

Jain, Andrea. "Who Is to Say Modern Yoga Practitioners Have It All Wrong? On Hindu Origins and Yogaphobia." *Journal of the American Academy of Religion* 82, no. 2 (2014): 427–471.

Jain, Andrea. *Selling Yoga: From Counterculture to Pop Culture.* New York: Oxford University Press, 2015.

Jamilla, Nick. "Defining the Jedi Order: *Star Wars'* Narrative and the Real World." In *Sex, Politics, and Religion in Star Wars: An Anthology*, edited by Douglas Brode and Leah Deyneka, 147–163. Lanham: Scarecrow Press, 2012.

Janes, Craig. "Buddhism, Science, and Market: The Globalisation of Tibetan Medicine." *Anthropology & Medicine* 9, no. 3 (2002): 267–289.

Johnson, Andrew Alan. "Authenticity, Tourism, and Self-Discovery in Thailand: Self-Creation and the Discerning Gaze of Trekkers and Old Hands." *Sojourn: Journal of Social Issues in Southeast Asia* 22, no. 2 (2007): 153–178.

Jones, Steven E. "Dickens on *Lost*: Text, Paratext, Fan-based Media." *The Wordsworth Circle* 38, no. 1/2 (2007): 71–77.

Joshi, K. S. "On the Meaning of Yoga." *Philosophy East & West* 15, no. 1 (1965): 53–64.

Kabbani, Muhammad Hisham. *Classical Islam and the Naqshbandi Sufi Tradition.* Washington, D.C.: The Islamic Supreme Council of America, 2004.

Kapchan, Deborah A. "The Promise of Sonic Translation: Performing the Festive Sacred in Morocco." *American Anthropologist* 110, no. 4 (2008): 467–483.

Kaschewsky, Rudolf. "The Image of Tibet in the West before the Nineteenth Century." In *Imagining Tibet: Perceptions, Projections, and Fantasies*, edited by Thierry Dodin and Heinz Räther, 3–20. Somerville, MA: Wisdom Publications, 2001.

Khabeer, Su'ad Abdul. "Rep That Islam: The Rhyme and Reason of American Hip Hop." *The Muslim World* 97 (2007): 125–141.

King, Richard. "Orientalism and the Modern Myth of 'Hinduism.'" *Numen* 46, no. 2 (1999): 146–185.

King, Richard. *Orientalism and Religion: Postcolonial theory, India, and 'the mystic East.'* New York: Routledge, 1999.

Kitiarsa, Pattana. "Beyond Syncretism: Hybridization of Popular Religion in Contemporary Thailand." *Journal of Southeast Asian Studies* 36, no. 3 (2005): 461–487.

Knabb, Joshua J. and Robert K. Welsh. "Reconsidering A. Reza Arasteh: Sufism and Psychotherapy." *The Journal of Transpersonal Psychology* 41, no. 41 (2009): 44–60.

Knudson, Sarah. "The Purchase of Enlightenment." *Contexts* 10, no. 2 (2011): 66–67.

Kopano, Baruti N. "Soul Thieves: White America and the Appropriation of Hip Hop and Black Culture." In *Soul Thieves: The Appropriation and Misrepresentation of African American Popular Culture*, edited by Tamara Lizette Brown and Baruti N. Kopano, 1–14. New York: Palgrave Macmillan, 2014.

Korom, Frank J. "The Role of Tibet in the New Age Movement." In *Imagining Tibet: Perceptions, Projections, and Fantasies*, edited by Thierry Dodin and Heinz Räther, 167–182. Somerville, MA: Wisdom Publications, 2001.

Kraptchuk, Ted and David Eisenberg. "Varieties of Healing, II: A Taxonomy of Unconventional Healing Practices." *Annals of Internal Medicine* 135: 196–204.

Kvaerne, Per. "Tibet Images among Researchers on Tibet." In *Imagining Tibet: Perceptions, Projections, and Fantasies*, edited by Thierry Dodin and Heinz Räther, 47–63. Somerville, MA: Wisdom Publications, 2001.

LadyBee (Christine Kristen). "The Outsider Art of Burning Man." *Leonardo* 36, no. 5 (2003): 343–348.

Larasati, Diyah. "Eat, Pray, Love Mimic: Female Citizenship and Otherness." *South Asian Popular Culture* 8, no. 1 (2010): 89–95.

Lee, Joohyun and Hong-bumm Kim. "Success Factors of Health Tourism: Cases of Asian Tourism Cities." *International Journal of Tourism Cities* 1, no. 3 (2015): 216–233.

Lee, Sander. "See You In Another Life, Brother: Bad Faith and Authenticity in Three *Lost* Souls." In *The Ultimate Lost and Philosophy: Think Together, Die Alone*, edited by Sharon Kaye, 120–141. Hoboken: Wiley, 2011.

Lewis, Franklin D. *Rumi Past and Present, East and West: The Life, Teachings and Poetry of Jalâl al-Din Rumi*. London: Oneworld, 2008.

Lewis, Reina. "Uncovering Modesty: Dejabis and Dewigies Expanding the Parameters of the Modest Fashion Blogosphere." *Fashion Theory* 19, no. 2 (2015): 243–270.

Lipton, George A. "Secular Sufism: Neoliberalism, Ethnoracism, and the Reformation of the Muslim Other." *The Muslim World* 101, no. 3 (2011): 427–440.

Llamas, Rosa and Russell Belk. "Shangri-La: Messing with a Myth." *Journal of Macromarketing* 31, no. 3 (2011): 257–275.

Lofton, Kathryn. *Oprah: The Gospel of an Icon*. Berkeley: University of California Press, 2011.

Logan, Dana W. "The Lean Closet: Asceticism in Postindustrial Consumer Culture." *Journal of the American Academy of Religion* 85, no. 3 (2–17): 600–628.

Lopez, Donald S. *Prisoners of Shangri-La: Tibetan Buddhism and the West*. Chicago: University of Chicago Press, 1998.

Lopez, Donald S. "The Image of Tibet of the Great Mystifiers." In *Imagining Tibet: Perceptions, Projections, and Fantasies*, edited by Thierry Dodin and Heinz Räther, 183–200. Somerville, MA: Wisdom Publications, 2001.

Low, Gail Ching-Liang, "White Skin, Black Masks: The Pleasures and Politics of Imperialism." *New Formations* 9 (1989): 83–103.

Low, Gail Ching-Liang. *White Skins/Black Masks: Representation and Colonialism*. New York: Routledge, 1996.

Lucia, Amanda. "Innovative Gurus: Tradition and Change in Contemporary Hinduism." *International Journal of Hindu Studies* 18, no. 2 (2014): 221–263.

MacCannell, Dean. *Empty Meeting Grounds: The Tourist Papers*. New York: Routledge, 1992.

Maghbouleh, Neda. *The Limits of Whiteness: Iranian Americans and the Everyday Politics of Race*. Stanford: Stanford University Press, 2017.

Malhotra, Ashok Kumar. *Instant Nirvana: Americanization of Mysticism and Meditation*. Oneonta: Oneonta Philosophy Series, 1999.

Malhotra, Ashok Kumar. *An Introduction to Yoga Philosophy: An Annotated Translation of the Yoga Sutras*. Aldershot, Hampshire: Ashgate, 2001.

Mann, Gurinder Singh, Paul David Numrich, and Raymond B. Williams. *Buddhists, Hindus, and Sikhs in America: A Short History*. New York: Oxford University Press, 2008.

Mannur, Anita and Pia K. Sahni. "'What Can Brown Do for You?' Indo Chic and the Fashionability of South Asian Inspired Styles." *South Asian Popular Culture* 9, no. 2 (2011): 177–190.

Marmor-Lavie, Galit, Patricia A. Stout, and Wei-Na Lee. "Spirituality in Advertising: A New Theoretical Approach." *Journal of Media and Religion* 8 (2009): 1–23.

Martin, Richard and Harold Kota. *Orientalism: Visions of the East in Western Dress* (Exhibition Catalogue). New York: The Metropolitan Museum of Art, 1994.

Maxwell, Thomas P. "Considering Spirituality: Integral Spirituality, Deep Science, and Ecological Awareness." *Zygon* 38, no. 2 (2003): 257–276.

Mbembe, Achille. *On the Postcolony*. Berkeley: University of California Press, 2001.

McClintock, Anne. *Imperial Leather: Race, Gender, and Sexuality in the Colonial Contest*. New York: Routledge, 1995.

McDaniel, Justin Thomas. "Liberation Materiality: Thai Buddhist Amulets and the Benefits of Selling Sacred Stuff." *Material Religion* 11, no. 3 (2016): 401–403.

McKay, Alex C. "'Truth,' Perception, and Politics: The British Construction of an Image of Tibet." In *Imagining Tibet: Perceptions, Projections, and*

Fantasies, edited by Thierry Dodin and Heinz Räther, 67–89. Somerville, MA: Wisdom Publications, 2001.

McKenzie, John S. "Right Business, Right Consumption: Controlling Commodification and Guiding Consumption in a Tibetan Buddhist Organization in Scotland." *Social Compass* 62, no. 4 (2015): 598–614.

McMahan, David L. *The Making of Buddhist Modernism*. New York: Oxford University Press, 2008.

McManus, Elizabeth Berkebile. "Protecting the Island: Narrative Continuance in *Lost*." *Journal of the Fantastic in the Arts* 22, no. 1 (2011): 4–23.

Meyer, David S. "Star Wars, *Star Wars*, and American Political Culture." *Journal of Popular Culture* 26, no. 2 (1992): 99–115.

Mickey, Ethel L. "'*Eat, Pray, Love*' Bullshit: Women's Empowerment through Wellness at an Elite Professional Conference." *Journal of Contemporary Ethnography* (2018): 1–2.

Midal, Fabrice. *Chögyam Trungpa: His Life and Vision*. Boston: Shambhala, 2012.

Miller, Bruce. *Rumi Comes to America: How the Poet of Mystical Love Arrived on our Shores*. Decatur: Miller eMedia, 2017.

Mirdal, Gretty M. "Mevlana Jalāl-ad-Dīn Rumi and Mindfulness." *Journal of Religion and Health* 51, no. 4 (2012): 1202–1215.

Mitra, Semontee. "Merchandizing the Sacred: Commodifying Hindu Religion, Gods/Goddesses, and Festivals in the United States." *Journal of Media and Religion* 15, no. 2 (2016): 113–121.

Mittell, Jason. "*Lost* in a Great Story: Evaluation in Narrative Television (and Television Studies)." In *Reading Lost: Perspectives on a Hit Television Show*, edited by Roberta Pearson, 119–138. New York: I.B. Tauris, 2009.

Møllgaard, Eske. "Slavoj Zizek's Critique of Western Buddhism." *Contemporary Buddhism* 9, no. 2 (2008): 167–180.

Morgan, David. *Visual Piety: A History and Theory of Popular Religious Images*. Berkeley: University of California Press, 1998.

Morris, Carl. "'Look into the Book of Life': Muslim Musicians, Sufism and Postmodern Spirituality in Britain." *Social Compass* 63, no. 3 (2016): 389–404.

Moors, Annelies. "NiqaBitch and Princess Hijab: Niqab Activism, Satire and Street Art." *Feminist Review* 98 (2011): 128–135.

Naraindas, Harish. "Of Relics, Body Parts, and Laser Beams: The German Heilpraktiker and His Ayurvedic Spa." *Anthropology & Medicine* 18, no. 1 (2011): 67–86.

Neuhaus, Tom. *Tibet in the Western Imagination*. New York: Palgrave Macmillan, 2002.

Newbury, Michael. "*Lost* in the Orient: Transnationalism Interrupted." In *Reading Lost: Perspectives on a Hit Television Show*, edited by Roberta Pearson, 201–220. New York: I.B. Tauris, 2009.

Osto, Douglas. *Altered States: Buddhism and Psychedelic Spirituality in America.* New York: Columbia University Press, 2016.

Ourvan, Jeff. *The Star Spangled Buddhist: Zen, Tibetan, and Soka Gakkai Buddhism and the Quest for Enlightenment in America.* New York: Skyhorse Publishing, 2003.

Palmer, Edward Henry. *Oriental Mysticism: A Treatise on Sufistic and Unitarian Theosophy of the Persians.* London: Nord Press, 1969.

Payne, Richard. "In Defense of Ritual." *Buddhadharma* 16, no. 3 (2018): 76–83.

Pechilis, Karen. "Understanding Modern Gurus." *International Journal of Hindu Studies* 21 (2017): 99–106.

Pedersen, Paul. "Tibet, Theosophy, and the Pyschologization of Buddhism." In *Imagining Tibet: Perceptions, Projections, and Fantasies*, edited by Thierry Dodin and Heinz Räther, 151–166. Somerville, MA: Wisdom Publications, 2001.

Pfadenhauer, Michaela. "In-Between Spaces, Pluralism and Hybridity as Elements of a New Paradigm for Religion in the Modern Age." *Human Studies* 39 (2016): 147–159.

Pike, Sarah M. "Selling Infinite Selves: Youth Culture and Contemporary Festivals." In *Religion and the Marketplace in the United States*, edited by Jan Stievermann, Philip Goff, and Detlef Junker, 191–214. New York: Oxford University Press, 2014.

Plate, S. Brent Rodriguez. "Star Wars." *Frequencies.* January 9, 2012. http://frequencies.ssrc.org/2012/01/09/star-wars/ (accessed 1/22/20).

Plate, S. Brent Rodriguez. "What the *Lost* Finale Is Really About." *Religion Dispatches*: May 22, 2010.

Pleasant, Maranda. "Marrakech, Morocco." *Mantra Yoga + Health*, May/July 2017.

Pollock, Dale. *Skywalking: The Life and Films of George Lucas.* New York: Da Capo Press, 1999.

Powers, John. *Introduction to Tibetan Buddhism.* New York: Snow Lion Publications, 1995.

Rakow, Katja. "Religious Branding and the Quest to Meet Consumer Needs: Joel Osteen's 'Message of Hope.'" In *Religion and the Marketplace in the United States*, edited by Jan Stievermann, Philip Goff, and Detlef Junker, 215–239. New York: Oxford University Press, 2014.

Rasch, William. "Enlightenment as Religion." *New German Critique* 108 (2009): 109–131.

Rawlinson, Andrew. "A History of Western Sufism." *DISKUS* 1, no. 1 (1993).

Richardson, Hugh E. *Tibet and Its History*. London: Oxford University Press, 1961.

Rocha, Cristina. *Zen in Brazil: The Quest for Cosmopolitan Modernity*. Honolulu: University of Hawaii Press, 2006.

Roberts, Allen F. and Mary Nooter Roberts. "A Saint in the City: Sufi Arts of Urban Senegal." *African Arts* 35, no. 4 (2002): 52–73, 93–96.

Roof, Wade Clark. *Spiritual Marketplace: Baby Boomers and the Remaking of American Religion*. Princeton: Princeton University Press, 2001.

Root, Deborah. *Cannibal Culture: Art, Appropriation, and the Commodification of Difference*. Boulder: Westview Press, 1996.

Ruthven, Malise. *The Divine Supermarket: Shopping for God in America*. New York: William Morrow and Company, 1989.

Said, Edward. *Orientalism*. New York: Vintage, 1979.

St. John, Graham. "Civilised Tribalism: Burning Man, Event-Tribes and Maker Culture." *Cultural Sociology* 12, no. 1 (2018): 3–21.

Sanders, Joshunda and Ana Mouyis. "Eat, Pray, Spend: Priv-Lit and the New, Enlightened American Dream." Bitchmagazine.com. *Bitch Magazine* October 22, 2010: n.p.

Schedneck, Brooke. *Thailand's International Meditation Centers: Tourism and the Global Commodification of Religious Practices*. New York: Routledge, 2015.

Schimmel, Annemarie. "Mystical Poetry in Islam: The Case of Maulana Jalaladdin Rumi." *Religion & Literature* 20, no. a (1988): 67–80.

Schmidt, Leigh Eric. *Consumer Rites: The Buying and Selling of American Holidays*. Princeton: Princeton University Press, 1995.

Schopen, Gregory. "Archaeology and Protestant Presuppositions in the Study of Buddhism." *History of Religions* 31, no. 1 (1991): 1–23.

Seabrook, John. "Letter from Skywalker Ranch: Why Is the Force Still with Us?" In *George Lucas: Interviews*, edited by Sally Kline, 190–215. Jackson: University Press of Mississippi, 1999.

Sedgwick, Mark. *Western Sufism: From the Abbasids to the New Age*. New York: Oxford University Press, 2017.

Sellers-Young, Barbara. *Belly Dance, Pilgrimage, and Identity*. New York: Palgrave Macmillan, 2016.

Senay, Banu. "The Fall and Rise of the *Ney*: From the Sufi Lodge to the World Stage." *Ethnomusicology Forum* 23, no. 3 (2014); 405–424.

Shah, Idries. *The Sufis*. New York: Doubleday, 1964.

Sherry, John F. and Robert V. Kozinets. "Comedy of the Commons: Nomadic Spirituality and the Burning Man Festival." *Consumer Culture Theory* 11 (2007): 119–147.

Shirazi, Faegheh. *Brand Islam: The Marketing and Commodification of Piety*. Austin: University of Texas Press, 2016.

Shippee, Steven R. "Trungpa's Barbarians and Merton's Titan: Resuming a Dialogue on Spiritual Egotism." *Buddhist-Christian Studies* 32 (2012): 109–125.

Shohat, Ella and Robert Stam. *Unthinking Eurocentrism: Multiculturalism and the Media*. New York: Routledge, 1994.

Sijapati, Megan Adamson. "Sufi Remembrance in the Meditation Marketplace of a Mobile App." In *Anthropological Perspectives on the Religious Uses of Mobile Apps*, edited by Jacqueline H. Fewkes, n.p. London: Palgrave MacMillan, 2019.

Silva, Sónia. "Art and Fetish in the Anthropology Museum." *Material Religion* 13, no. 1 (2017): 77–96.

Silva-Jelly, Natasha. "Oprah For President?" (Interview) *Harper's Bazaar*, March 2018.

Sinha, Vineeta. *Religion and Commodification: 'Merchandizing' Diasporic Hinduism*. New York: Rutgers, 2011.

Skegaard, Søren and Giana M. Eckhardt. "Glocal Yoga: Re-appropriation in the Indian Consumptionscape." *Marketing Theory* 12, no. 1 (2012): 45–60.

Smith, Jonathon Z. *Imagining Religion: From Babylon to Jamestown*. Chicago: University of Chicago Press, 1982.

Smith, Jonathon Z. *Drudgery Divine: On the Comparison of Early Christianities and the Religions of Late Antiquity*. Chicago: University of Chicago Press, 1990.

Smith, Jonathon Z. *Map Is Not Territory*. Chicago: University of Chicago Press, 1993.

Srinivas, Smriti. "Highways for Healing: Contemporaneous 'Temples' and Religious Movements in an Indian City." *Journal of the American Academy of Religion* 86, no. 2 (2018); 473–525.

Srivastava, Vinay Kumar. "Religion and Development: Understanding Their Relationship with Reference to Hinduism: A Study Marking the Centenary of Weber's Religions of India." *Social Change* 43, no. 3 (2016): 337–354.

Steinbrink, Malte. "'We Did the Slum!': Urban Poverty Tourism in Historical Perspective." In *Tourism and Geographies of Inequality: The New Global Slumming Phenomenon*, edited by Fabian Frenzel and Ko Koens, 19–40. New York: Routledge, 2015.

Strauss, Sarah. "The Master's Narrative: Swami Sivananda and the Transnational Production of Yoga." *Journal of Folklore Research* 39, no. 2/3 (2002): 217–241.

Suzuki, Shunryu. *Zen Mind, Beginner's Mind.* Edited by Trudy Dixon. New York: Weatherhill, 1972.

Takacs, Stacy. "Monsters Everywhere: Spooky TV and the Politics of Fear in Post-9/11 America." *Science Fiction Studies* 36, no. 1 (2009): 1–20.

Taylor, Charles. *A Secular Age.* Cambridge: Harvard University Press, 2007.

Tello, Julieta. "Creating Your Nurturing Personal Sanctuary." *Mantra Yoga + Health*, May–July 2017, 40–41.

"The O List." *The Oprah Magazine*, March 2018.

Therrien, Catherine. "Quest Migrants: French People in Morocco Searching for 'Elsewhereness.'" In *Contested Spiritualities, Lifestyle Migration and Residential Tourism*, edited by Michael Janoschka and Heiko Hass, 108–123. New York: Routledge, 2014.

"The Seven Chakras." *Hinduism Today* 33, no. 1 (2011): 114–115.

Thomas, Owen C. "Spiritual but Not Religious: The Influence of the Current Romantic Movement." *The Anglican Theological Review* 88, no. 3 (2006): 397–415.

Tickell, Alex. "Footprints on the Beach: Traces of Colonial Adventure in Narratives of Independent Tourism." *Postcolonial Studies* 4, no. 1 (2001): 39–54.

Tillich, Paul. *Systematic Theology, Vol. 3.* Chicago: University of Chicago Press, 1963.

Timalsina, Sthaneshwar. "Encountering the Other: Tantra in the Cross-cultural Context." *The Journal of Hindu Studies* 4 (2011): 274–289.

Ting Zhen Ee, Amanda Evangeline and Christian Kahl. "My Mind and Soul Suspended on a Ticket to Self-Discovery. Now Boarding, Koh Phi Phi!" *Procedia Social and Behavioral Sciences* 144 (2014): 5–14.

Tourage, Mahdi. "Performing Belief and Reviving Islam: Prominent (White Male) Converts in Muslim Revival Conventions." *Performing Islam* 1, no. 3 (2012): 207–226.

Trungpa, Chögyam. *Cutting Through Spiritual Materialism.* Boulder, CO: Shambhala, 2002.

Twair, Pat McDonnell. "ABC-TV's Hit Series, '*Lost*,' Features Sayid, Sensitive, Appealing Iraqi." *Washington Report on Middle East Affairs* 24, no. 3: 44, 52.

Tweed, Thomas. *The American Encounter with Buddhism 1844–1912: Victorian Culture and the Limits of Dissent.* Bloomington, IN: Indiana University Press, 1992.

Urry, John. *The Tourist Gaze: Leisure and Travel in Contemporary Societies.* London: Sage Publications, 2002.

Vandenburg, Tycho and Virginia Braun. "'Basically, It's Sorcery for Your Vagina': Unpacking Western Representations of Vaginal Steaming." *Culture, Health & Sexuality* 19, no. 4 (2017): 470–485.

Versluis, Arthur. *American Gurus: From Transcendentalism to New Age Religion.* New York: Oxford University Press, 2014.

Vial, Theodore. *Modern Religion, Modern Race.* New York: Oxford University Press, 2016.

Warikoo, K. "Shrines and Pilgrimages of Kashmir." *Himalayan and Central Asian Studies* 21, no. 1 (2017): 49–60.

Watson, C. W. "A Popular Indonesian Preacher: The Significance of Aa Gymnastiar." *The Journal of the Royal Anthropological Institute* 11, no. 4 (2005): 773–792.

Wharton, Annabel Jane. *Selling Jerusalem: Relics, Replicas, Theme Parks.* Chicago: University of Chicago Press, 2006.

Wharton Annabel Jane. "Relics, Protestants, Things." *Material Religion* 10, no. 4 (2014): 412–430.

Wheeler, Kayla Renée. "The Ethics of Conducting Virtual Ethnography on Visual Platforms." *Fieldwork in Religion* 12, no. 2 (2017): 163–178.

Wilkins-LaFlamme, Sarah. "How Unreligious are the Religious 'Nones'? Religious Dynamics of the Unaffiliated in Canada." *Canadian Journal of Sociology* 40, no. 4 (2015): 477–500.

Williams, Ruth. "*Eat, Pray, Love*: Producing the Female Neoliberal Spiritual Subject." *The Journal of Popular Culture* 47, no. 3 (2014): 613–633.

Wilson, Jeff. *Mindful America: The Mutual Transformation of Buddhist Meditation and American Culture.* New York: Oxford University Press, 2014.

Winslow, Luke A. "The Imaged Other: Style and Substance in the Rhetoric of Joel Osteen." *Southern Communication Journal* 79, no. 3 (2014): 250–271.

Yoshihara, Mari. *Embracing the East: White Women and American Orientalism.* New York: Oxford University Press, 2003.

Yusuf, Hamza. *Purification of the Heart: Signs, Symptoms, and Cures of the Spiritual Diseases of the Heart.* Bridgeview, IL: Starlatch, 2004.

Zaehner, Robert Charles. *Mysticism Sacred and Profane: An Inquiry into Some Varieties of Praeternatural Experience.* New York: Galaxy Books, 1961.

Zaidman, Nurit, Ofra Goldstein-Gidoni, and Iris Nehemya. "From Temples to Organizations: The Introduction and Packaging of Spirituality." *Organization* 16, no. 4 (2009): 597–621.

Zarcone, Thierry. "Rereadings and Transformations of Sufism in the West." *Diogenes* 47, no. 187 (1999): 110–121.

Zebiri, Kate. "'Holy Foolishness' and 'Crazy Wisdom' as Teaching Styles in Contemporary Western Sufism." *Religion & Literature* 44, no. 2 (2012): 93–122.

Žižek, Slavoj. *The Puppet and the Dwarf: The Perverse Core of Christianity*. Cambridge, MA: MIT Press, 2003.

Žižek, Slavoj. "The Prospects of Radical Politics Today." In *Slavoj Žižek, The Universal Exception: Selected Writings* (vol. 2). Edited by Rex Butler and Scott Stephens, 237–258. London: Continuum, 2006.

INDEX

References to images are in *italics*.

INDEX

INDEX

INDEX